About the Author

The second eldest of eight children George Browning grew up on a small English dairy farm and migrated to Australia aged 18 to work as a groom on a poll Hereford stud.

He began studying for the ministry aged 20, graduating with First Class Honours. After eight years in parochial ministry he returned to the same College as Vice Principal and lecturer in Old Testament, thus beginning a life time interest in OT studies and research. After another 10 years of parochial ministry, in 1985 he was consecrated a Bishop in Brisbane where in addition to his Episcopal ministry he was also Principal of St Francis Theological College.

In these years he developed a passion for social justice, being involved initially in indigenous issues and more latterly in environmental justice. Appointment to Canberra as its Anglican bishop in 1993 saw him develop advocacy skills at a national level and a passion for justice as an integral expression of Christian faith.

At the 1998 Lambeth Conference of Anglican bishops in the UK he was appointed Chair of the Environment section of the conference and subsequently elected inaugural convener of the International Anglican Communion's environment network.

He remains an ardent social justice advocate, these days focusing on two issues; environmental justice and the cries for justice of the Palestinian people. He shares with the rest of his family responsibility for the trust in memory of his mother, the Barbara May Foundation, which is building hospitals for women's health in rural Ethiopia

SABBATH AND THE COMMON GOOD

PROSPECTS FOR A
NEW HUMANITY

GEORGE VICTOR BROWNING

First published in 2016 by Barrallier Books Pty Ltd,
trading as Echo Books

Registered Office: 35-37 Gordon Avenue, West Geelong, Victoria 3220,
Australia.

www.echobooks.com.au

National Library of Australia Cataloguing-in-Publication entry.

Creator: Browning, George, 1942- author.

Title: Sabbath and the Common Good : prospects for a new humanity
/George Browning.

ISBN: 9780994418425 (paperback)

Notes: Includes bibliographical references.

Subjects: Human ecology--Religious aspects--Christianity. Environmental
degradation--Religious aspects--Christianity. Environmental degradation--Moral
and ethical aspects. Social evolution--Philosophy. Civilization--Philosophy.Dewey
Number: 261.88

Book and cover design by Peter Gamble, Ink Pot Graphic Design, Canberra.
Set in Garamond Premier Pro Display, 12/17 and Minerva, Scalptura.

www.echobooks.com.au

Front Cover:*The front cover illustrates the Fibonacci sequence seen in the pine cone,
against a background of bees' comb. Both illustrate the order, efficiency and fecundity
present in nature which humanity, at its best, has tried to mimic.
We are only beginning to understand the rhythms, sequences and order which we share
with the whole created order and are reluctant to take responsibility for the chaos of
which we are capable when this order is ignored or overruled.
(The most famous use of the Fibonacci cone can be seen at the Eden Project in Cornwall).*

Contents

Part 2–Biblical Theology: Unfolding Sabbath from Creation to Christ

Part 3–Sabbath and the Human Vocation

Acknowledgements

I am grateful for the many sources of inspiration that have contributed to the genesis of this book.

Having grown up on the land and having commenced my working life in this context I am intuitively aware that the health of the land and the health of humanity are inextricably bound together.

I am in debt to the international Anglican Communion for appointing me the initial convenor of its Environmental Network (2005—2009). Through this appointment I have been privileged to meet inspiring leaders across the globe and to witness first hand the already devastating consequences of environmental change, especially in some of the poorest places on earth.

I was privileged to share responsibility for input and discussion about the environmental crisis at the 1998 and 2008 Lambeth Conferences. Both conferences called for the development of a sabbath based ethic in response to the crisis.

I am indebted to my father, John Browning, for intuitively knowing that the practice of sabbath is at the heart of Christian living. This book is in part a desire to flesh out this intuition for him as a demonstration that God 'reigns' in sabbath.

I am very grateful to Dr Heather Thomson, Professor James Haire and Professor Stephen Pickard for their wisdom and guidance: also to Mr Alan Wilson who has painstakingly checked the text and references.

The biblical text is taken from the New Revised Standard Version (NRSV). Consistent with this text, sabbath is referred to in the lower case unless circumstances demand otherwise.

Finally, I have written for my grandchildren (and their remarkable grandmother with whom I have had the privilege of sharing life's journey for 50 years), conscious of the reality that the choices available to them in the future are dependent upon environmentally ethical living in the present.

FOREWORD

For at least four decades it has been the contention of environmental science that the biosphere faces a crisis. The growing consensus is that this crisis is not simply a reflection of the well documented cycle of natural variation, but that its intensity is escalated by post industrial human activity.

This situation presents the Christian community, with a moral dilemma. Can the Christian community tolerate activity which threatens human and non-human life with a more fragile, less equitable and less sustainable future? The answer must be 'no'.

Christian belief and action is predicated on love of God and love of neighbour. Contemporary love of neighbour must act to transform a global community where current advantage and power is disproportionately exercised by a minority and disadvantage is experienced, or predicted to fall, upon the majority poor, generations yet unborn and upon the natural environment.

Responding to social or moral issues, Anglicans have been traditionally encouraged to seek direction from scripture which calls for the triumph of common good over self interest as an expression of the human calling under God.

Sabbath is a biblical framework for global common good and a reliable basis upon which the human vocation in the 21st century can be renewed. This work argues that sabbath, with roots in the primeval creation narrative, reveals the manner of God's engagement with the created order. Further, it argues that the manner in which humanity is to respond to God in the context of the environmental crisis, is to include the whole created order in the category of neighbour deserving of love care and equity.

PART 1
CRISIS AND COMMON GOOD

Living in the midst of these technologically aggressive human societies we cannot expect to draw attention [to the suffering of the planet] without incurring some of the rejection, perhaps even wrath, that has always been the lot of the prophetic community.[1]

CHAPTER 1

THE ENVIRONMENTAL AND THEOLOGICAL CONTEXT

The supreme reality of our time is our indivisibility as children of God and our common vulnerability on this planet.[2]

That there is an environmental crisis[3] has been the proposition of a growing body of scientific research for decades. This does not mean that details relating to the perceived crisis are not contested, they are, particularly the scale of human causation. It is also important to understand that the science is an analysis of what has occurred, not a prediction of what will occur, although of course what has occurred has a direct bearing upon what will occur. The crisis is multifaceted. It involves serious decline to bio-diversity, desertification, water shortages, pollution of earth, air and water, increasing intensity to significant weather events, and unsustainable exploitation. However, the factor gaining most attention, because of its current and projected effect, is global warming.[4] Attention given to global warming is promoted from opposite directions. On the one hand, global warming is considered a serious threat. Its immediate effects are said to be already felt, while in the future its potential is perceived to seriously undermine the total biosphere, including human flourishing. On the other hand, despite the science, the reality of global warming and its relationship to the human footprint is contested in the public discourse. From those who have a strong vested interest in unlimited exploitation, it is denied.[5] In the public discourse there is confusion between what can rightly be called 'fact' and what should more appropriately be called 'opinion'.[6]

It is not within the remit of this exploration to defend or challenge the science. The science is widely accepted internationally and has bi-partisan political support in Australia. While there may be widespread agreement about the science, no such political agreement exists as to an appropriate, let alone adequate, response to the science: a situation which has been a catalyst for this book. If there is an environmental crisis and if this crisis is largely, if not totally, caused by humanity then this truth poses a significant challenge to Christian ethics and morality. It has always been a Christian view that: the earth[7] is the Lord's and all that therein is (Ps. 24:1), (1 Cor. 10:26). It has also been a long held Christian view[8] that humanity is charged with the task of stewardship,[9] of caring for the earth. Given these two fundamental propositions, the Christian community cannot simply turn a blind eye to the crisis, or, on the other hand, consider it to be the problem of others. The scale of the crisis implicates all human beings as participants. All are contributors to the problem; all must consider themselves participants in an effective response, and all must live with the future in mind as argued in Chapter 6.

Denying the science of climate change that has a 95%[10] consensus from scientists across all continents is not plausible and, given the seriousness of their findings, it is irresponsible. The 2013 report from the Intergovernmental Panel on Climate Change made the following points:

- Warming of the climate system is unequivocal and since the 1950's many of the observed changes are unprecedented over decades to millennia. The atmosphere and oceans have warmed, the amounts of snow and ice have diminished, sea level has risen and the concentrations of greenhouse gases have increased.[11]

- Each of the last three decades has been successively warmer at the earth's surface than any preceding decade since 1850.[12]
- Ocean warming dominates the energy stored.[13]
- The rate of sea level rise since the mid-19th Century has been larger than the mean rate for the two previous millennia.[14]
- The concentrations of carbon dioxide, methane and nitrous oxide have increased to levels unprecedented in the last 800,000 years. CO_2 levels have increased by 40% since preindustrial times.[15]
- Human influence on climate systems is clear. This is evident from the increasing greenhouse gas concentrations in the atmosphere, positive radiating forcing, observed warming and understanding the climate system.[16]
- Limiting climate change will require substantial and sustained reductions of greenhouse gas emissions.[17]

Scientists say it is their task to examine and present the facts as best they are able; it is the task of others to determine what should be done in relation to these facts. Response to the scientific data places the environmental crisis within a political and economic context.

Political and Economic Context

Responding to the environmental crisis involves acknowledging and dealing with the size of global population, the rate of human consumption and the level of technological exploitation. Such acknowledgement and consequent action is proving very difficult to achieve in liberal democracies where the rights of individuals are treated as sacrosanct and any impingement upon perceived economic rights are strongly resisted. 'Modern liberalism, individualism and capitalism are profoundly intertwined'.[18]

Capitalism is dependent upon growing consumption, an outcome of a market driven economy's need for profit and growth. Capitalism has become the ubiquitous mode of international trade. While China, the largest emerging world economy, continues to be governed by a communistic ideology, nevertheless its growing influence upon the world is based upon capitalist, consumer driven principles. While capitalism is first and foremost the economic driver of the first world, it creates client states in the 'majority world'.[19] It can be said that 'market' driven capitalism is the world's heartbeat.[20] But can capitalism deliver anything other than financial profit?

> The key question today is global and urgent: how can capitalism in the 21st century deliver the three overarching goals sought by societies around the world: economic prosperity, social justice and environmental sustainability?[21]

World capitalism is usually referred to as 'neoclassical economics'. This term refers to a market driven economic approach in which supply and demand determine prices, and a profit producing balance is sought between income constrained consumers and cost constrained producers. It is this context, as much as the environmental crisis itself, in which the Christian Gospel is to be lived and proclaimed. It is in this context that a plausible Christian ethic should challenge customs and expectations which are inconsistent with the 'kingdom narrative' Jesus proclaimed.

Critics of growing economic inequity argue that neoclassical economics has been further refined since the 1970's into what is called 'neo-liberalism'.[22] This period, since the rise of Reagan and Thatcher, has seen regulation reduced, CEO salaries spike, and tax paid by the rich shrink in the US from a highest bracket of 51.2% of income in 1955, to a highest level of 16.6% of income in 2007. 50% of wealth in the US is held by 1% of the people.[23] This period has also seen:

The global economy become suddenly so large—$70 trillion a year and doubling in size roughly every 20 years—that the earth's air, water, land, and climate are all under threat. Our global response to date has been so obtuse, so absurd, so short-sighted, that it almost seems that humanity has a death wish.[24]

The sacrosanct principle of the 'market' is exponential growth.[25] What is most feared in any country, or indeed the global market, is recession, let alone depression. The health of all the major countries of the world is judged not on factors of human well-being but on the percentage growth of their GDP (Gross Domestic Production). Because responding to environmental issues is argued by industry as an unnecessary impost upon the cost of production, almost all political parties, in most countries, lack the political will to enact legislation that would lessen the impact of the human footprint within their country. In this work I do not have the space to argue that conversion to a carbon neutral economy is both technically and economically possible within a generation. This case has been made.[26] Resistance to such transition by conglomerates wedded to the status quo, their capacity to lobby government, and, through advertising, persuade the general public that caring for the environment is an unnecessary expense, has so far made journeying even to the first rung on the ladder in this transition politically fraught.

In his *Foolishness to the Greeks*, Lesslie Newbigin reflects upon neoclassical economics as a system devoid of ethics:

> As the principle of the division of labour gained ascendancy, the market moved into central place as the mechanism that linked all the separate procedures with each other and the consumer. The modern science of economics was born. Economics was no longer part of ethics. It was not concerned with the purpose of human life. It was no longer about the requirements of justice and the dangers of covetousness. It became the science of the working of the market as a self operating mechanism modelled on a Newtonian Universe.[27]

The Newtonian commitment to cause and effect plays out in this economic theory through the assumption of exponential growth. The exponents of the theory argue for a 'drip down effect', indeed many of the world's poor have been pulled out of poverty, especially in Asia. However, at the same time the wealth gap between the rich and the poor has greatly increased. Growing inequity within wealthy nations, and between wealthy and poor nations, means that at the very least such an assumption must be challenged.[28] Those who benefit most from the prevailing economic orthodoxy resist strategies that aim, on the one hand, to reduce human inequity, and on the other, to factor environmental cost into the productivity equation. The market seeks to minimise expense and maximise price thus maintaining profit.

In contemporary public discourse the 'economy' has become shorthand for all that is healthy or unhealthy in human life. But what is 'economy'? Williams argues: "Economy' is, in its origins, simply a word for housekeeping. ... In light of its origins, the word gives growing force to the question, 'what for'?"[29] This question was at the forefront of the minds of the bishops at successive Lambeth Conferences (see Chapter 2). The bishops insisted investment should be for the benefit of society as a whole, that the prevailing economic system be imbued with moral principles. In constantly changing national and international circumstances, the bishops considered it the obligation of government to legislate reform; minimising inequity, guarding against exploitation. This sense of obligation led logically to the argument of later conferences that an economic system that threatened environmental sustainability should be reformed.

The human economy has become so pervasive, affecting all aspects of life on the planet, that in the year 2000 the Dutch Nobel Prize winning atmospheric chemist, Professor Paul Crutzen, proposed that the earth has now moved from the Holocene to the Anthropocene era.[30] By this he meant that the earth is no longer simply host to a number of species of which humanity is one, albeit the dominant species, but that the earth is now being transformed and shaped by the activities of this one species. He noted in particular that because of human activity natural extinction is now happening at 1000 times the historically observed rate and that we have now entered what some scientists are calling the sixth period of mass extinction.[31]

For this to have occurred humanity has, consciously or unconsciously, considered itself to be apart from the world rather than part of the world, and has allowed its earth-changing activities to accelerate without giving thought to the consequences of these activities for the earth and indeed for humanity itself.

Valuing 'mastery' over 'mutuality' within the natural order absolves humanity from the accountabilities that must apply were humanity to understand itself a partner within the family of creation. The context from which this book has its genesis is a Western culture, over which Christianity initially exercised considerable influence, but in which human activity is now increasingly divorced from a sense of responsibility for 'sustaining and renewing the life of the earth.'[32] This situation stands in stark contrast to pre-industrial society or most indigenous societies that retain their traditional values.[33] In the United States of America and in Australia economically driven politics is lobbied aggressively in a tenacious battle to defend the status quo of maximum economic growth. The necessity of exponential economic growth is a narrative that has come to dominate the public mind across the political divide. The truth of this narrative is assumed and seldom questioned. This work researches a different narrative—a narrative that sustainability is more important than growth and that cooperation for common good is a greater guarantor of human and non-human well-being than competition driven by individual self-interest. The urgency of this task is well stated by Moltmann:

> If man and nature are to have any chance of surviving, especially
> in view of the ecological crisis and the progressive destruction of
> nature brought about by both Christianity and natural science,

then we must both revise the understanding of man present in the traditional doctrine of creation: have dominion over the earth (Gen. 1:28), as well as the understanding of man present in the Cartesian natural science: master and possessor of nature.[34]

Finally, individualism is deemed by many[35] to be a particular feature of modern industrialised society and the ideology that undergirds the economic principles of the free market, with its overriding and ubiquitous commitment to exponential growth. Christian values support and encourage the flourishing of the individual, but a flourishing within the life of a healthy community. Christian values do not support the flourishing of an individual independently of the communities to which all belong, least of all at the expense of those communities. These communities now include the global human community, together with generations yet unborn. That accountability also includes the ecological community of the non-human creation. If expectations of continuous exponential growth are unsustainable, as many economists now argue,[36] and if the expectations of individuals for accumulating personal wealth are allowed to override commitment to 'Common Wealth,'[37] then commitment to 'individualism' has become a stumbling block to a sustainable future for all human beings and is self-defeating. Individualism exalts the right of personal freedom; however if individual actions on a vast scale (the world is now populated by 7 billion people)[38] put a sustainable future for all at risk then it is legitimate to ask what personal freedom means in this context. If freedom means the right of individuals to do whatever they want then we must agree with Paul Ricoeur that 'evil is an invention of freedom.'[39] Freedom must always be understood to exist within the constraints of a relational world. In a relational world individual actions are constrained by the necessity of justice towards others and indeed toward the non-human creation. Ricoeur, expanding the arguments of Kant and Plato states:

> If injustice can be the figure of radical evil, it is because justice is
> not one virtue out of many but the very form of virtue, the unifying
> principle which makes the soul, from being several, into one.[40]

Jesus' teaching on the 'Kingdom of God' assumes a relational world sustained by a relational God. Thus it is a 'Gospel' matter that economic order be redefined to assure the greatest possible good for human and non-human creation alike. The challenge facing humanity in the 21st century is not to increase market competition in the hope of expanding economic growth, but to achieve a level of human global cooperation which will enable health, stability and sustainability for human and non-human creation alike, for this and future generations.

Christianity and the Environmental Crisis

While neo-classical economics has produced some positive outcomes, the context of the Church's contemporary mission is that economic orthodoxy also produces outcomes contrary to Gospel values, outcomes of considerable human injustice, but more particularly outcomes of serious environmental and ecological degradation. In response to this situation, the international Anglican Communion developed a five point mission statement,[41] and subsequently established its own environmental network to guide its decision making bodies, especially the meeting of Primates and the Anglican Consultative Council.

The mission statement mandates responsibility for challenging and transforming unjust structures and for sustaining and renewing the life of the earth. This is a contribution to these missional priorities by developing a narrative upon which behavioural change might be enacted.

The home of capitalism is the West, with a culture and history profoundly influenced by Christianity. Being the 'home' of both (capitalism and Christianity), the question has to be asked: 'has Christianity contributed to capitalism and the individualism that lies behind it,' or even more dramatically: 'is Christianity the major reason for its global dominance'? The question is important. Responding to the environmental crisis means not simply attending to 'changing light globes'[42] and 'planting more trees,'[43] but rethinking consumption as the necessary driver of economic life. If consumer driven acquisitiveness is a logical outcome of Christianity in the 20th and 21st centuries then there is little point in arguing for an ethical response to the environmental crisis from a Christian theology. If on the other hand the proposition that consumer acquisitiveness as a 'definer of human identity'[44] is in fact the antithesis of the Gospel, Christianity has a significant counter cultural role. Christianity must demonstrate its difference to the prevailing culture, not simply for its own sake, but so that it might speak prophetically to the global community. Jesus said 'you cannot serve God and wealth' (Mtt. 6:24). An acquisitive, consumer driven society, a society which equates the 'good life' with the 'goods life' says, 'Yes we can.' If it can be shown that, unintentionally, Christianity has been sympathetic to an ideology that is essentially the antithesis of Christian belief, considerable attention needs to be given to reforming or realigning Christian praxis, so that it more faithfully reflects core belief and values. It needs to do this so that it might be an agent of positive transformation for the whole human family and for the total biosphere which yearns for a sustainable future.

The two most well known figures to claim that Christianity has been a significant contributor to the rise of an aggressive consumerism have been Lynn White and Max Weber.

Lynn White's[45] 1967 highly publicised paper, places the blame for human over-exploitation of the natural environment at the foot of the Christian community, while Max Weber, in his *The Protestant Ethic and the Spirit of Capitalism*,[46] (1904), claims that contemporary individualism owes its origins to the Reformation. White claims that Christianity is inexorably linked to exploitation because of the weight it gives to the first creation narrative and the apparent commission to humanity to: 'be fruitful and multiply and fill the earth and subdue it and have dominion' (Gen. 1:28). Because the history of Christianity and the development of western culture share much in common, he argues that Christian belief has been instrumental in forming the ideas and assumptions of the West's consumerist culture. While weight needs to be given to White's argument it ought also to be said that for the majority of Christian history avarice was deemed to be one of the 'deadly sins' and that the accumulation of 'wants' in excess of 'needs' undermined the human calling.

Weber's[47] argument is that Protestantism is greatly influenced by what he believes to be Calvin's doctrine of double predestination: that is to say a teaching that some are fore-ordained to salvation and others to damnation. He argues that, following the Reformation and the rejection of the institutional Church as the individual's source of grace and salvation, each individual had to secure their own salvation through faith alone and that demonstration of this salvation was observed in material prosperity. Protestantism, especially that which came to be the foundation of the United States of America, was driven, he argues, by the need of individuals to work hard to demonstrate God's blessing. While there is some weight in Weber's argument, indeed the 21st century 'prosperity Gospel'[48] is a demonstration of it; the real story is far more nuanced.

In his *The Unintended Reformation* Brad Gregory makes a different argument. It is that Christianity's influence upon consumerism was quite unintended, occurring despite the Church's essential opposition to avarice and unnecessary acquisitiveness. His argument is that the unresolved doctrinal divisions of the Church left each denomination, or sect, in a position of needing to demonstrate that adherence to their rule was a source of blessing and that this blessing was observable:

> Not Reformation teaching as such, but rather the doctrinal
> disagreements and concrete religio-political disruptions between

magisterial Protestants and Catholics would create the conditions
for an ideological *volte-face* concerning acquisitiveness.[49]

Avarice has always been condemned by the Church.[50] The great
monastic movements of the medieval period were born out of eschewing
materialistic values. Ironically the mendicant way of life was itself very
attractive to wealth![51] Those who were wealthy through position and
privilege sought association with these movements as a vicarious means
of identifying with values that were not personally followed. Prior to the
Reformation usury was considered incompatible with Christian values.[52]
If money was lent to those in need to secure some basic necessity, only that
which had been lent could be recovered. Even beyond the Reformation
usury was considered incompatible with the Christian imperative to
care for one's neighbour, and was not widely practised. While many were
wealthy, the medieval period did not reflect a capitalist society. Ensuring
that none went hungry was an outcome of *caritas,* love of neighbour.

Great reformers such as Luther and Zwingli also condemned avarice.
While the Reformation placed more emphasis upon the individual, the
necessary obligation of caring for one another remained.

> Magisterial Protestant reformers regarded economic behaviour as
> part of Christian morality, condemned avarice as sinful, preached
> detachment from material possessions, insisted on care for the
> poor and excoriated those who selfishly prioritized their individual
> desires above the common good.[53]

Gregory's argument is that focus on material wealth was an
unintended outcome of the unresolved divisions, political and
theological, of the Reformation. Because, he argues, doctrines remained
unresolved and competition and rivalry emerged from these differences,
it became necessary to demonstrate the 'rightness' or 'rightfulness'
of denominational adherence through the material prosperity of
membership.[54]

Rather than Christianity intentionally influencing the materialistic direction of modern society, the opposite is more likely to be the case. 'The market and inherited Christian morality were increasingly divorced, which removed the ethical restraints inhibiting the eventual formation of a full-blown capitalist and consumerist society.'[55] For centuries in 'Christian Europe', the Church and the State were partners. At their best the virtues of Christianity were adopted by the State. At its worst seductive power in the hands of leaders in both Church and State meant that the 'caritas ethic' was taught to the faithful but hidden behind the trappings of power for those in authority. As the partnership between Church and State waned following the Reformation, and as Enlightenment attitudes towards institution and authority began to dominate, a different institution emerged as the junior partner of government in the exercise of power—the market. Today the junior partner has in some circumstances become the controlling master.[56] Following the global financial collapse of 2008 the state found itself bailing out the banks. The lobbying power of massive multi-nationals appears to be beyond the capacity of governments to resist.[57] Many very large companies do business and largely avoid accountability beyond the judicial limits of any single state.

> Increasingly the 'common good' now means simply the state controlled sum of all pleasures by individuals pursuing ever more plentiful material goods, as produced by the market's benevolent invisible hand.[58]

Even if Christianity is not 'responsible' for the emergence of a consumerist, capitalist society as argued by White and Weber, significant challenges still remain. There is need for the reemergence of a theology which will undergird a counter-cultural way of life to capitalistic, consumer-driven acquisitiveness: a way of life which can be attractively transformative: a way of life which can lead to an equitable and sustainable life for humanity and the whole biosphere into a multi-generational future.

Theological and Ethical Context

Creation, what is believed about it, and how this belief influences the practical living of Christian people should not be a peripheral matter; and yet it appears to have become so. Some sectors of the Christian community overtly resist the notion that responsibility for environmental issues should be a Christian mandate, claiming that at best such concerns are a distraction from the core business of 'saving lost humanity.'[59] The Church's contemporary obsession with personal morality over issues of global and social justice[60] is further evidence. It is not that personal morality is not important, rather that it has come to overshadow global concerns for justice.[61]

Christian teaching in relation to the earth is that it is God's dwelling place,[62] that God imbues creation with sacredness, or value, in its own right, for its own sake. It is not simply a resource whose sole value is to be understood in terms of its usefulness to humanity. The Church also witnesses to the universal reign of God, a reign in Christ that heralds a 'new creation.' 'The kingdom of God embraces the whole of creation ... the life Jesus brings is the harbinger and beginning of the bodily life of the new creation.'[63] Of necessity therefore the Church must look again at creation's bearing to God in light of the environmental crisis and humanity's increasing tendency to value creation simply as a human resource.

A creation-based theology presents a relational view of the world, and as such provides a much needed corrective to the market-driven individualism which so dominates western, materialistic and economic culture. Dan Hardy argues that western societal forms are in disarray and that the corrective is not to look first at a theology of redemption:

> Rather than trace the social transcendental, as the element which underlies all society and thus informs social pragmatics, to God's specific act of redemption in Christ; it should be traced to the Logos of God operative in creation. This divine ordering is what ultimately implants in the human condition the 'being-with' which is natural to it.[64]

Kevin Treston makes the same point:

> A major theological enterprise in the twenty-first century should
> be the reframing of the Christ story within God's revelation in
> Jesus and within the context of creation. Redemption theology
> and creation theology are two faces of the one experience of God's
> revelation through Christ in creation. Both theologies point to
> restoring and living a 'life in abundance' within creation.[65]

Treston's 'life in abundance *within* creation,' contrasts with a 'prosperity gospel' which promises individual advantage *from* creation on the basis that individual prosperity is a sign of God's favour. The one emphasises what is to be shared within the community of creation, the other emphasises what is to be personally isolated from creation.

A commitment to human redemption that does not embrace a commitment to the redeeming and sustaining of the created order reduces the Church and its mission to a status less than that which it claims for itself. 'Respect for the living material world and human self-respect belong together. The restoration or salvation of one is bound up in the other.'[66]

Hardy and Treston do not argue for the removal of redemption theology from its central position in Christian preaching and exposition, but to place it in the relational context of creation. This is also my goal, not the minimisation of redemption theology, but its understanding in the light of creation. Redemption theology is embedded in a narrative of salvation history, of God 'working his purposes out as year succeeds to year.'[67] The possibility of salvation history assumes, *a priori*, a material world of time and space influenced by the reign of God. The nature of that created world informs the reason for, and the outcome of, redemption. Thus, unless redemption theology is informed by creation theology, a theology that assumes the unity and relationality of creation, it falls into the trap of an over emphasis upon the individual.

What the Church believes about creation and what it believes about an ideal human society are intertwining claims to truth arising from an understanding that creation is 'a single house.' Since the industrial revolution a new human society has been recreated out of the pre-industrial feudal system, with an emphasis upon the freedom, autonomy, and rights that individuals can claim. This period, influenced by the Enlightenment, has not been anti-religious, but it has developed an ideology of human reason and autonomy without reference to a meta-religious narrative. Lesslie Newbigin argues that the Enlightenment spawned two distinct worlds.

> The public world is the world of facts upon which every intelligent person is expected to agree—or be capable of being persuaded. The private world is the world where we are free to follow our own preferences—a world in which there is no right or wrong in life style.[68] ... The response of the Christian Church post the Enlightenment has been to retreat into the private world.[69] It has secured for itself a continuing place at the cost of surrendering the crucial field.[70]

Christians living in this culture are inevitably shaped by it. 'To surrender the crucial field' is to allow gross inequity to go unchallenged in the name of profit. Surrendering the crucial field is to turn a blind eye to injustice. 'What is at stake is our continuance as a species capable of some vision of universal justice.'[71] To surrender the crucial field is to remain silent when self interest prevails over common good. Rowan Williams warns:

> No process whose goal is the limited or exclusive security of an individual or interest group or even national community alone can be regarded as unequivocally good in Christian terms because of the underlying aspiration to a state of security in isolation.[72]

To surrender the crucial field is to live with an assumption that the Christian faith has nothing to contribute to matters of public policy and nothing to contribute to a vision for the emerging shape of global society.

An ideal society is one in which respect and honour are attributed to all members of the house, human and non-human. 'We must begin by recognising that our ecological crisis is part of a crisis of what we understand by our humanity; it is part of a general process of losing our 'feel' for what is appropriately human.'[73] If our starting point is to believe that what is appropriately human is domination and exploitation we will end up in a very different place to a destiny driven by a view that what is appropriately human is respect, honour, and service of the other.

> To set an example of modest unostentatious living ... provide moderately for the needs of those dependent upon him; after doing so, consider all surplus revenues as trust funds ... the man of wealth thus becoming the mere trustee and agent for his poorer brethren.[74]

Williams makes much of a connection between the environmental crisis and what he perceives as a crisis of the human vocation, exemplified by the dominance of self interest. 'The world is less than it might be as long as humans remain less than they might be'[75] is a good example of his argument in both books and lectures. Given its values, Christianity could be rightly accused of culpability in terms of the evolution of human society if it is not modelling what humans might be, or worse, complying with human self awareness that is less than it ought to be. Moltmann poses the question: 'Is Christianity a factor in the ecological crisis'?[76] His answer is 'yes' if Christianity assumes 'dominion' to be the human calling. 'Yes' if creation is to be viewed anthropomorphically, valued only from a human perspective. But above all 'yes' if Christianity's monotheism strips nature of its mystery, preparing the way for its secularisation and degradation into human property.[77]

Attention has already been drawn to Lynn White's essay. He argues that the Enlightenment may have distanced modern society from the influence of institutional Christianity; nevertheless vestiges of its doctrinal heritage remain very much alive in western commercial and exploitative behaviour. He cites the exploitation of physical creation as his primary example and argues that such an attitude arises from a Christian world view that physical creation has no purpose other than to serve human purpose and that Christianity is the most anthropocentric religion the world has ever seen.

> Our science and technology have grown out of Christian attitudes towards man's relation to nature which are almost universally held not only by Christians and neo-Christians, but also by those who regard themselves as post-Christian. ... More science and more technology are not going to get us out of the present ecological crisis until we find a new religion, or re-think our old one.
>
> Both our present science and our present technology are so tinctured with orthodox Christian arrogance toward nature that no solution for our ecological crisis can be expected from them alone. Since the roots of our trouble are so largely religious, the remedy must also be essentially religious, whether we call it that or not.[78]

Neither White's critique, nor Weber's assertion, can axiomatically be drawn from Protestantism or Christianity generally. However, at the commencement of the 21st century, Christianity appears to accept and be embedded in the prevailing economic structures of our time. If the Church's teaching and values have unwittingly contributed to human exploitation of non-human creation, then the Church faces a double task. It must first examine its own theological 'backyard'. It must ask whether its teaching has had unintended consequences, if not in the mind of the teachers, then in the mind of the hearers. It must do this while at the same time contributing, by word and example, to a theology for an equitable and sustainable future.

Has Christianity's retreat into the private world become terminal in the mind of wider world, if not in its own? Are the worlds of religion and science now parallel universes? In recent years well known Anglican (priest) scholars who combine science and theology such as Alister McGrath[79] and

John Polkinghorne,[80] have argued that science and Christianity are not only compatible, but that they should inform one another. Together, they argue, science and Christianity should contribute to a new understanding of the place of humanity within the non-human creation.

McGrath and Polkinghorne are respected in the fields of both science and faith, and serve as strong counter-points to a world view in which science and religion share no common ground. Polkinghorne argues that not only is humanity part of creation, but that the process of evolution gives to all life and to humanity in particular the capacity to form and reform itself in response to the creation of which it is a part. He argues that belief in God who 'chose' to give life the capacity to 'remake' itself, makes for a richer and more dynamic belief than devotion to God who has created a static universe, with the final shape and form of life having been pre-determined.[81] In this respect Polkinghorne follows the argument of Pierre Teilhard De Chardin[82] who asserted that creation needs the evolution of the human mind.

The work of Polkinghorne and McGrath go some way to counter White's argument that Christianity is responsible for the excesses of human exploitation. Chapter 3 examines the Genesis narrative upon which White's argument is based, and argues that set within the biblical narrative as a whole his view that humanity is divinely ordained to 'gain mastery over nature' cannot be supported. White's critique may well rest on a misunderstanding, even a distortion of scripture, however the fruits of that distortion remain. I seek to establish a theology which will undergird a responsible twenty-first century environmental ethic.

The Sabbath and Creation Theology

While belief in God as creator is the first affirmation of the creeds, what this means has been open to many interpretations. A literal, historical, interpretation of the Genesis narrative concludes that creation was an activity of God at the beginning of time. On the other hand, a christologically focussed view of creation concludes that creation continues in the unfolding purposes of God in Jesus. 'Process theology' understands God both as infinite and unchanging, but also 'affected' by the unfolding consequences of creation.

Many have written a treatise on creation theology and its bearing upon the environmental crisis.[83] I have chosen to explore sabbath[84] as a theological and ethical framework linking creation and redemption theologies. If, as already suggested, the environmental crisis could be more properly understood as a crisis of the human vocation, I am exploring sabbath as a window through which the human vocation might be understood afresh in light of our current crisis. Through the window of sabbath I am arguing that:

1.   The nature of God revealed in Jesus and the nature of God revealed in creation is the same and that the Christian vocation to imitate Christ has implications beyond human to human interaction into engagement with the non-human creation.

2.   The Christian doctrine of the Trinity is reflected in creation; therefore an appropriate relationship of mutuality between humanity and the natural order must undergird hope for the future flourishing of creation, of which humanity is part.

Chapters 3 and 4 unfold sabbath in the biblical narrative. Chapter 3 focusses on sabbath as a window into an understanding of the universal reign of God, especially in light of the Genesis creation account (Gen. 2:1-4). Chapter 4 explores sabbath in the early Church and as interpreted by Jesus: it points to the universal reign of God being accomplished in Jesus, and the human vocation being fulfilled in him.

The theologian to have most developed a theology of Sabbath as a responsible ecological attitude is Jürgen Moltmann.[85] However, in the development of his various propositions, Moltmann has drawn significantly on the earlier work of Karl Barth. It is difficult to develop a theology of sabbath and its significance to the human vocation in light of the current environmental crisis without reference to Barth.

Chapters 3 and 4, and to a lesser degree Chapter 5, engage with Barth and his doctrine of creation. Notwithstanding Barth's influence, this engagement warrants justification in light of the widespread perception that he rejected natural theology. Most other supporting documents in the book are drawn from contemporary theologians, with a preference, for Anglican theologians.

The need for explanation is heightened in light of the strong critique Barth received from respected Anglican voices at Lambeth Conferences in the mid 20th century. Charles Raven, writing after the 1930 Lambeth Conference, criticised Barth's focus on the transcendence of God, 'making any fulfilment of God's reign on earth utterly irrelevant.'[86] William Wand made similar assertions at, and following, the 1948 Conference:

> Under the leadership of the continental theologian Karl Barth an attempt was made to obliterate all traces of natural theology from Christian teaching and to assert the strongest possible dualism between Christ and the world. ... At the 1948 Lambeth Conference the Bishops composed their report on the *Nature of Man* remaining true to the Anglican tradition, rejecting the Barthian view.[87]

A more prominent disagreement (split) with Barth occurred in 1934 in correspondence initiated by the eminent Swiss theologian, Emil Brunner. Brunner believed Barth had gone too far in his insistence that from the perspective of Christian theology knowledge of God can come only from revelation in Jesus. Brunner argued that it is reasonable to expect that the creation will reveal the hand of the creator. Barth argued that revelation is a matter of grace through faith, not reason.[88]

It is likely that Wand, Raven, and the English Church generally were responding to Barth's commentary on Romans rather than to his magisterial work on creation which was not published in English until 1958. Barth does not allow natural theology to be a contributor to a theology of salvation, to hold a position prior to Christian Revelation.[89] However, he neither explicitly nor implicitly supports a dualism between

Christ and the world. Indeed the core of his argument is that creation finds its focus in Christ, and, critically for my work, Christ is the fulfilment of sabbath. It is because Christ is the *logos* of God, through whom all things came to be and in whom all things are redeemed, that natural theology has to be taken seriously. As Moltmann describes it:

> For a time natural theology was considered to be a rival to revealed theology, and in the 1930's Karl Barth fought against it. But natural theology is neither a rival to revealed theology nor its preliminary stage; it is its necessary consequence.[90]

On the one hand Barth's theology is fashioned out of the specific context of dire human conflict in the first half of the 20th century; and yet on the other hand he is a systematic theologian who proposes an inclusive theological framework beyond any particular human context. 'Karl Barth is a systematic theologian in the respect that nothing written in one place is said to be without implicit or explicit reference to other theological themes.'[91] It is perhaps inevitable that his particular context will, wittingly or unwittingly, be reflected upon a canvass which is intended to be beyond any particular time or place. For example, Barth devotes a major section of his theology of creation to the notion of 'covenant' for which creation is described as the 'external instrument'. The intended or unintended consequence is to imply that creation exists to serve the redemptive purposes of God for humanity. Colin Gunton expresses it well:

> Because commitment to human salvation is in some way written in the heart of God in a way that commitment to creation is not, the created order as a whole is given a rather instrumental place in the works of God as but the outer basis of covenant. This brings human creation into undue prominence.[92]

Also, while there is no doubt about the prominence given by Barth to human salvation, indeed it is hard to read the scriptures without totally agreeing with this emphasis, nevertheless he does not see any place for humanity other than in partnership with the totality of creation.

The termination of creation is not its completion. That is to say it is not completed because it is concluded, but because on the presupposition of this conclusion God rested on the seventh day. The completing of creation is the joyful readiness in which the Creator and the creature, the Master and the work that he has set before him are conjoined, and together anticipate the common history which now commences.[93]

It has also been long contended that Barth is a 'universalist' in that his theology of redemption is argued ontologically, that is to say, that in the resurrection Christ assumes for all humanity the nature or destiny of the second Adam. The 'universalist' tag given to Barth is countered by the question he poses in relation to sabbath and with which Chapter 3 commences. 'Will the human race keep the Sabbath or not? Will it enter into its promised rest or not'?[94] Speaking between the two world wars Barth is addressing the future destiny of humanity under the oppressive shadow of human misery and conflict. His rhetorical question requires no change at the commencement of the twenty-first century as humanity balances its appetite for material prosperity with an environmental imperative for health and sustainability.

Barth's context was specifically of inter-human conflict, while that of today is the broader context of humanity and the total biosphere. Were Barth speaking today, rather than in the context of Europe's conflicts, he would no doubt have different emphases to make. There remain however several reasons why I recognise my indebtedness to him.

1. Sabbath is rooted equally in creation and redemption as illustrated by the distinctions within the fourth commandment[95] in the two decalogues. (Exodus situates the fourth commandment within creation while Deuteronomy places it in the context of redemption—the Exodus). Therefore, it is contended, creation and redemption 'speak to one another'. Kathryn Tanner sums up Barth's position

thus: 'What God does in redemption reflects God's activity in creation.'[96] In Chapter 7 it is argued that the 'kenosis', so obvious in the redemptive activity of God in Jesus, is also the mark of God's activity in creation, celebrated in sabbath and as a consequence informs the human vocation.

2. Sabbath is a theological assertion and equally an ethical requirement, not simply a requirement upon the Jewish people, but a requirement inherent within creation and therefore universally applicable. It is an ethical requirement that informs the human vocation. The connection between theology and a lived life is a constant theme of Barth's writing.

3. Any theology that does not bear on ethics, broadly conceived— that is to say any theology without bearing on a life lived before God—is not Christian theology.[97]

4. Sabbath rest is essentially about God's dwelling with creation and of the need of creation, especially humanity within creation, to so restrict its desire for independent autonomy that it finds its 'rest' in fellowship with God and with the whole created order. Barth's theology of creation emphasises the fellowship or community of creation that comes about as a result of God's dwelling with it. Tanner again reflects Barth: 'Although God might have remained alone without detriment to God's fullness and splendour, God freely chose to be with another who is not God by creating the world.'[98]

5. Sabbath can only be fully understood in Jesus. From the beginning Sabbath was made for him, in the same way that creation was made in him and through him. This contention is vital to the argument of this book: If sabbath is truly fulfilled in Jesus, if it is that which shapes his proclamation of the Kingdom of God, then sabbath must shape the Church's self-understanding. For

Barth, Christ is the starting point for all theological excursions. In relation to creation one does not start there (as in natural theology) and work forward to Christ, but the starting point is Christ who illumines the meaning of creation.

6. When beliefs about providence [and creation] stem from Christ, rather than move to him, providence [and creation] become not the immanent movement of created powers but those arrangements of the world that reflect God's prior intention for the world in Christ, arrangements that reflect God's primary intention to draw the world toward himself.[99]

7. The unique contribution that I am endeavouring to make to the body of knowledge is not just that environmental/ecological responsibility is core to the Church's mission, not just that the whole of creation is included in God's redemptive purposes. Many others have made this argument. The unique contribution is that sabbath provides a theological and ethical grounding for this commitment because sabbath is fulfilled in Jesus. Sabbath fulfilment shapes what Jesus meant by the Kingdom of God. Surprisingly, few Christian commentators make any reference to sabbath as they muster their arguments for a theological/biblical undergirding of environmental stewardship. While Barth's systematic theology is not directed towards an environmental context requiring a Christian response, he gives considerable attention to sabbath, its place as the climax of creation and its fulfilment in Jesus, as the quotations in Chapters 3 and 4 illustrate. Indeed, Barth's creation and sabbath material is remarkable given that he is not in the midst of ecological and creation debates; he is in the midst of human survival/redemptive salvation in the world of Nazism and communism (1940's and 1950's).

In recent times Barth has become the spokesperson for the 'intelligent evangelicals' (he was not always thus). Given a theology of creation has not always been a priority to evangelicals it is also remarkable how, in the evangelical context, he exegetes creation and sabbath rest in relation to concepts of redemption. Like all human beings who endeavour to explore the nature of God, Barth sees through a glass darkly. Nevertheless, he has been a towering influence in 20th century theology and his influence remains, despite the necessity for further elucidation in a vastly changed world context.

Similarities to Barth's approach can be found in the writings of the internationally known Jewish scholar and theologian, Abraham Heschel. He refers to sabbath as a gift, a gift through which heaven and earth meet. 'The Sabbath is given unto you, not you unto the Sabbath'.[100] 'The Sabbath and eternity are one—or of the same essence'.[101] His words reflect the well known words of Jesus, the one who fulfils sabbath; the one in whom heaven and earth specifically meet: 'The sabbath was made for humankind, not humankind for the sabbath' (Mark 2: 27).

I am endeavouring to develop an understanding of sabbath theology and practice which can free humanity from the captivity and consequences of competitive individualism and provide a pathway to a shared, sustainable, and equitable future—to a vocation reclaimed. This understanding is in stark contrast to the negative slavishness of sabbath encountered and criticised by Jesus. Sabbath is not about how one day in seven is to be lived, rather it is an insight into how all life is to be lived: indeed an insight into the very purpose and destiny of that living.

I explore sabbath theologically as an insight into the divine intention that earth might be embraced by heaven. A theological insight that speaks of the blessing and sanctification of the whole created order through the rest or indwelling (shekinah)[102] of God. I also explore sabbath as an ethical mandate, celebrating the relatedness of all things and the requirement, particularly from humanity, that the implications of that relatedness be respected in the service of 'common good'.

Creation and the Common Good

'Common good' has a long pedigree in scripture and in Christian history. Chapter 2 establishes the place of common good as a foundational principle, undergirding Anglican theological and ethical response to social issues, through the debates, reports and resolutions of successive Lambeth Conferences. Sabbath and the notion of common good are embedded in the ethics of the Old Testament as outlined in Chapter 3. In the New Testament, the early Christian community was said to 'hold all things in common' (Acts 4:32). Holding all things in common was seen to be a mark of Christian identity.

The notion of 'common good' has roots both within philosophy and religion. Within philosophy, 'good' or more particularly 'common good' has no necessary dependence upon religious belief. It was a notion that arose in the writings of philosophers such as Plato, Aristotle and Cicero.[103] In the writings of Aristotle, particularly in his concept *eudaimonia*[104], good is associated with virtue. That which is good is also virtuous. For Aristotle *eudaimonia* was akin to 'well-being' rather than 'happiness', although happiness might flow from well-being. Common good in this sense is a notion that relates to an ideal or desired state of both individual and social human fulfilment.

Within the Christian tradition, 'God is the consistent basis for goodness which is God's creative intention, reflecting God's character.'[105] This goodness is specifically mediated through Jesus Christ. 'For Thomas [Aquinas] the highest good is God, the next highest is the common good of the universe.'[106] Moral philosophy, as articulated by Thomas Aquinas, dominated Christianity until the Reformation. It was founded upon Aristotle's notion of 'virtue',[107] the chief of which being *caritas* (love).[108] 'Thomas emphasises that each individual must be understood amidst our complex web of relationships.'[109] This 'teleological virtue ethic'[110] assumed the notion of a 'common good', with appropriate and consistent application both within Church and within politics. Distinction between the two was not made.[111] Despite the widespread promulgation of the philosophy, in medieval life there appeared to be a complete lack of application of the ethic amongst those who taught it in the leadership of the Church and of the State.

The Reformation, activated in part because of the lack of application of the ethic, rejected the notion of a universally applicable virtue based ethic,[112] claiming that the medieval credibility gap between ethic and practice resulted not so much from human wilfulness, but from 'wrong doctrine'. The Reformation set out to reform the doctrine and by implication the praxis.[113] The Reformation insisted upon a moral code based upon rules drawn from scripture. The difficulty then, as of now, is that there are differences of opinion as to how scripture is to be read and interpreted, leading Christians of different traditions to prioritise different rules to obey.[114] Practicing *caritas* (love) as the most desired virtue was replaced with 'obedience' to scripture. The loss of an overarching majesterium, post the Reformation, and following the Enlightenment, has led western liberal democracies to replace commitment to 'common good' with a view that the role of the State is to protect individual human rights.

> A transformation from a substantive morality for the good to a formal morality of rights constitutes the central change in Western ethics over the past half a millennium, in terms of theory, practice, laws and institutions.[115]

When Thomas Jefferson uttered his: 'we hold these views to be self-evident: that all men are created equal; that they are endowed by their creator with certain inalienable rights; that amongst these are life, liberty, and the pursuit of happiness'[116] he accepted that in natural law, under God, certain rights could be assumed universal. Now that liberal democracies are largely secular, that assumption is no longer valid and an ethical code based upon individual rights becomes the protection of that which each individual deems appropriate for her or himself.

This point is made by the contemporary philosopher Alasdair MacIntyre.[117] He claims that abandonment of Aristotle's *eudaimonia* and its application in the Christian tradition, its replacement with a commitment to a 'moral code' based upon individual rights, leads inexorably down a track to nihilism.[118] He comes to this conclusion on the basis of an inner incoherence in the individual rights philosophy. On the one hand there is a rejection of a teleological virtue ethic, a refusal to accept that humanity shares a common destiny and is therefore subject to a quality of life dictated by that destiny. On the other hand there is a desire for a code which protects individuals from the inhumanities they inflict upon one another.

If there is a loss of understanding that human beings share a common (divinely intended) destiny, that there is no common virtue to which all humans can or should aspire, then 'good' is reduced to a relative concept and any idea of 'common good' becomes hard if not impossible to sustain. 'The common good is inconsistent with a pluralist society like ours. Different people have different ideas about what constitutes the 'good life' for human beings.'[119] If common good exists, it exists in a more utilitarian sense, being a condition of society which facilitates the protection of individual rights. The Old Testament scholar Walter Brueggemann writes: 'The great crisis amongst us is the crisis of 'the common good' the sense of community solidarity that binds all in a common destiny ... We face a crisis of the common good because there are powerful forces amongst us to resist the common good, to violate community solidarity and to deny a common destiny.'[120] He goes on: 'The resistance to the common good has cultic, moral and economic dimensions.'[121]

A desire for the 'common good', and particularly for political intervention in the name of 'common good', the hope of the environmental movement, is viewed suspiciously by self-interest as an undesirable attempt to impose a sectarian view point upon individuals who should be protected from illegitimate incursions into their right to make life choices as they deem fit. This point, its prevalence in western political discourse, and a thoughtful reflection upon contemporary American life is addressed by Mary Keys.[122] 'The state becomes a bureaucracy in the service of appetite aimed above all at the promotion of economic life and comfort.'[123]

Contemporary political reluctance to claim any voice for Christianity in public dialogue confirms a 'dominant western narrative for ever greater individual liberation from resented impositions, with religion interpreted primarily as a form of oppressive social control.'[124] So, is an appeal to 'common good' an inappropriate appeal in a contemporary western pluralistic society, an appeal doomed to irrelevance and failure?[125]

I am arguing that a sense of common good that emerges from Christian theology is doing no more but no less than reinforcing the imperative that has now developed with escalating urgency from the world of science: that while we might live within a pluralistic world of human culture, tradition, and expectation, we live in a single world of interdependent existence. I am using the concept of 'common good' in a particular way, to draw together the imperatives placed upon humanity by the work of contemporary science and a theological concept that Anglicans have consistently drawn upon when dealing with social or ethical issues. Put simply it is the concept of *oikos*[126] or that of a single house. 'We now have to realise we do not live on the earth, but quite literally within the earth.'[127] Within this single house 'the creation sabbath points towards the goal, which is the indwelling of God in the completed creation, the cosmic *shekinah.*'[128]

From the perspective of science, as already shown, we humans are urgently to understand and live within the limits inherent in the complex relationality of all things.[129] Science warns humanity of the serious consequences to be faced by future generations of human beings, quite apart from the impact upon diverse species and eco-systems, if large scale human exploitative activity continues as if somehow human activity exists 'apart from' and without consequence to the total biosphere.[130]

From a theological perspective, Christians generally and Anglicans in particular (see Chapter 2) have drawn upon the theology of *oikos* or a single house as a basis of moral theology. It is an application of the ethical and moral consequences that flow from believing that through the cross and resurrection Jesus creates a single, redeemed community that crosses all previously contrived boundaries, neither 'Greek nor Jew, Bond or Free, Male or Female' (Gal. 3:28). Indeed this community is nothing less than a 'New Creation'. I am using a sabbath based theology of creation, a theology fulfilled in Jesus and given an eschatological 'now and not yet' imperative, to argue that this single house is not simply a single house of humanity, but of the whole created order. Therefore 'common good' must be understood as embracing the entirety of 'all that is not God', that the 'common good' of humanity is not different to but is embraced within the 'common good' of all creation.

> We human persons need each other within communities. We human communities need each other within the community of humanity. We, humanity, need nature within the community of creation. We, the creation, need God, our Creator and Re-creator.[131]

While in the past a moral philosophy of 'common good' has related almost exclusively to the human arena, I am arguing for a sense of the common good that includes the whole of the created order, of good that is common to all, of good sought for a part of creation which can only be found in relation to the whole of creation. The ethics that flow from a sabbath creation theology imply the necessity of living within limits. The ethics imply that: 'we face a choice between a society where people accept modest sacrifices for common good, or a more contentious society where groups selfishly protect their own benefits.'[132]

In making this argument I am both implicitly and explicitly arguing for a refinement by the Church of the marks of its constancy, the classical marks: 'One, Holy, Catholic and Apostolic.'[133] In particular that 'common good' as it applies to humanity within the context of all creation must lift the mark of 'catholicity' beyond a purely anthropocentric interpretation to be expressive of that wholeness God intends within the 'New Creation' for the whole created order, a catholicity that embraces all, past present and future.

Conclusions

The environmental crisis cannot be adequately addressed if 'good' is defined only in terms of individual human rights, nor if 'values' are replaced by 'value'; if all activity is reduced to an economic value. The environmental crisis cannot be adequately addressed if human activity assumes that there are many houses in which to live, rather than a single house embracing the whole created order. Nor is it likely to be addressed at the level of national and international politics alone. It requires the active participation of all aspects of civil society and most particularly the pro-active participation of all communities of faith.

While a focus on 'sabbath' as a descriptor of creation which is common for all contributes towards a universal response, applicable to all faiths and to none,[134] the arguments in this book are specifically addressed to the Anglican community. While the environmental crisis did not specifically appear in national and international Church debate until the 1960's, international Anglicanism in the 19th and 20th centuries faced and debated many global issues with potential threat to all humanity. The following chapter examines principles which guided those debates, through the Lambeth Conferences, to establish similar principles that might be relied upon in addressing the environmental crisis today. As will be shown, a key principle was reference to the 'common good'.

CHAPTER 2

THE ANGLICAN CONTEXT: A LAMBETH PERSPECTIVE

Man is on the verge of abrogating his prerogative as the creator of society and reducing himself to nothing but its victim. ... Rich or poor, strong or weak, clever or stupid—it makes no difference, no person, no institution, no nation can be entirely self-sufficient any longer.[135]

Chapter 1 has set the environmental crisis in the context of a critical social challenge facing global humanity in the 21st century. How a response to social issues is made, or avoided, throws light upon societal and individual values, even upon a human sense of self identity. Christianity has responded to social issues over two millennia out of its sense that the incarnation dignifies humanity, and out of a belief that in Christ a new community has been formed inclusive of the whole created order.

Over time, Anglicans have developed identifiable principles upon which to base a response to social issues, principles that, in the present context, can be applied to the environmental crisis. But how is 'being Anglican' to be understood, what might constitute an Anglican, international, perspective in the contemporary world? For the Roman Catholic Church, for example, a similar basis for such a discourse would be the documents of the Second Vatican Council and more recent Catholic Encyclicals. These command a centrist authority from a Church whose roots pre-date sovereign states. On the other hand, the Anglican Church, like most Protestant Churches, is shaped by the requirements of sovereign states. Shaping Anglican global communion in this context has been significantly served for over 140 years by drawing together national Episcopal leadership to the Lambeth Conferences every ten years.

It was as a result of the Church of England's worldwide expansion in the eighteenth and more particularly the nineteenth century that the term 'Anglican' took a geographically 'universal' perspective. This expansion presented the Church with an entirely new set of problems. The Church's special status and identity in England[136] could not easily, least of all automatically, be transferred to countries with their own legitimate form of government, although initially an attempt to do so was made through Letters Patent from the Crown.[137] As this attempt quickly broke down anxiety arose, especially in South Africa, the United States and Canada, as to how the church could claim to have retained its 'catholic order' and what this might mean, theologically, liturgically, ecumenically, and in moral and ethical discourse, when it could no longer rely on the spoken and unspoken historical and theological mores inherent in being the established 'catholic' Church of England.

It was in response to this dilemma that the Lambeth Conferences began and have continued (every ten years)[138] to the present day. The conferences are not 'ecumenical councils'. They do not decide matters of theological orthodoxy, nor do they attempt to govern, or direct, the life of autonomous national churches. The conferences gather those who have been elected, or appointed, to lead autonomous Anglican dioceses, through the office of the episcopate, in the expectation that they (and by implication their churches) be in fellowship with one another through mutual respect and trust in the mores, tradition and theological inheritance implicit in the office of the Archbishop of Canterbury. The Anglican Church is a 'Communion', not a confessional Church. The conferences have, over the years, built an understanding of what such communion means. As early as 1888 it was declared, through the 'Lambeth Quadrilateral', that a minimum requirement for Anglican identity be adherence to the four pillars of the quadrilateral.[139] This quadrilateral is the cornerstone of the 'Fundamental Declaration' in the constitution of the Anglican Church of Australia.[140]

Notwithstanding the quadrilateral, the nature of Anglican 'communion', unity, and authority continues to be a matter of conversation and development, helped by ongoing ecumenical dialogue such as that with the Chalcedonian Orthodox. The Virginia Report[141] of 1997 referred to Anglican 'communion' as 'a complex and still evolving network of authority.'[142] The Lambeth Conferences were referred to as: 'embodying the Pauline concept of the Church as a body. Each part of the body is different, but every part is necessary to the body.' The Windsor Report of 2004, called in the midst of controversy over the Church's dealing with homosexuality and female episcopate, urged the Church to heed its four instruments of unity (in historical order):

> The Archbishop of Canterbury
> The Lambeth Conferences (1867)
> The Anglican Consultative Council (1971)[143]
> The Primates Meetings[144] (1978)[145]

Over 140 years, the conferences have grappled with social issues from working class poverty arising from the industrial revolution, to the Great Depression and two World Wars. The earliest conferences had to deal with the exclusive assertion to catholicity inherent in the First Vatican Council and the Roman Catholic claim of Papal infallibility (1870). Latterly conferences have dealt with issues of social inclusion, and the interrelated issues of human poverty, sustainability, and environmental degradation resulting both from human ignorance and human greed. While the Lambeth Conferences have not in themselves either sought to legislate for the whole Anglican Communion, or indeed claimed a definitive theological stand on a given issue, they have in the course of their papers and sermons, debates and resolutions, provided a guide to the manner in which Anglicans approach social and moral conundrums from a theological perspective and out of a fundamental assumption that being Anglican is to be part of the 'Holy, Catholic Church.'[146] The Lambeth Conferences have remained the primary, representative, vehicle for conversation on matters of concern for the Churches, inclusive of every diocese throughout the Anglican Communion. In latter years the representative nature of the conference has widened to include some leading clergy and lay people from across the communion.[147]

It is for these reasons that the Lambeth Conferences have been chosen as a vehicle to explore an 'Anglican perspective' to social and ethical issues generally, and by implication, to the specific ethical issues presented by the environmental crisis. It is not the aim of this chapter to search for an Anglican 'position' on this matter, but to research, from the Lambeth material, general guidelines as to how such a position might be sought.

Lambeth Origins

Lambeth origins are briefly outlined in Appendix 4. The origins have a bearing upon what might be considered an adequate response to the environmental crisis because:

1.   While centralised authority was requested, it was rejected, meaning greater reliance is placed upon mutual trust and respect in 'communion', and confidence placed in the principles upon which such communion is predicated. An Anglican response to the environmental crisis that is more than simply the opinion of some members of the Church must be convincingly based upon principles that have wide if not universal acceptance within the Anglican Communion.

2. While the presenting reason for calling the first conference
    was a crisis over the order of the Church, the underlying issue
    was the interpretation of scripture, and what it might mean to
    exist under the authority of scripture. An Anglican response to
    the environmental crisis must be founded in scripture.

Lambeth Content

Successive Lambeth Conferences have debated 874 resolutions;[148] these resolutions have focussed on the following general areas:

The order of the Anglican Church[149]

In the early years the focus related to issues (like the Colenso affair)[150] that arose as a consequence of the rapid expansion of the Church outside the boundaries of the United Kingdom. In more recent years the focus has been upon the ordination of women, first to the priesthood and more recently to the episcopate. Other issues have included liturgical revision and the capacity of the Church to encompass doctrinal difference.

The relationship between the Anglican Church and other Churches[151]

The first conference began, in its declaration, by deeply regretting the sorry divisions of the Christian Church and every Conference since has fielded discussion, received reports, and moved resolutions of encouragement that differences be overcome. In the last two conferences the relationship between Christianity and other faiths has become increasingly more significant.

Matters of Marriage, Sexuality, Gender and Personal Piety

The early conferences strongly supported prohibition of marriage after divorce, grappled with polygamy in the growing African Churches, and decried any activity on 'The Lord's Day'. More recent conferences have been dominated by discussion on homosexuality. This discussion has impinged upon 'order' in the Church through its implications for ordination.

Evangelism

The early conferences focussed upon the evangelisation of the 'heathen' in the new territories that had come under

British colonial rule.More latterly the focus has been upon evangelism in the 'first world', particularly countries such as Britain and Australia where Christianity is perceived to be in decline. This focus came to a climax at the 1988 Lambeth Conference in its call for a 'Decade of Evangelism'.

Social Issues

This is the area of interest to those who seek widely acceptable principles upon which to respond to the environmental crisis. The issues fall into two general categories:

issues of regional, or local concern, and
generic issues of global impact.

Environmental issues were not specifically addressed until the 1968 conference. However, human behaviours that have subsequently been shown to seriously impact the environment were addressed from the very beginning, for example:

1.   Economic competition which favours individuals at the expense of common good were considered inconsistent with Christian belief.[152]

2.   Rhetoric that presents consumerism, materialism, as a source of meaning and human fulfilment, were seen as demeaning.[153]

3.   Economic health was not to be treated as a goal independently from the goal of human dignity, equity and well-being. (From 1978 onwards this assertion is extended to include ecological well-being).[154]

4.   The Christian view of humanity was considered within the context of community without division or boundary, therefore activity which sets one group or nation against another or advantages one group or nation at the expense of another cannot be tolerated.[155]

5. While industrialisation and new technologies have brought extraordinary advancement in standards of living and human health, at the same time these same developments were seen to carry significant downsides that need to be addressed.[156]

While successive Lambeth Conferences, with some exceptions, have not been reticent to raise issues they believe affected the health, harmony, equity, and well-being of humankind, what appears lacking is a cogent theological and ethical foundation, with sufficient authority, to engage the whole church in the ethical issues emanating from the environmental crisis.

The Lambeth Conferences of 1998 and 2008 specifically requested the development of such a foundation. The resolution on 'creation' at the 1998 conference asks for the 'development of a theological and biblical framework to undergird the Church's response to the environmental crisis' and prays for the 'recovery of the Sabbath principle as part of the redemption of time and the restoration of the divinely intended rhythms of life.'[157] The record of the 2008 Lambeth Conference, 'Lambeth Indaba', records: 'Theologies of creation, sabbath, stewardship and 'enough' need to be developed for general use.'[158]

A cogent ethical and theological foundation, based upon consistent and carefully constructed argument from Lambeth material, is made more difficult in light of the fact that since 1978 there appears to have been little knowledge of, or reference to, the findings of previous Lambeth Conferences. 'Bishops at the most recent Lambeth conferences seem strangely unaware of what their predecessors have resolved and taught.'[159] This disconnection has left contemporary Lambeth bishops struggling adequately to ground their response to the environmental crisis in an historically developed biblical and theological foundation. 'This strong sense of building the teaching from one Lambeth Conference to the next disappeared almost without trace in 1998.'[160]

What follows is the outcome of research into this perceived loss of theological continuity. It argues that each Lambeth Conference reinforced theological guidelines that are pertinent in response to the environmental crisis. While not specifically about the environment, these guidelines include the following:

1. At the first and every subsequent Lambeth Conference the bishops sought to assert the primacy of scripture in all things, including that which undergirds Anglican response to social issues. A response to the environmental crisis must have a biblical foundation.

2. At the first and every subsequent Lambeth Conference the bishops sought to lay claim to the Church's essential catholicity. A response to the environmental crisis must be shown to reflect that which is core to Christian teaching and practice.

3. At the first and every subsequent Lambeth Conference the bishops wrestled with the tension that exists between the desire for individual human flourishing and the biblical mandate for interdependence, the promotion of 'common good'. This struggle is at the heart of the environmental crisis.

4. At the first and every subsequent Lambeth Conference the bishops wrestled with the concept of 'human vocation'. Acknowledging the weakness of human nature, they sought to understand and apply ethical precepts which could have avoided the sometimes catastrophic predicaments of their time. Given the current level of human dominance and control, understanding how humans can enhance ecological diversity and fecundity is vital.

Each of these themes is explored in the promotion of the sabbath principle in later chapters. Here I examine each in turn in relation to the Lambeth Conferences.

Lambeth and the Primacy of Scripture

The Anglican Communion has always cherished scripture and given it a central place in its life. This emphasis was historically summed up in Article 6 of the 39 Articles,[161] *Holy Scripture containeth all things necessary for salvation,* and is confirmed by the way scripture is heavily drawn on in its liturgical life. In recent times deep divisions over women's ordination and wider questions over gender and sexuality are perceived to have their root not in the issue per se, but in different ways that scripture is read. The 2008 Lambeth Conference focussed on scripture reading as a means of assisting the bishops to listen to one another over diverse ways in which scripture is interpreted, even amongst their own membership. The goal was to come to a greater understanding of how to 'handle the diversity of opinions in relation to moral and ethical issues.'[162] While from an Anglican perspective ethical, moral or social issues cannot be appropriately addressed without an adequate biblical foundation, how that foundation had come to be interpreted was perceived to be at the heart of the Church's deep divisions. It is therefore important to state the premises which are being relied upon and which are assumed to be 'Anglican'.

Colenso, Science and Biblical Criticism

When the first Lambeth Conference met in 1867, its main concern was the oversight of the rapidly growing colonial Churches and the desire, on the part of some, for an international synod which, in matters of doctrine and order, could dictate to and in certain circumstances repeal the resolutions of national, regional and diocesan synods. However, behind the agenda set by Archbishop Longley was the deeper issue of what breadth in diversity of understanding the Anglican Communion could tolerate in matters of biblical reading and reflection. Mark Chapman sees this as the ongoing dilemma within the heart of Anglicanism. 'It was 'this question of limits' [referring to the issues of universal redemption raised by Colenso and Benjamin Jowett's essay in *Essays and Reviews*[163]] that became a central concern both within and between the Churches of the Anglican Communion.'[164]

The most recent Lambeth Conference (2008), reflecting the same question, called for a study of how the Bible is read and reflected upon throughout the Anglican Communion. This call was mandated by ACC-14[165] meeting in Jamaica in 2009.[166]

While all subsequent Lambeth Conferences accepted the authority of scripture as given, the Lambeth Conferences of 1897, 1958, and 1998 made scripture a matter of critical examination and sought to further clarify the use of scripture in worship, teaching and especially as a guide for navigating the troubled pathways of a rapidly changing world. Differences of theological stance almost invariably relate to differences of biblical interpretation.

The Conference of 1897 commissioned a committee under the chair of the then Bishop of Gloucester to 'consider and report upon the subject of the critical study of Holy Scripture.'[167] Before and after Colenso there had been considerable growth in biblical historical and literary criticism and also a struggle to integrate biblical insight with the rapidly expanding field of scientific knowledge. The committee states:

We have come to realise with new conviction:

- the variety, the fullness, the continuous growth shown in the Bible, and that the Bible is a Divine Library rather than a single Book.
- the permanent value of the several books of the Old and New Testaments, when each is placed in their historical environment, and in relation to the ruling ideas of the time.[168]

Perhaps the most important paragraph of the report is:

Your committee desire in the first place to record their unfaltering conviction that the Divine authority and unique inspiration of the Holy Scriptures cannot be injuriously affected by the reverent and reasonable use of criticism in investigating the structure and composition of different books. They affirm that the Bible in historic, moral, and spiritual coherence, presents a Revelation of God, progressively given, and adapted to various ages, until it finds its completion in the Person and teaching and work of the Lord Jesus Christ. This revelation, as interpreted and applied under the guidance of the Holy Ghost, constitutes the supreme rule and ultimate standard of Christian doctrine.[169]

More than one hundred years later, the report of the study *Bible in the Life of the Church*, which had been sought by the 2008 Lambeth Conference; records remarkably similar findings:

1. Christ is the Living Word of God

2. The *Old Testament* is the foundation of Christian Scripture

3. The *Bible* is to be taken as a whole and has within it great depths of spiritual meaning.

4. There are many different literary genres in the *Bible*, which are to be distinguished carefully and consistently.

5. An accurate reading of the *Bible* is informed not threatened, by sound historical and scientific understanding: the God who inspires scripture as a true witness is the same God who created the world.

6. The *Bible* must be seen in the context of the world in which it was written and also brought into conversation or confrontation with our worlds in order to discern God's will for us today.

7. We listen to the scriptures with open hearts and attentive minds accepting their authority for our lives and expecting that we will be transformed and renewed by the continuing work of the Holy Spirit.[170]

The biblical foundation developed in response to the environmental crisis has attempted to be true to these principles. Sabbath is argued from the perspective of its fulfilment in Jesus. While 'creation' is the '*Sitz im Leben*' of sabbath, there is a progressive understanding of the origin and application of sabbath, even within the Old Testament. Sabbath needs to be understood and reinterpreted in a changing contemporary context, that lives might be transformed and renewed by it.

In his priestly ministry, Dewi Morgan[171] built a reputation as a bridge between the Church and the secular world. Because of this, his *Lambeth Speaks*, written after the 1958 Lambeth Conference, commands attention. While he makes the slightly exaggerated claim that 'the only previous occasion when the Bible was mentioned on the agenda [of a Lambeth Conference] was 1897,'[172] in his comments upon the report, *The Holy Bible its Authority and Message*[173] he notes Lambeth's claim that 'It is through the Bible that the modern world can come to understand itself'.[174]

The Bible was given pre-eminent place at the 1958 conference, resulting in no less than 12 resolutions. The bishops met in a context of greatly increased scientific discovery and technological advancement. However, they believed that the crisis caused by a clash between a literal understanding of scripture and modern critical analysis was over. 'It was in the nineteenth century that the clash between belief in the Bible as the inspired word of God and modern critical and historical studies became acute.'[175] 'It is our conviction however that the Bible has come though this travail with its authority not damaged but enhanced.'[176]

To claim, as did the conference of 1958, that the Bible is a prism through which we can make sense of our world appears too confident in a contemporary, technologically inspired context. It also seems too confident to a contemporary world which largely perceives a bible based faith at best to be irrelevant and at worse a dangerous perversion of scientific truth. However it is in the spirit of this claim that my argument is developed, inspired by Anglican leadership both before and after 1958.

Rowan Williams argues that reliance upon scientific technology alone will not sufficiently equip humanity to meet the environmental challenges of the twenty first century. He argues that values beyond materialism must be drawn upon. 'If we lived rationally we should be taking instant action about those features of our present life which are making the human future more precarious.'[177] In the third section of his *Faith in the Public Square* which he entitles 'Living with Limits', Williams argues that the biblical narrative speaks of a web of interdependent relationships in which each individual will discover fulfilment and 'wealth' not through accumulation and 'ownership', but through a response which is self giving. 'God's self-forgetting and self-sharing love is what animates every object and structure and situation in the world, and that no response to the world that is not aware of this is either truthful or sustainable.'[178]

F.D. Maurice had much earlier claimed that the Bible, a child of the Church, speaks to and of the world because the Church is itself a microcosm of the world.

> The Church contains the elements of which the world is composed. In the Church, these elements are penetrated by a uniting, reconciling power. The Church is therefore human society in its normal state; the world, that same society irregular and abnormal. The world is the Church without God; the Church is the world restored to its relation with God, taken back by him into the state for which he created it.[179]

In 1897, while Bishop of Birmingham, Charles Gore spoke of kenosis being not simply the hallmark of Christ's redemptive activity, but also the prism through which the world should be understood. The scriptures, climaxing in the revelation of God as 'self-giving', were important to Gore as the source of health and vitality for the Church in its engagement with the world. 'The canon of scripture was formed, in order that the Church may be kept constantly in touch with the original revelation, on the maintenance of which its healthy life depended.'[180]

The 1958 Lambeth Conference, having received the report *The Authority and Message of the Bible*,[181] then received and passed 12 resolutions. The resolutions which are most pertinent to principles which might undergird an environmental response are resolutions 1, 2 and 8.

Resolution 1
The Bible: The conference affirms its belief that the Bible discloses the truths about the relation of God and man which are the key to the world's predicament and is therefore deeply relevant to the modern world.

Resolution 2
The Bible: The church affirms that our Lord Jesus Christ is God's final word to man, and that in this light all Holy Scripture must be seen and interpreted, the Old Testament in terms of promise and the New Testament in terms of fulfilment.

Resolution 8
The Bible: The conference acknowledges gratefully the work of scientists in increasing man's knowledge of the universe, wherein is seen the majesty of God in his creative activity. It therefore calls upon Christian people to learn reverently from every new disclosure of truth and at the same time to bear witness to the biblical message of God and Saviour apart from whom no gift can be rightly used.[182]

In summary we can say that:

1. An Anglican response to an ethical or social issue must be founded in scripture.
2. The God who inspired scripture is the same God who created the world; therefore scientific discovery should be embraced as complimentary to biblical revelation.
3. The Bible should be read and reflected upon for the light it throws on the difficulties and complexities of life in this or any age. It is the medium through which the world can understand itself.

4. The Bible's continued interpretation enables every new context to come under the microscope of God's intended fulfilment in Jesus, 'the living word' of God.

Lambeth and Catholicity

The importance of this section lies in the Anglican claim to be part of the universal (catholic) church. This claim lifts the application of a theological proposition or an ethical mandate, beyond the limited parameters of Anglicanism into potential application within the universal Church. From its Greek etymology we understand catholicity to mean universal. 'The Greek word *katholikos* means concerning the whole (*kata*— concerning or about; *holos*—the whole, entire, universal).'[183] The word is given particular meaning in the context of belief. 'Catholic in the sense of 'orthodox' became enshrined in the Vincentian Canon: 'the catholic faith is that which is believed everywhere, always, by everyone.''[184]

The claim that the Anglican Church is part of the One, Holy, *Catholic* Church, that it is a custodian of belief that could/should be 'believed everywhere, always, by everyone', has been a constant theme of the Lambeth Conferences. As noted in the introduction to this chapter, debates at every conference about the Church's 'order', and ecumenical debates deriving from concern over church division, have all been grounded in the Anglican Church's belief in its 'catholic nature', as the starting point.

From 1867 to 1958 each Lambeth Conference concluded with the circulation of an encyclical letter which began: 'We Bishops and Archbishops of the Holy Catholic Church.'[185] Indeed, the encyclical letter of 1948 went on to claim: 'The Anglican Communion is part of the Holy Catholic Church.'[186] The Lambeth Conferences began at a time when the Roman Catholic Church was asserting its claim to universality.[187] While not overtly responding to these claims there can be little doubt that the bishops attending the conferences felt the pressure of the

Roman Catholic Church's claim to unique, divine, universal, authority and wished to reinforce the 'catholic' inheritance of Anglicanism. Chapman claims: 'the word Anglican [in the establishment of the Anglican Communion] was used as a synonym for catholicity rather than Englishness.'[188]

Resolution 11 of the 1888 Conference (the adoption of what became known as the Lambeth Quadrilateral) was a key plank in asserting the 'catholicity' of the worldwide Anglican Communion. The words of the quadrilateral had their origin in the American Protestant Episcopal Church, through the influence of the American Episcopalian, William Reed Huntingdon. Huntingdon described what he called the 'true Anglican position'. This he claims, like the City of God in the Apocalypse, may be found to be four square. He thus describes the fundamental principles of Anglicanism under four points using the analogy of a quadrilateral derived from Augustine.'[189] 'Huntingdon's four points were taken as constitutive of the Church Catholic at the General Convention of the American Episcopal Church held at Chicago in 1886.'[190]

In 1888 the Bishops adopted a slightly revised version of the Chicago Quadrilateral, intending the quadrilateral to be no more, but no less, than a benchmark to encourage union. Lambeth turned the quadrilateral into prescriptive articles of faith to define Anglican membership.

> A crucial difference, however, was that instead of simply seeing the four points as inherent parts of the deposit of faith and order, the Lambeth resolution regarded the four points as 'articles' and therefore constitutive of Anglicanism and the wider Catholic faith. Huntingdon's Anglican principle thereby became less a clamour for reconciliation and more a description of those Churches which could be accepted as members of the Anglican Communion.[191]

The first point of the quadrilateral, reflecting article 6 of the 39 Articles,[192] became: 'The Holy Scriptures of the Old and New Testaments as 'containing all things necessary for salvation'[193] and as being the rule and ultimate standard of faith.'[194] The Ecumenical Councils, reflecting the catholic tradition of the Church, argue that the biblical standard is summarised by the ancient creeds.[195] The first statement of belief within the creeds is belief in God as Creator, but what are the implications of this belief in our contemporary context? The following chapters argue that scripture intends us to understand that the relationship between God and creation is to be understood in the light of sabbath. As such, I argue this as the 'catholic' position.

The 1930 Lambeth Conference defined Anglicanism by resolution 49 as follows:

> A fellowship within the One Holy <u>Catholic</u> and Apostolic Church with Dioceses, Provinces or Regional Churches in Communion with the See of Canterbury.
>
> 1. They uphold and propagate the Catholic and Apostolic faith as set out in the Book of Common Prayer
> 2. They are particular or national Churches
> 3. They are bound together not by a central legislative and executive authority but by mutual loyalty sustained through the common counsel of bishops in conference.

The Conference set out the ideals for which the Church of England [the Anglican Church] has always stood. 'They are the ideals of the church of Christ. Prominent among them are an open Bible, a pastoral priesthood, a common worship, a standard of conduct consistent with that worship and a fearless love of truth.'[196] It is the last, 'a standard of conduct consistent with that worship and a fearless love of truth', that has led the Anglican Church to express its catholicity through the championing of moral and ethical issues.

Paul Avis, quoting Bishop Charles Gore, successively Bishop of Worcester, Birmingham, and Oxford (1853–1932), argues that Anglican catholicism is commitment to, and life lived in, the grace of God revealed in scripture:

> Anglicanism therefore bears witness to a scriptural Catholicism, 'a catholicism in which scripture is enthroned in the highest place of controlling authority ... which is rational and can court the light of all genuine enquiry; which is free to deal with the new problems and wants of a new time.'[197]

Few influenced the direction of Anglicanism more significantly at the end of the nineteenth century and the early decades of the 20th century than Bishop Gore. Gore understood Anglicanism to be deeply incarnational and its catholicity 'based upon the catholic character of Christ and upon his universal function in creation and redemption.'[198] The 'incarnational' character of Anglicanism,[199] understands catholic Christianity, not as a calling out of the world but as immersion in the world, for its transformation in Christ's name.

Gore became very concerned for the social implications of the Gospel and was frustrated by the Church's fixation on governance and doctrinal orthodoxy. He was to say: 'Christian religion is not first a philosophy or a system of ideas, but a 'way of life'.'[200] He became a strong proponent of socialism:

> Gore used the term socialism very much as Maurice, Kingsley and Westcott had used it before him, to describe a general attitude towards the relation of the individual to society. ... He was not campaigning for economic socialism and he entirely repudiated Marxist materialism as a basis for social reconstruction.[201]

His social engagement led to perhaps his most influential insight into catholicity. [He] 'held that the Church had too often lost sight of the social and ethical meaning of Catholicism being inordinately preoccupied with doctrinal orthodoxy in the east and with government in the west.'[202] Gore insisted that catholicity must be concerned with the social and ethical implications of Christ's life and teaching. Gore's definition implies that catholicity is demonstrated and affirmed in the Church and in the individual by how life is lived as much as by what is taught and believed.

In recent times this position has been well articulated by the Old Testament scholar, Walter Brueggemann when he says: '[the Gospel] is an insistence that the love of God happens in praxis, not in thought or piety and that 'knowledge of God' is a relational reality.'[203]

In his opening address to the 1968 Lambeth Conference Michael Ramsey stated: 'as the work of unity advances there will come into existence united churches not describably Anglican but in communion with us and sharing with us what we hold to be the unshaken essence of catholicity.'[204] He describes what he means by this in his 'The Gospel and the Catholic Church':

Catholicism always stands before the Church door at Wittenberg to read the truth by which she is created and by which she is also judged. 'The true treasure of the Church is the Holy Gospel of the glory and grace of God.'[205]

Ramsey, the quintessential 'Catholic' Anglican, was deeply concerned that what was believed was also experienced and immersed in the love and grace of God, which alone has the power to transform the world.

Establishing a basis for catholicity is important, for, as Benjamin Myers expresses the theology of Rowan Williams: 'Catholicity is not just one of the marks of the church's identity; it is the church's whole rationale, its form of life, its mode of encountering the world.'[206] If sabbath is an expression of catholicity, then attending to the relationships at the heart of creation must shape the Church and its mission. Sabbath fulfilled in Jesus means that in him the relationships inherent in creation are actualised. Williams' point is that in Jesus 'the rationale of all other relations is made plain.'[207]

> The message of Christ's resurrection continually draws the Church beyond itself, into a world whose lines of division have been abolished. The catholicity of the Church, therefore, is simply its capacity to accommodate human beings in the full range of their humanity.[208]

Timothy Gorringe makes the same point:

> God is encountered in the bringing of order out of chaos, in the
> reconciliation of persons and communities and in hope that God's
> glory will finally irradiate all things and that everything we do
> should be shaped by that hope. ... It follows that Christian Ethics is
> an imaginative engagement with the stories and ruminations which
> give distinctiveness to this particular community. In regard to any
> issue Christians will interrogate contemporary sciences with these
> stories and interrogate the stories with the sciences.[209]

Anglicanism's claim to full catholicity is at the heart of its DNA.
Anglicanism, as demonstrated through successive Lambeth Conferences,
insists that catholic teaching (theology) lead its membership to
transformative action and witness in the world. In our contemporary
context this involves commitment to a theology of creation, embracing
the whole world, a theology that I am arguing should be pursued
through the lens of sabbath which compels an ethical response to the
environmental crisis.

Lambeth and the Common Good

'We live in an absolutely interdependent planet and we are going to
live in a joint community that works at this, or the bright day is done. And
thereafter the dark.'[210] With these words Dame Barbara Ward addressed
the 1978 Lambeth Conference and in so doing highlighted a theme that
has run through Lambeth Conferences from the outset. Namely, that while
the Gospel message undergirds the necessity of diversity, and especially the
flourishing and uniqueness of every individual human being, 'individualism'
is a cancerous expression of this focus. 'Individualism', successive Lambeth
Conferences claim, is associated with the inequities and social evils that
beset the world at a personal, regional, national and international level. In
Lambeth Essays on Faith, Daisuke Kitagawa[211] spelt out the dilemma faced
by contemporary society which has seen extraordinary advancement

in the flourishing of individuals, but has yet to face up to the consequences
of rampant self-interest at a personal, national and international level.

> Individualism, or the doctrine of the sovereignty of the individual
> with his inalienable rights to life, liberty and the pursuit of happiness,
> as well as the innate capacity to know right from wrong, is the doctrine
> of laissez-faire economics or a society controlled by the free market
> and rationalism with its corollary, the belief in automatic progress of
> man's society was the bedrock on which classical democracy stood.
> The manner in which these propositions have been discredited in the
> last century is a story all too familiar to us.[212]

If propositions undergirding the idea of the sovereignty of the
individual were discredited 40 years ago and the intervening period has
demonstrated the environmental consequences of continuing with such an
ideal, the urgency of a different narrative is self apparent.

The individual and the common good

The 1888 report and commendation to the Churches of the Anglican
Communion on socialism,[213] was not about political or economic ideology,
but the Gospel imperative for equity and justice, for common good.

> Gore insisted [Lambeth 1908] there is nothing in the socialistic idea
> of the constitution of society which is antagonistic to Christianity
> and that its main idea is closely allied to the Christian idea.
> Furthermore the Gospel indicts the present social organisation
> and the official church with a prophetic wrath because they allow
> poverty and degradation. The legitimate church upholds an ideal
> of social obligation and fellowship upon which to model reform.[214]

The bishops consistently highlighted the self-destructiveness of
greed, the shallowness of accumulation beyond reasonable personal need,
and they condemned the misuse of power which made the wealthy richer
and subjugated the poor to greater poverty. In their commendation of
'socialism' to the Churches of the Anglican Communion, the Bishops in
their encyclical letter said in part:

> Excessive inequality in the distribution of the world's goods, vast accumulation and desperate poverty side by side, these suggest many anxious considerations to any thoughtful person, who is penetrated with the mind of Christ. ... To study schemes ... whereby ... a peaceful solution of the problems without violence or injustice, is one of the noblest pursuits which can engage the thoughts of those who strive to follow the footsteps of Christ.[215]

The 1888 conference report defined socialism as 'associated production, with a collective capital, with the view to an equitable distribution.'[216] The report went on to say: 'between Socialism thus defined and Christianity there is obviously no necessary contradiction.'[217] The report encouraged clergy: 'in sermons and lectures, to set forth the true principles of society showing how property is a trust to be administered for the good of humanity and how much of what is good and true in socialism is to be found in the precepts of Christ.'[218] Archbishop William Thomson of York gave the final address in St Paul's Cathedral, London. He spoke at some length of socialism and the need to redress the imbalance industry has created, which has provided great wealth to some while keeping others in poverty. 'Let us speak of avarice as our Lord and his Apostles speak of it as deadly sin; let us explain the sinfulness of luxury; let us charge wealth with its proper trusts.'[219]

Because socialism is now burdened with political and economic baggage that associates it with communism, it is not a definition that is at all helpful in the contemporary world. However, the moral and social imperative that lies behind the language used in 1888 remains as relevant and as urgent as it was then. Perhaps more relevant, for the problems associated with individualism have now been shown to have dire consequences of inequity and injustice between human beings, while similar inequity and injustice now prevails within the whole created order.

The next conference at which the issues of individualism and the common good were substantially addressed was the conference of 1920 and particularly in the report of the committee appointed to consider the *opportunity and duty of the Church in regard to industrial and social problems.*[220] A summary position of the report is that it is:

> ... foolish to despise individual enterprise and unduly to fetter individual liberty. But the dominant principle in a rightly ordered society will be cooperation for the common good rather than competition for private advantage.[221] .... Cooperation for the common good is the goal towards which the industrial journey of society should be directed.[222]

The 1920 conference had followed quickly on the heels of the 'Great War'. The scars of that war cast a shadow over the bishops who attended the conference, a shadow not simply caused by the war itself but emanating from their analysis that the weaknesses inherent in the human condition, if not corrected, would continue to impact the post war period. The report commences with a damning exposé of the state of industrial society and of Christianity's inability to influence it.

> It has been commonly held that different individuals, different sections or interests or classes must pursue their own self interest, and that the result of that pursuit would be the best possible condition of society as a whole. Experience has shown this doctrine is false. ... The great prophet of that false doctrine was Germany.[223]

It is difficult to argue that Christianity has as much, let alone more, influence upon the values and priorities of contemporary society as it did in 1920. The 1920 report went on to link the failure of social impact to an inadequate missiology, an inadequate evangelistic understanding, a thinking that 'turning to Christ' is only a matter for the individual.

> What then is the right aim? ... No self regarding purpose will suffice: a self centred individual security or a Church-centred corporate selfishness is equally insufficient. ... It must include the extension everywhere of the knowledge of God's sovereignty of love and the claim that his sovereign sway shall govern every part of life. ...

> We do not deny that the primary business of the Church is to deal
> with the individual ... but we want that conversion to be real and
> complete. The converted life is Christ centred not self centred.[224]

It is significant that the 1920 conference linked spiritual and material
individualism. If the focus of Christian mission is primarily, let alone
exclusively, individual salvation, an appropriate focus on common good, on
the good of creation, slips easily from view.

The bishops attending the 1920 conference could not have foreseen the
collapse of the stock market on 29 October 1929, heralding years of bitter
worldwide depression. Their encyclical letter following the conference,
however, hinted at the upheaval they foresaw if competition held sway over
the Gospel imperative of cooperation.

> Today we are confronted by a worldwide upheaval and embittered
> antagonism in social relations the course of which none can foresee.
> We seem to be involved in an internecine conflict between capital
> and labour in which each aims at an exclusive supremacy. ... Every
> trade or profession ought to be producing something that men
> want and ought to want. ... The message of Christianity in this
> matter is to make men see that here they can and must 'in love serve
> one another'.[225]

As the 1920 bishops found it impossible to predict the immediate
outcome of human self centeredness, least of all a calamitous outcome
within ten years. So too, in our contemporary context, it is impossible
and inappropriate to predict specific environmental outcomes from
current economic self centeredness. However, that each year we add to
the environmental debt, and that the debt must be paid, is as much the
terrifying conclusion of science as it must be the warning of those who
profess the Christian faith.

The 1948 Lambeth Conference, in its encyclical letter to the world
and the church, condemned insistence upon rights as an expression of
individualism when not combined with a commitment to responsibility

or duty. 'To insist only on rights turns them to wrongs unless the insistence is matched with faithful discharge of the duties which men owe to God ... to society ... and to each other.'[226] This theme, of the necessary relationship between the individual and the community (human and non-human) to which they belong, has remained constant.

Following the 1988 Conference a 'Two-Thirds World' reflection was written. The major theme of this conference had been 'evangelism', resulting in the promulgation of a 'Decade of Evangelism'. This reflection questioned the influence that an exaggerated emphasis upon the individual was having even, perhaps especially, on the promulgation of the Gospel amongst those who as yet had not accepted it, or perhaps had not heard it.

> Some of us are particularly concerned about the highly individualistic approach in evangelism in the West which is often conducted in exactly the same manner in other parts of the world, with the result that converts are being isolated and even alienated from their families and communities.[227]

This 1988 reflection echoes the 1920 warning that focus on the individual, independently of the community(ies) to which they belong, undermines the Gospel imperative of relationality. Spiritual and material well-being has a communal focus. Living 'for the other' is necessary for the health and well-being of human communities, we now know the same principle applies within the wider environmental community to which all humans belong and in which all humans hope to thrive.

Nation States and the Common Good

The idea of a nation state is relatively recent and, at least potentially, presents a challenge to Christianity which, in its catholic identity, is committed to equity and justice within the 'brotherhood' of all humanity. A situation in which a Christian enjoys citizenship of a nation that seeks advantage at the cost of others, or which tolerates let alone contributes to gross inequity, places the Christian at odds with her/his governing authorities. This is potentially, if not already, the reality when appropriate action to mitigate environmental damage is ignored or denied by national politics.

Twentieth century enterprise, technology, communication and trade have created a global world. It is the appropriate hope of every sovereign state to take advantage of this global environment for national self interest. However an ideal in which all share equitably the benefits of such a world is undermined by two realities:

1. The opportunity for advantage in a competitive model is not equal for all.

2. Recent environmental history has shown that few are prepared to take responsibility for the challenges and problems that a global world has created unless it is in perceived national self-interest to do so.

International conferences called to address the accelerating environmental crisis have consistently floundered on the hurdle of national self-interest, despite the fact that, unresolved, the environmental crisis is an obvious threat to the self-interest of every nation on earth. That 'individualism' wears national clothing has long been an observation of Lambeth Conferences. Following the 'Great War', the bishops of the 1920 Lambeth Conference had the following to say in their encyclical letter to members of the Anglican Communion:

> Each of us belongs by his birth to some one of the many nations of the world. But every Christian belongs by his second birth to one holy nation which is God's own possession. When loyalty to his own nation comes into conflict with loyalty to that holy nation of which Christ is king, a Christian must have no doubt as to which loyalty must give way.[228]

This statement addresses as clearly as any can the theological as well as the ethical imperative inherent in the Gospel that where there is conflict, the Christian is bound to stand for that citizenship which enhances and strengthens equity for the whole human family. The 1920 conference was too early to appreciate the impact that national self interest would have ecologically, however the encyclical letter went on to say: 'no selfishness in the world has been so persistent or so ruthless as national selfishness.'[229]

From 1958 onwards concern for catastrophic consequences of 'national individualism' concerned the bishops at each and every subsequent conference. Dewi Morgan's *Lambeth Speaks* provides useful insights into the minds of the Bishops at the 1958 Conference. He quotes: 'today is the day of confusion when man by his science can make darkness light, but by his sins has made the light dark.'[230] This quotation is similar to the comment of Professor Will Steffen, Chair of the Australian Climate Commission, referred to in Chapter 1, that the future of humankind at the close of the 21st century is not contingent upon further technological innovation, but overcoming the worst traits of human behaviour. The worst of this behaviour is often tied to the behaviour of human beings within nation states. Morgan again: 'frequently [human] pride is not in natural hills and valleys but in an unnatural concept called the 'state'. ... Dr Toynbee's definition of nationalism is a 'spirit which makes people feel and act and think [they are] part of any given society as if it were the whole of society.''[231]

The 1958 Lambeth report, *The Reconciling of Conflicts between and within Nations,* states: 'Nationalism can be so often perverted. Where it becomes the expression of political, racial, or cultural supremacy it denies the sovereignty of God and security of mankind.'[232]

The 1968 Lambeth Conference lamented the same theme of a global world which lacked the political will to address its most pressing problems. The conference report, *Renewal of Faith,* opines 'The organs of government are national, but our problems are global and must be faced globally.'[233] The difference this time is that the Lambeth Conference specifically addressed the signs of environmental degradation and ecological stress at the hands of an exploding global human population that seemed unaware of the pressure it was placing on natural resources and a Christian community which seemed unaware of its vocation as stewards.

> In his relation to God's creation, over which he seems to exercise control, man is in danger of failing to recognise that he is a trustee, a steward who must render account. This may be seen for example in his pollution of air, soil and ocean, and his scant regard for the balance of nature, or the needs of future generations, and his tendency, without disciplined restraint, to use the animal creation for his own ends. A theology of creation needs to be worked out which sees Christ, the agent of all creation, as inaugurating a cosmic redemption.[234]

This call for an adequately articulated theology of creation to undergird human moral responsibility in light of the environmental crisis increased in intensity in all following Lambeth Conferences, climaxing in the calls emanating from 1998 and 2008.

Bishops attending the 1978 conference were circulated a set of preparatory papers,[235] which set the tone for resolutions at the conference. Hugh Montefiore, the Bishop of Birmingham, submitted a paper entitled *Nationalism and Internationalism* in which he addresses the theme with which we are now all too familiar. He pointed out that the idea of nation states, or 'nationalism', is not a form of governance that has a long history, nor is it a form of governance that must necessarily be the only way in which a democratically free world population should chose to live and express their citizenship:

> Nationalism was invented in Europe less than two hundred years ago and has since spread over the world ... originally and essentially it is the doctrine that mankind is naturally divided into nations and that they constitute natural units of political sovereignty. ... Nature has decreed, so it is believed, that nations and states should be co-terminus.[236]

He then went on to decry the impotence of world political order that seems incapable of addressing the problems which affect the future of all humanity, issues which often find their origins amongst the prosperous, but are manifested amongst the poor.

> In this day of advanced communication, when the nations of the world are closer than ever before, virtually every important influence in the lives of men is international. Yet man's loyalty remains with the nation state. The more closely people become interdependent, the more they react by turning to their national traditions.[237]

Montefiore appropriately draws attention to the paradox that, on the one hand if an individual, or nation, lacks confidence or esteem in its engagement with others, it will be defensive and unproductive; yet on the other hand, too much confidence can lead to arrogance, leaving important matters of cohesion, equity and justice unaddressed.

> Just as an individual must have sufficient self-esteem if he is to engage in fruitful personal relationship with others, so a corporate entity such as a nation must have sufficient self esteem if it is to play its proper role in world affairs.[238] And yet nationalism in itself gives no answer to the areas of human need, kinship, cohesion and economic function.[239]

Barbara Ward, in her address to the 1978 conference, expressed hope that humanity might learn to cooperate out of necessity, very much as our ancient forebears had learnt cooperation was essential for survival.

> New insights may persuade us in time to live together not as angry separate envious tribal groupings but as a planetary people rationally dedicated to the care and maintenance of our only home. ... The new vision is more in the sense and movement of the beatitudes than our past proud certainties ... here lies the beginning of wisdom.[240]

Clearly Barbara Ward's address and Montefiore's paper had a considerable impact upon the 1978 conference, for Resolution 1, 'Today's World', stated in its prologue:

> On the one hand there are great potentialities for advancement in human well being, but there are also real possibilities of catastrophic disaster if present attitudes and the expectations of individuals do not change and if vital problems of society are not confronted by governments and through international co-operation.[241]

The 1988 Lambeth Conference had become even more aware of the looming environmental crisis as scientific consensus affirmed interdependence within the natural order and the necessity of humankind to work internationally for the common good. In his opening address Archbishop Robert Runcie stressed science's emphasis upon the necessity of cooperation for the common good.

> Scientists today would wish to stress the interdependence and balance of nature rather than a misunderstood, competitive, evolutionary theory. So I would urge strong Anglican support for the world conference on Peace, Justice and the integrity of creation.[242]

As the conference went to work, its committee, 'Christianity and the Social Order', paid particular attention to the tension that exists between the Church's commitment to the spiritual and material health and well-being of individuals, and enhancing healthy communities to which all individuals belong.

> The way forward will be found ... in new forms of mutual interdependence and the sharing of power between the individual and society, whereby society works for the good of the individual and the individual works for the good of society. ... The mission of the Church is twofold: to seek the renewal of society through the renewal of the individual, and to seek the renewal of the individual through the spiritual renewal of society.[243]

The 1998 conference became pessimistic about governmental will to act for global common good because of nationalistic priorities. 'World governments will not prioritise these issues because of perceived political cost.'[244] 'Despite this [awareness of ecological degradation and disproportionate price being paid by the poor] the social and political resolve to create a more ecologically sustainable way of life has not materialised.'[245] In light of this pessimistic analysis, the Bishops resolved that there was even greater onus of responsibility upon the Churches, and faith communities generally, to take control of the moral and ethical argument. They hoped to mobilise the loyalty of faith communities beyond the narrow confines of personal or national self interest, for the sake of a globally sustainable and ethical future.

> This then becomes a challenge for the world's faith communities. It is a challenge for those of us who inherit the Biblical story. Our Gospel is not anthropocentric, it is God-centred, it is life centred, it is Logos centred and it is Jesus Christ centred.[246]

Conclusion

From a theology of the indivisibility of the whole created order under the sovereignty of God, and the unity of all things in a new redeemed community in Christ, successive Lambeth Conferences have emphasised the need for humanity to understand itself as one family, seeking common good. The conferences have consistently highlighted the dangers of individualism, expressed both personally and nationally. The later conferences extended their warning about the impact of both personal and national individualism upon the non-human creation.

From the 1978 conference onwards, the Bishops have noted that while theology and science have converged in their understanding of global interdependence, political will has not kept pace. Environmental harmony and sustainability is not being addressed in political decision making. In light of this political reality Lambeth Conferences have emphasised the responsibility of civil society to lead. This leadership will be driven by belief in the imperative of common good.

Lambeth and the Human Vocation

Christian vocation is a calling to develop character, after the mind of Christ (Phil. 2:5); rather than commit to any specific action or profession. Fulfilling this vocation is not simply to please God, but to experience the fulfilment which God intends. The vocation of the descendants of Abraham (Christian, Jew and Muslim) is not to seek personal blessing, but to desire to be a blessing to the world (Gen. 4:3). The human vocation is described in Micah as: 'to do justice, and to love kindness and walk humbly with your God' (Mic. 6:8). Rowan Williams in his Ebor lecture[247] links this vocation with the environmental crisis when he suggests: 'ecological questions are increasingly being defined as issues of justice.'[248]

This section examines ways in which human vocation was considered at successive Lambeth Conferences, through the social issues of that time, to gain an understanding of how the 'human vocation' might be applied to the environmental crisis. Williams' summary answer might be: 'Renewing the face of the earth then is an exercise not of imposing some private human vision on a passive nature, but of living in such a way as to bring more clearly to light the interconnectedness of all things.'[249]

Early conferences, social issues and the human vocation

The first conference of 1867 met for only four days and was primarily concerned with governance of the fast growing 'Anglican Communion' in light of the Colenso crisis. However, Archbishop Longley invited other agenda suggestions.

> 'The social application of the Gospel' was the 11th and final suggestion. It was suggested by Bishop Whipple of Minnesota who was unable to come and the item lapsed. Not until 1888 did this subject get on to the agenda of a Lambeth Conference.[250]

In 1888 Bishop James Moorehouse,[251] in a context of post-industrial inequality, presented the topic of socialism as an expression of the Christian calling: 'it indicated that cooperation is the true solution of the difficulty.'[252] The argument of Moorehouse was that because God has created an interdependent, relational world, the motivation of each employer and worker (indeed of all human beings) should be focussed upon the contribution to be made, through work and production, to society as a whole rather than upon self interest and profit.

It was in 1897 however that the role or vocation of humanity in an industrialised world became a significant part of the Lambeth agenda. 'The committee on industrial problems under the chairmanship of Bishop Percival of Hereford emphasised four principles: brotherhood, labour, justice and public responsibility.'[253]

1. The principle of brotherhood. This principle ... proclaims that men are members one of another, [and] should act in all relations of life as a constant counterpoise to the instinct of competition.

2. The principle of labour. That every man is bound to service, the service of God and man ... this service is obligatory on all.

3. The principle of justice. The social order cannot ignore the interests of any of its parts and must be tested by the degree in which it delivers happy, useful and untrammelled life.

4. The principle of public responsibility. A Christian community is morally responsible for the character of its own economic and social order and for deciding to what extent matters affecting that order are to be left to individual initiative and to the unregulated play of economic forces.[254]

These four principles amplified what the 1888 conference had meant by socialism and were considered sufficiently significant by future conferences to be used as a benchmark for comment on social and economic matters. They speak directly to a Christian view of the 'human vocation' as it applies to the environmental crisis:

1. We are members not simply of one another, but of the whole creation. We are called to work cooperatively for its health and wealth being.

2. All contribute according to their means and opportunity. The environmental crisis is not the problem of government, or business, or industry alone. It is the problem of us all and all must contribute to its redemption. The greatest responsibility falls upon those who through wealth, or position, are able to exercise most influence.

3. As already noted, justice is at the heart of a biblical notion of human vocation. Environmental justice addresses growing indebtedness experienced by the natural order, its increasing inability to sustain diversity and its failing capacity to regenerate in the face of expanding human exploitation. Environmental justice also has a human face (addressed in Chapters 6 and 7) in a situation where the poor of the current world together with generations yet unborn carry a burden of diminishing health and opportunity, not of their making.

4. The principle of public responsibility was referenced through the statement: 'A Christian community is morally responsible for the character of its own economic and social order and for deciding to what extent matters affecting that order are to be left to individual initiative and to the unregulated play of economic forces.'[255] In public discourse it is the responsibility of all human beings to understand and respond to the underpinnings of contemporary life which impact environmental health and well-being—and which must be changed.

The 1920 Lambeth Conference has sometimes been described as the greatest of all Lambeth Conferences.[256] The bishops were clearly determined to address the immense post-war social issues, not least questions about human existence raised by the war itself. They did so in a manner which was strangely absent from the 1930 conference, despite the fact it met after the 'Wall Street Crash'. The 1920 report was entitled *Report of the committee appointed to consider the opportunity and duty of the Church in regard to industrial and social problems*.[257] The title reflected the prevailing view of the bishops that humanity's mission and specifically the Church's mission is shaped by context, a context which confers 'duty'. 'The primary duty of the Church (by which we mean the whole of society of Christian men) is to witness to the principles of Christ and his kingdom.'[258]

The committee report reinforced principles enunciated by previous conferences:

> We desire to reaffirm the finding of the 1897 Committee: 'Christian opinion ought to condemn the belief that economic conditions are to be left to the action of material causes and mechanical laws, uncontrolled by any moral responsibility.'[259]
>
> The principle of human value, with its insistence on the worth of the individual, needs to be complemented with the principle of human brotherhood, which teaches us that we are members one of another. The incarnation broke down the ancient barriers. Differences of race, of class, of sex, are transcended: 'we are one in Christ Jesus.'[260]

Post the bleak and dark years of war, the bishops were concerned that humanity was becoming immersed in consumerism and acquisition as escapism with the consequence that real human identity was being lost. 'We cannot accept the theory, which is indeed repudiated by modern economists that man is to be regarded simply as an acquisitive animal.'[261]

The 1920 report proposed three principles:

1. Each must be given the opportunity for a full human life, because under God all human beings are of infinite value.

2. All must work together for the common good because we are all brothers of Jesus Christ.

3.   All must care for one another. 'If one member suffers all
members suffer with it'.[262]

The conference's emphasis upon duty as an expression of human vocation
has implications for the contemporary response to the environmental crisis.
The appeal was based upon the principle of responsibility, enunciated first
in 1897. The conference affirmed that responsibility exists because we are
'members one of another', we are responsible for what we do, or neglect to
do, for and with each other. It exists because we have an intergenerational
responsibility, choices made or opportunities missed have a future impact.
Intergenerational responsibility was perceived to be important in this
post-war context; it remains a crucial theme in the context of depleted
environmental health. It is addressed in following chapters.

'Enough' and debt

Economic priorities are a guide to how human vocation is prioritised,
particularly if material prosperity is given attention above social harmony
and well-being.

The 1978 conference focus on 'enough' is important, not least because
the evangelical stream of the Church engaged in environmental issues
through the leadership of the evangelical Bishop of Winchester, John V.
Taylor, who in 1975 had published his influential *Enough is Enough*.[263] (This
subject is explored further in Chapter 7). Each of Taylor's chapters began
with a quotation from the illusions created by Charles Lutwidge Dodgson
(Lewis Carroll) in *Alice's Adventures in Wonderland*.[264] Taylor chose these
quotes to highlight proportional absurdity; that is to say, the absurdity of
economic greed which exceeds need and unnecessarily diminishes a finite
environment. The conference picked up this theme in its first resolution:
'we need to challenge the assumption that 'more is better' and 'having is
being', which add fuel to the fire of human greed.'[265] Resolution 2 went
on: 'we appeal to leaders and governments of the world to participate
actively in the establishment of a new economic order'. The resolution

made no attempt to describe what this 'new order' might look like. Taylor, in his chapter, *The Cheerful Revolution*,[266] suggests that the 'new economic order' will come about through choices each individual makes not to be 'conned'[267] by consumerist society, and to choose differently. If humans think more highly (more grandly) of themselves than they ought (Rom. 12:3), then the absurdity of unnecessary wealth, of growth that outstrips need, will be unrecognised.

Taylor's theological arguments are an articulation of what he calls the 'shalom of God'. This shalom, this contentment, well-being, harmony, Taylor argues, is made possible through a celebration of 'enough'. His argument is reinforced by Brueggemann, who, in *Journey to the Common Good* argues that gratitude, which feeds a mindset of abundance leads to neighbourliness; a sharing through which all are enabled to experience a sense of 'enough'.[268] From this theology and its ethical requirement, Chapter 7 attempts to draw some parameters or guidelines that might shape that proposed new order. For Taylor, understanding 'enough' is necessary for human self understanding.

The 1998 conference met in the context of a new millennium, and, drawing on the jubilee image of release, focussed its attention on the alleviation of third world debt. The consideration was titled *International Debt and Economic Justice*.[269] The report and its resolutions drew on familiar theological themes: the commonality of all humanity under God, the primacy of 'common good' over self centred individualism, the incompatibility of any form of debt with the generosity of God, and the obligation to 'share one another's burdens' in the community of Christ.[270] The report went on to argue that third world debt was an unjust burden upon the shoulders of those who, most often, had not chosen to create it and that it condemned innocent people to generational impoverishment.

The issue of debt forgiveness, raised so significantly in this conference, applies to the struggle for environmental sustainability;

the overshoot now measured at 140% annually,[271] is what is referred to as our accumulating environmental debt.[272] The argument, and the subsequent outcome of debt forgiven, serves to underscore the reality that a moral argument can be persuasive, even in the face of hardnosed monetary policy. The Lambeth Conferences consistently argued that morality must always take precedence over acquisitiveness in human enterprise.

In the matter of economics and the human vocation, there remains one trend that has not escaped the critique of the bishops, the trend towards a virtual economy. Williams' critique in the *Financial Times* following the 'Occupy Movement Sit-in' at St Paul's Cathedral is an important expression of concern.[273] This concern is more fully articulated in his *Faith in the Public Square*:

> The move away from a realistic focus on productivity/added value
> and towards the virtualised economy of money transactions has
> been deeply seductive, and, over a limited time-frame, spectacularly
> successful in generating purchasing power.[274]

The seriousness of this trend lies in its assumption that humanity can morally transfer 'wealth' from the virtual world to the 'real' world of human interaction when what is being transferred is not related to production or to 'value-added'. It artificially elevates human capacity to further exploit the environment.

Technology and the Human Vocation

Technological innovation has completely changed both the human and the non-human landscape since the commencement of the industrial revolution. That this change has brought advantage to humanity is clear. That it has caused suffering is also without dispute. "Technology' cannot be abstracted from that which produces it and it produces.'[275] The last forty years in particular have highlighted the damage that technological advancement can wreak upon non-human creation simply through the increased capacity it delivers to exploit the natural environment, whether the intention is well meaning or not. 'Both economic growth and technological optimism—natural allies—are versions of the delusion that there are no limits to what we can have and do.'[276] Technology can be utilised for purposes that are both benign and malignant. The pedestal upon which technology is customarily placed as the saviour and solver of all human problems and dilemmas has been consistently challenged by the bishops over the last 140 years on three grounds:

1. **Technological progress cannot/should not be the measure of human progress**

There appears to be an assumption within the technologically developed world that technological progress is inevitable, that it is always to be welcomed, and that problem solving through technology is the vocation of contemporary humanity. Rowan Williams challenges this assumption:

> We have the worst of all worlds intellectually speaking; an assumption that the human mind and will are separate from the material world so that they can impose their material needs upon it and a further assumption that to describe the problem solving function of the human brain is to describe thinking in the only way that matters.[277]

The point Williams makes is important. If as Moltmann says: 'persons become persons only in community and a human community exists only in personal relationships'[278] then technology can only contribute to human progress if it serves as a conduit to the building of relationships between human beings, and between human beings and the non-human creation. Technological advances that *have* wealth creation as their sole objective, serve to reinforce a notion that human vocations that increase wealth should be more generously rewarded than vocations that serve community building and the 'common good'. This notion has been subject to critical analysis by successive Lambeth Conferences.

A few references serve to make this point:

The pre-eminent report of the 1948 Conference was *The Christian Doctrine of Man*. The Conference report was framed with the Second World War as its immediate backdrop. In part it says:

Man is responsible to his creator for the use which he makes of the 'raw material', all drawn from the bounty of the earth in industrial and agricultural activity. God commits it to him on trust, to be used for the setting forward of his purpose—'the glory of God and the relief of man's estate'. Because this great truth has been ignored, man is becoming more and more the slave of his own machines and the rhythms they impose upon his mind and his social life.[279]

The 1958 conference dealt with the consequences of industrial innovation in its report of *Conflicts between and with Nations* and in its report on the *Family in Contemporary Society*. The former reflected:

The committee is convinced that now is the time for the Church to make some new and imaginative attempt to study and define more closely the direction in which it should move towards a deeper penetration into industrial society in all its aspects.[280]

While it is true that Bishops such as George Bell of Chichester (1929–1958), Ernest Burgmann of Canberra (1934–1960) and John Moyes of Armidale (1929–1964) did engage industrial society in the way imagined in the resolution, and Rowan Williams in the present era has consistently done so, the majority of the Church has failed to do so.

The 1968 conference considered the impact that rapid expansion of technology has had on a community of faith, inferring that trust in relationships was being replaced by trust in material technology. The report, *Renewal of Faith*, expresses it succinctly:

The growth of technological change and urbanisation has altered man's basic assumptions about himself and the world. He finds himself more and more in control of the environment and less and less in need of God. ... Consequently the society that is emerging from contemporary changes may rightly be called a 'secular society'.[281]

Concern about the rise of a 'secular society' could be understood as a defensive position by a Church that perceives its influence and membership to be on the wane. Indeed the last forty years has seen plenty of evidence that the Church has turned inward and that the focus of its energy has been its membership and survival. However, the statement of 1968, which in various forms is repeated in debate and reports in subsequent conferences, should be read in more positive light as deep concern for humanity and its place within the non-human creation. Such concern is the heart of the Gospel, reflecting Jesus' concern for the world expressed poignantly in his weeping over Jerusalem (Luke 19:41-44). In the preparatory papers for the 1978 conference Kosoke Koyama has the following to say:

> Technology has given man powerful tools to exact efficiently from the cosmos specific benefits for man. Technology is an administrative relationship of man to the cosmos. It does not make a dialogical symbolic relationship between man and the cosmos.[282]

> How can we have technological abundance and yet keep an enchanted world? How can we continue *dialogue* in the world of *application*?[283]

Koyama's contribution to the 1978 debate was condensed into the strongly worded *resolution 1* of the conference. Statement 5 of the resolution reads: 'We may need to contemplate a paradox—an increasing use of appropriate technology, while returning, where possible to many of the values of pre-industrial society.'[284] What the bishops meant by this is not clear. However, it can be assumed that what they had in mind was a challenge to contemporary convention that individuals should be encouraged to pursue self-interest through technological innovation, and instead should covet a way of life in which human interdependence and sense of community is more highly valued. That interdependence is the natural state of the cosmos and that technology has the capacity to put individual human self-interest in front of this 'natural order' was taken up by Robert Runcie in 1988.

> We seem to be discovering that individualism is not enough. ... The real world is not like that. So the questioning pursuit of the goal

of economic liberalism has led to the recent collapse of the money markets and the painful rediscovery of our interdependence. .... This interdependence, this inability of any nation to be an island is of course known...so we wake to the truth that interdependence is not the wild idea of dreamers, but simply the way things are.[285]

2.   Technology: a tool for service not of power or control

The argument by Lynn White and others that Christianity has wittingly or unwittingly contributed to both the acceptance and the encouragement of human power (dominion) over non-human creation has been discussed in the introductory chapter. That this influence continues to bear weight is argued by Moltmann in a recent publication:

> What are the interests and values governing our scientific and technological civilisation? To put it simply: the main concern is the boundless will for domination which has driven men and women to seize power over nature, and continues to do so. ... Why has this come about? The deepest reason is found in the religion of modern men and women: in Western Europe, ever since the renaissance, God has always been interpreted in an increasingly one-sided way as the 'Almighty'.[286]

Moltmann's point is that the popular understanding of 'almighty' as 'all powerful' does not appropriately reflect what the 'reign of Jesus' means, and is therefore misleading in terms of enlightening human vocation.

This point was taken up quite extensively by the 1920 Lambeth Conference in the report of the Committee appointed to consider the *Opportunity and Duty of the Church in regard to Social and Industrial Problems*. The report was damning of the established Church of England, both in England and overseas, in that its prophetic life did not disturb secular industrial society. 'We cannot claim a good record with regard to labour issues: since the beginning of the industrial revolution only a minority of the members of our Church have insisted on the social application of the Gospel.'[287] Picking up the 1897 principle of brotherhood, that regard and respect for one another should be fundamental to all human endeavour, the 1920 report went on to say:

> The corollary of this principle of brotherhood, in relation to our industrial system is that we must regard industry, not chiefly as a means of private profit or class advantage, but as an opportunity of service, ' for the glory of God and the good of man's estate.'[288]

As already noted, the 1958 conference produced a report entitled *Family in Contemporary Society*. This report concerned itself with undue power being exercised by industry over its employees resulting in adverse intrusion into family life: 'the greater the power exercised by those who control industry over the life of the total community, the more scrupulous and tender in conscience must they be in the exercise of that pervasive power.'[289] In this statement and others already referred to, the conference argued that industry and technological innovation always brings with it moral as well as technical and economic considerations. Left to itself, industry will not unreasonably judge the success or failure of its enterprise on profit. From where is the moral critique to come? Within a democratic society the instrument for regulating industrial practice in light of moral principle is government. Given a tendency by government in western democracy to be reticent to interfere in the 'freedom of the market' the burden of responsibility on faith communities to exercise this prophetic voice becomes more urgent.

The 1978 Conference was considerably helped by the quality of its preparatory papers. Koyama's essay has already been referenced. In relation to technology and power he had this to say: 'Technology is about control. ... That which is controlled cannot be called holy. Does not technology by its very function foster secularisation'?[290] Koyama's point is surely an exaggeration, for cannot the motivation of technology be service and not control? However, his point that control is the antithesis of holiness is taken up in part 2 of the book. In the meantime, it is important not to underestimate that humans find power seductive, and in relation to the environmental crisis are reluctant even to admit that giving up some measure of control is life giving, not life diminishing.

3.   **Reliance on technology becomes a reliance upon secular materialism**

There is now an expectation that each generation will be materially wealthier than the one that preceded it. "Progress' remains a basic assumption of the western way of life.'[291] Restraint is the antithesis of consumerism and the mantra of exponential growth. As Moltmann has observed:

> Technologies and sciences are always developed from particular human interests and concerns; they are never value free ... Lost is the wisdom of self restraint and the preservation of equilibrium between culture and nature which was observed earlier in 'pre-modern' or non-European societies. ... This gives rise to the decisive questions of the present time. Is the industrial society unavoidably the 'end of nature'? Or must nature be protected from industrial society?[292]

Moltmann is vulnerable to the retort frequently injected by vested interests that nature's needs are being placed above human needs. A false choice: to choose for the natural environment is in fact to choose also for humanity. As Daisuke Kitagawa succinctly argues:

> Man is at once a child of nature and a child of society. Man is however not merely an integral part of mother nature but is capable of studying, analysing and transcending it, as Reinhold Niebuhr has definitively explicated in his *Nature and Destiny of Man* ... it simply means he can be an intelligent collaborator with, or manipulator of, the forces of nature.[293]

The 1978 conference, in its first resolution, forecast: 'such [ethical] decisions will not be easy to make ... creative solutions will require technical knowledge and moral insight. ... Decisions will be not only difficult but unpopular.'[294] This projection has become painfully realised in the environmental debate where any restraint upon industry is rigorously opposed, even in the face of the argument of science that to ignore restraint is to put sustainability at risk.

Moltmann's cautionary imperative that simply because humanity has the technical capacity to undertake large exploitative undertakings does not mean they should be pursued, was echoed in the 1948 Lambeth report on the *Christian Doctrine of Man*:

> Because there are so many things which applied science has taught men how to do, it does not follow that it is right to do them. ... There are few more desperate needs at the present day than the bringing of technical discovery into true line with ethical direction.[295]

The capacity of technology to give humanity leverage for greater exploitation and expanding inequity has long been observed by successive Lambeth Conferences. This point was made very clearly in the report, *Renewal of Faith*, at the 1968 conference: 'Technology produces great benefits for man, but its misuse prevents the realization of its tremendous potential for human good. It has been exploited to make the rich richer and the poor poorer.'[296] A similar argument was made at the 1958 conference:

> Industry, on any decent or Christian principle of social obligation cannot be content to argue: 'Our only job is to produce and to pay the market price for such labour as we can attract'. It has a further obligation towards its employees, towards their family life and towards the local and national community of which it is a part.[297]

A piece of technology is simply that, but as a tool affecting human and non-human well-being it is open to moral critique. As the 1920 conference stated; 'we are bound to bring the principles of the Gospel to bear on [all human conditions] whether they obtain at home or in the remote regions of the earth.'[298]

Creation and the human vocation

While an understanding of the complexity of the environmental crisis and humanity's role within this crisis was quite late, nevertheless hints can be found as early as 1888 in the final Eucharistic sermon preached by the Archbishop of York.[299] The Archbishop declared that the world was subjected to constant change, but through change humanity was to anticipate fulfilment—to live in hope. He spoke of the various geological eras, the rise and fall of empires and the coming of God's revelation in Jesus, a revelation of hope, of a new and renewed humanity in and through which the whole creation could realise its redemption. But, he declared, human greed, selfishness, and an inability to understand the 'brotherhood' of all humanity, even within the Church, has prevented this hope of redemption from being realised.[300] Specifically the Archbishop said: 'The creation is still waiting for a redemption of which man shall be, in a measure, the instrument.'[301] Strikingly, Archbishop Thomson named division within the church as an impediment, not simply to its evangelistic capacity, but to its role in imaging the human vocation to be servants of the whole created order. Much later, David Jenkins,[302] when working for the World Council of Churches, addressed the same issue, the role of humanity in a divided world. He said:

> The question: 'What is man'? May be shifted to 'What resources do men and women have and what resources might they have for living hopefully and creatively with the questions which their life in the world puts to humanity.'[303]

Jenkins, and Williams after him, saw the environmental question not as a problem external to humanity but a problem that lay at the heart of what it means to be human.

The 1920 conference repeated the theme of Archbishop Thomson's sermon, speaking of God's activity within the whole of creation and warning the church against a false dualism in its missiology, the temptation to afford to 'spiritual' matters greater gravity than attention afforded material or physical reality.

> If the Church is to contend that the first things which are spiritual must come first, its members must not forget that our Lord, who won the victory in the spiritual sphere, intended that victory to cover the whole of life.[304]

The 1948 conference, in its report on *The Doctrine of Man* argued that humanity is, in very essence, part of the whole created order. The report said:

> As a creature, man is a child of nature. ... The environment to which
> he must adjust himself is at once natural and spiritual. ... Our need
> for bread, our need for one another and our need for God are all
> interdependent. ... Man is a creature, not the Lord of creation. He
> is therefore responsible before God for what he does to the world
> and how he uses it.[305]

This was quite a remarkable statement to come before the mid-point of the 20th century. It was taken up and built upon at the 1968 conference which prepared its attendees by providing them with a potted record of the debate and resolutions of previous conferences.[306] As noted, sadly, this appears to be the last time such an effort was made, leaving contemporary bishops, with few exceptions, ignorant of the work of their predecessors and therefore not in a position to build upon it. The *Report on Renewal of Faith* called for a restatement of Christian vocation in light of the novel moral and ethical problems of the contemporary age, in order that Christian mission might be more effective.[307]

The 1968 report resulted in the first specific resolution on the environment to emerge from a Lambeth Conference:

> Resolution 6 The conference urges all Christians in obedience to
> the doctrine of creation to take all responsible action to ensure
> man's responsible stewardship over nature; in particular in his
> relationship with animals, and with regard to the conservation of
> soil, and the prevention of the pollution of the air, soil and ocean.[308]

The 1978 conference became increasingly aware of the environmental threat, calling humanity to lay to heart the dangers in which it was placing non-human creation by ignoring its finite nature and by refusing to accept limitations to the human exploitative ambition for control. Point 11 of the conference's first resolution read:

> The resources of our planet are limited; delicate ecological balances
> can be disturbed by modern technology, or threatened by the toxic
> effects of human ingenuity. ... Alternative sources of power must be
> harnessed for use.[309]

In preparation for the 1978 conference Koyama drew on the covenantal
theme to counter the trend he perceived to be developing in contemporary
consciousness that creation was losing its 'enchantment', being reduced to a
resource controlled by humanity for technological advancement.

> The biblical image of the covenant of God does not suggest an
> 'efficient technological posture'. ... The biblical world is not a lonely
> world, it is an enchanting world. The basis for this enchantment is
> that God ... engages in dialogue with man. He does so within the
> context of creation, the cosmos. Man is surrounded by the eikon of
> the cosmos and the logos of God.[310]

Between 1978 and 1988 the issue of environmental responsibility
had become such a significant matter that it was considered necessary to
add one further 'mark' to the official mission statement of the Anglican
Communion. So, to the mandate of preaching the gospel, nurturing new
believers, caring for those in need and addressing unjust structures was
added a fifth mark: 'To strive to safeguard the integrity of creation and
sustain and renew the life of the earth.'[311]

The 1988 conference considered environmental issues in its report
Christianity and the Social Order. In so doing, the report made the important
observation that human poverty and environmental degradation are
connected. Human poverty threatens the environment because the poor do
not have the luxury of choices that might mitigate environmental damage,
while on the other hand, environmental damage accentuates human poverty.
The report noted: 'A proper understanding of the doctrine of creation carries
with it important ethical considerations about the behaviour of humanity
in relation to technology and the environment.'[312] In its work since its
establishment in 2004, the Anglican Communion Environment Network has

continued to make the link between environmental degradation and human poverty, calling on Church organisations which deal with international aid to include environmental considerations in their mandate.

The 1988 conference, in its resolution 40, identified four interrelated issues as being a threat to the planet:

> (a) unjust distribution of the world's wealth, (b) social injustice within nations, (c) the rise of militarism, (d) irreversible damage to the environment; and therefore:
>
> a) Calls upon each province and diocese to devise a programme of study, reflection and action in which the following elements should play a part:
>
> As a matter of urgency, the giving of information to our people of what is happening to our environment, and to encourage them to see stewardship of God's earth for the care of our neighbours as a necessary part of Christian discipleship and a Christian contribution to citizenship.[313]

(The full resolution can be found in Appendix 2).

'In light of the ecological crisis,'[314] the 1998 conference attempted a comprehensive theology of creation in its report, *Called to Full Humanity*.[315] More than ten years later Rowan Williams makes the same connection between 'full humanity' and ecological understanding and sensitivity: 'If we are locked into a way of life that does not honour who and what we are because it does not honour life itself and our calling to nourish it, we are not even going to know where to start in addressing the environmental challenge.'[316] The 1998 theological outline began in affirmation of the 'creation covenant' (Gen. 9, Isa. 11:24, 32), suggesting that through the covenant God 'binds all living things and the earth itself into a web of inter-relatedness'. The report emphasised the duty of human beings to 'keep' (Gen. 2:15) the earth and suggested that *radah* (dominion) (Gen. 1:26) should be understood in this light.[317] The report asserts that the (creation) covenant is renewed in Jesus, the Logos who 'became flesh, dwelt amongst us and in his life death and resurrection reveals that to be fully human is to be in communion with God and the created order.'[318]

The report went on to describe 'the Sacrament of Creation' as the 'deep communion' between God and creation. The report amplified its meaning by quoting St Basil: 'the Father, the original cause ... the Creator of all things; the Son, the creative cause ... the one through whom all things were made; the Spirit, the implementing cause ... the 'Creator of Life.'[319] In a different context, but with the same sense of urgency, 1998 recalls the 1920 call to 'sacred duty': 'to care for and love [creation] as a vehicle of God's own presence and revelation.'[320]

This sense of duty flowed into an urgent call for the exercise of a moral voice: 'There is little time. World Governments will not prioritise these [environmental] issues because of perceived political cost.'[321] The report concluded its introduction by noting that the Archbishop of Canterbury (George Carey) had said that ecological challenges were unlikely to be met satisfactorily 'without moral and spiritual motivation nurtured by the Churches', but he also acknowledged that with few exceptions 'our contribution to public debate about environmental responsibility had often been patchy and undistinguished.'[322]

The report concludes with a call for the 'reinvigoration of [sabbath], the 'feast of enoughness', not as a nostalgic symbol of religious past, but as a feast of redemption and an anticipation of the ecological harmony and sustainable equilibrium of Christ's Kingdom.'[323] Chapter 4 makes the connection between sabbath fulfilled in Jesus and his proclamation of the 'kingdom', suggesting that Jesus' understanding and identification with the former enables his declaration of the latter.

The 2008 conference did its work in 'indaba' groups without plenary sessions, debating major reports, or moving resolutions. From these conversational groups, based on a common reading of scripture, this reflection emerged. 'While many agencies can engage with environmental issues, the Church must do so from the starting point of Scripture and a credible theology.'[324] The reflection continued: 'Theologies of creation, sabbath, stewardship and 'enough' need to be developed for general use.'[325]

Conclusions

An examination of Lambeth Conference materials indicates common principles have been applied in response to social issues over 140 years and that these principles apply to the environmental crisis. These principles indicate that engaging with environmental dilemmas is not only consistent with an Anglican ethos, but demanded by it.

An Anglican response to social or ethical issues must begin in scripture

Over the 140 year period of the Lambeth Conferences, science has radically changed human perceptions. However, this period has also encouraged Anglicans to be confident that science and scripture speak of the same world and reflect its truths differently, but complimentarily.

Believing that the Bible is a key to understanding and resolving the world's predicaments, the Church seeks, from the Bible, a theological and ethical understanding of the issues faced, that human responses might be life giving and life transforming.

An Anglican response to social or ethical issues is an expression of 'catholicity'

That which is core to the Church's identity and mission, what it must be and do to be true to itself, is an expression of its catholicity. Catholicity is the character of the undivided Church. The Lambeth material makes clear that the Anglican Communion understands itself to be an integral part of the 'One Holy Catholic Church'. As such the Church is not committed to its own brand of truth but to truth that has universal application.

The Anglican Church understands its catholicity to be expressed through the manner in which theology is brought into conversation or confrontation with human behaviour in a contemporary context. Responding to the environmental crisis and especially the human vocation in light of the crisis is an expression of this catholicity.

An Anglican response to social issues assumes that when self interest and the 'Common Good' are in conflict, common good must prevail

Commitment to 'Common Good' underpins an Anglican ethical response to social issues. For the Christian community, the priority of 'Common Good' flows from belief in the 'brotherhood' or commonality of all humanity under God. It is reinforced through faith in a boundary-less redeemed community, inclusive of the whole creation, born from the death and resurrection of Jesus.

Interconnectedness is a fundamental characteristic of creation. The bishops have argued that self interested individualism (including national individualism) is a significant cause of the world's intractable problems. Commitment to 'common good' serves universal well-being, while diminished commitment to common good diminishes all life.

An Anglican response to social issues asks 'what does it mean to be human'?

The bishops contend that post industrial society, increasingly dependent upon a mechanical analysis of the world, has lost a sense of enchantment and is less open to an ethical and moral judgement of human activity, especially economic activity. They reflected that human beings have a propensity to make secondary matters absolute (e.g. the economy) and to entirely miss that which is fundamental (e.g. health and harmony that flow from interconnectedness). They insist that human 'being' flows from belonging, not acquisition. No human activity, least of all technical innovation, should lie outside the purview of moral and ethical critique.

An Anglican response to the environmental crisis needs to be both theologically and ethically grounded

Over 140 years the Lambeth Conferences have expressed the notion that there cannot be two parallel worlds. The world of science and the world of the Bible are the same world, albeit understood through contrasting prisms. The conferences have stressed that scientific discovery should be welcomed as further illuminating the wonder and potential of a created world. From the outset the conferences have celebrated the Creator and creation, recognising the responsibility of humans as stewards. Since 1968 the conferences have specifically recognised that the environmental crisis is exacerbated by human greed and over-exploitation. The last five conferences have called for the development of a theological position and the implementation of ethical practice. The last two conferences have specifically called for a response framed around a theology of 'sabbath' and 'enough'.

The second and third parts of the book are developed in response to these conclusions.

Presenting an Anglican response to the environmental crisis, the second part focuses on scripture through the lens of sabbath to argue that humanity must understand itself as part of creation, not apart from it. The interconnectedness of creation and the sabbath ethic, developed in both the Old and New Testaments, demands that priority be given to service of the common good, for it is only through the well-being of the whole that the individual can hope to flourish.

The third part of the book examines the human vocation in light of a sabbath theology, focussing in particular upon the limits that humanity must accept to its exploitative ambition, if health and sustainability are to be secured for the whole environment.

PART 2
BIBLICAL THEOLOGY: UNFOLDING SABBATH FROM CREATION TO CHRIST

The Sabbath day is the day when God's presence with and in creation becomes evident. It symbolises that God's home is indeed on earth and that the earth can find rest, a sense of security and a home for all its creatures with God.[326]

Part 1 set the ecological crisis within both its environmental and theological contexts. It then examined an Anglican framework in which social issues, such as this crisis, have been historically examined, in light of the work of successive Lambeth Conferences. This examination revealed that social issues must be examined in light of scripture, they must be tackled with the assumption that common good will prevail, and they must be tackled in a manner which is empowered by a Christian understanding of the human vocation. Part 2 argues that a rediscovery of sabbath fulfils all of these objectives, that sabbath is at heart a celebration of common good, and that living its principles, its ethical mandates, is to live the human vocation.

This insight is well summarised in a quotation from Norman Wirzba: 'By understanding the sabbath, we better appreciate who God is and what the character of all created life is.'[327]

CHAPTER 3

SABBATH AND THE UNIVERSAL REIGN OF GOD

In the sabbath command God announces that he has limited himself, bounded his action, the condition of his satisfaction with the object of his love.[328]

This chapter examines sabbath belief and practice as developed in the Old Testament. It focusses on sabbath as a window through which we might better understand the nature of the universal reign of God, especially as illumined through Genesis 2:1-4. In turn, this provides background to Jesus' self-understanding of sabbath and his reinterpretation of its prevailing practice.

If sabbath is indispensable to Christian belief and practice, then Karl Barth's teasing question (referenced in Chapter 1) gives focus to human history yet to be written: 'Will the human race keep the sabbath or not? Will it enter into its promised rest or not'?[329] Given my proposition that allegiance to sabbath is allegiance to common good, how Barth's question is answered will be determined by the weight placed, both now and into the future, on human commitment to common good. The close connection between sabbath and common good have its roots in the Old Testament. To this we now turn.

While Sabbath is named in only 15 books of the Old Testament, its significance and practice in both Jewish and Christian tradition are considerable. It is embedded in the creation narrative. It appears in both decalogues. It is understood through the various legal prescriptions that deal with the weekly Sabbath, the Sabbatical Year and the Jubilee. Its reference is present in each septet. And above all it is the constant reference point for just and right actions in relation to land, others and to God. As discussed later in this chapter, the Chronicler, responding to Jeremiah, (2 Chron. 36:20-21) concluded that Israel's collapse and exile is directly related to its inability to act in accordance with sabbath principles. As Wirzba asserts: 'from a scriptural point of view, Sabbath observance is a matter of life and death. ... Given the gravity of this command, it is clear that there must be more to it than simply a break from our regular routines.'[330]

The Decalogue prescription of sabbath occurs in Exodus 20:1-17 and again in Deuteronomy 5:6-21. However, the context of these texts gives sabbath, and the argument for its loyalty in the lives of people, different emphases. In Exodus 20 the context for sabbath is said to be 'Creation', while in Deuteronomy it is said to be the 'Exodus', the iconic Old Testament act of redemption through which the Israelite nation was born. To Christians, creation and redemption are the twin activities of God, the avenues of God's engagement beyond the divine being (*opus Dei ad extra*).[331] What God purposes to create, God also purposes to redeem. Therefore, according to the decalogue(s), sabbath is central to our understanding of both. Given the nexus between sabbath, creation, and redemption it is axiomatic that sabbath must also contribute to human understanding of the nature of God.

Sabbath origins: Scholarly debate

While there are several references to sabbath in the pre-exilic period it is not clear that these references refer to a single developed practice. There is no clear evidence that in this period there was a weekly, popular, and widespread celebration akin to later practice. An assumption that from the very beginning 'sabbath' meant a weekly, cultic, religious celebration observed by all people is very difficult to confirm from the text. There is reference to its association with the Royal House in the seventh century, as indicated by the references in 2 Kings to the roster of guards and portals of the king's house that are apparently associated with the Sabbath:

> The covered portal for use on the Sabbath that had been built inside the palace and the outer entrance for the king he (Ahaz) removed from the house of the Lord. He did this because of the King of Assyria. (2 Kings 16:18).

> This is what you are to do: one third of you, those of you who go off duty on the sabbath and guard the king's house (another third being at the gate Sur and a third at the gate behind the guards) shall guard the palace; and your two divisions that come on duty in force on the sabbath. (2 Kings 11:5-7).

These verses indicate that sabbath may have been associated with a ceremony connected to the Royal Household. Gnana Robinson[332] argues that any pre-exile biblical reference to sabbath is a reference to royal full moon day celebrations on the 15th day of the month and it was not until after the fall of the Davidic kingdom that sabbath became widely associated with seventh day rest and a celebration of Yahweh's universal sovereignty.

Of the fifteen Old Testament books that mention the sabbath, the following have texts that link Sabbath and New Moon and or appointed feasts: Leviticus (23: 2-43), Numbers (28.1.—29.31), 2 Kings (4:23), 1 Chronicles (23:31), 2 Chronicles (8:13, 31:3), Nehemiah (10:33), Isaiah (1:13, 58:13, 66:23), Lamentations (2:6), Ezekiel (46:1), Amos (8:5), and Hosea (2:11). There are three major cultic calendars in the Hebrew Bible, Leviticus 23:2-43, Numbers 28:129:39 and Ezekiel 45:13-46:15. In both Ezekiel and Numbers the sacrifices prescribed for the New Moon are more demanding than those prescribed for the Sabbath.[333] The Leviticus calendar has no prescribed sacrifices for the Sabbath. Sabbath is completely missing from the listing of feast days in Ezra Chapter 3.

Victor Hamilton,[334] with many other scholars, makes the philological link between the Hebrew word for 'rest' and the Mesopotamian word for 'full moon': 'We are of the opinion that the Hebrew noun šabbāt, the completion of the week is to be identified philologically with AKK. šapattu, the day of the full moon, the fifteenth day of the lunar month'. Rainer Albertz pushes the development of sabbath as a weekly family celebration into the period of the Babylonian Exile.[335] He argues that prior to the exile, Sabbath was the cultic new moon festival celebrated by the priests, while amongst the people there was probably a rest day associated with an agricultural taboo. He suggests the two probably came together after the exile. Andreas Schuele[336] claims that the Sabbath Festival developed out of the celebration of the full moon and cites the absence of any reference to Sabbath in Deutero-Isaiah as an indication that if Sabbath developed in the exile, its universal practice was a gradual development. Schuele goes on to note that Trito-Isaiah (Isa. 56:2,6) defines sabbath keeping as 'doing good deeds, serving Yahweh, and loving his name, which Trito-Isaiah does not consider as exclusively Jewish virtues, but as something that every human being is, or ought to be, capable of doing.'[337]

A counter position is presented by E. Haag: 'šabbāt derives from the verb šābat in the specialised meaning 'celebrate', in the OT the noun šabbāt refers consistently to the weekly day of rest that is independent of the lunar phases and has no reference to the day of the full moon.'[338] This counter position is also supported by Paul Barker,[339] although Barker's argument seems to be generated by an assumption that because Sabbath is decreed by the Decalogue it must have been practiced in the pre-exilic period. He cites Hosea 2:11: *I will put an end to all her mirth, her festivals, her new moons and her sabbaths*, as evidence of a pre-exilic weekly festival. Few scholars, however, [would] agree the text supports such a position.

Heather McKay[340] argues that Sabbath was a household observance that became a day of communal worship no earlier than 200 BCE.

Margaret Barker[341] argues that Sabbath evolved into a day of worship for Jewish people in the Roman period. She argues that during the period of the Hebrew Scriptures there is no reference to Sabbath as a communal day of worship. She cites the Qumran texts as the first clear indication that Sabbath had taken on a communal observance in the singing of psalms and the teaching of the Torah. Richard Lowery[342] points to various views on both the origins of Sabbath and its cultic importance over many centuries to warn against an assumption that Sabbath has a single meaning in the Hebrew Scriptures.

It appears therefore from the textual references and the scholarship based on them that Sabbath may well have had its origins in the rhythms and cycles of the moon, originally pagan celebrations that honoured the mystical cycles of life upon which fertility and abundance were deemed to depend. Judaism replaced the honouring of nature with the honouring of the God who is its creator.

Judaism's developing monotheism demanded expression for belief that God is sovereign, not simply in relation to all nations, but over the created order. The Israelite understanding of God's sovereignty and God's presence are interconnected. As monotheism grew stronger so too grew the need to understand how God could be present beyond the Israelite people, indeed beyond the confines of Israel or Judah. A brief excursion into Israel's sense of God's journey and presence with them is necessary as background to the final development of the creation narrative and its crowning by sabbath, the 'rest' of God, post the exile.

Sabbath and Shekinah (The Presence of God)

> Observe the sabbath day to keep it holy as the Lord your God commanded you. Six days you shall labour and do all your work. But the seventh day is the sabbath of the Lord your God: you shall not do any work—you, or your son or your daughter, or your male or female slave, or your ox or your donkey, or any of your livestock,

or the resident alien in your towns, so that your male and female slave may rest as well as you. Remember that you were a slave in the land of Egypt and the Lord your God brought you out from there with a mighty hand and an outstretched arm; therefore the Lord your God commanded you to keep the sabbath day (Deut. 5:12-15).

While the Exodus Decalogue (Exod. 20:1-17) sets sabbath in the context of creation, the Deuteronomic Decalogue sets sabbath in the course of Israel's history, in the context of the unique and quintessentially redemptive activity of God—the Exodus. In the Deuteronomic Decalogue, the Exodus is the reason why the people are commanded to keep the Sabbath. Why? God purposes to act for the sanctity of the whole creation through a people he calls to himself. Deuteronomy declares that it is through the Exodus that God has come to 'rest' specifically with his people, to set them apart, not for their sake but in fulfilment of the promise to Abraham to make them a blessing to the nations. Because God chooses to rest with them, they must rest with God. 'In returning and rest you will be saved; in quietness and in trust shall be your strength' (Isa. 30:15).

During the 40 year journey through the wilderness God's presence, *shekinah*, or resting, is known in the 'pillar of cloud by day and the fire by night' (Exod. 13:21). The presence of God is subsequently secured or carried in the Ark of the Presence containing sanctified objects identified with God's providential grace: the tablets of stone upon which the commandments were written, jars of manna and Moses' rod that budded. The presence of God or *shekinah* travelled with them, being the source of their healing and victory during the wilderness wandering and the period of the Judges. Following the reign of David and the building of the temple under Solomon, God's resting was given a home in the Jerusalem temple from where the reign of God is established over the totality of creation. In *Creation*, Margaret Barker argues that the design of the temple mimics the eternal throne of God over the whole of creation and is the place to which all should come in recognition and thankfulness of that sovereignty.[343] Yahweh's presence in Jerusalem is the source of creation's hallowing, and his people are to be its instrument.

The loss of the temple was potentially catastrophic; it amounted to a loss of the presence of God: 'how could we sing the Lord's song in a foreign land?' (Psalm 137:4). In response to this crisis 'P',[344] the priestly editor in the post exilic period, radically posited the presence of God 'shekinah' within the primeval creation narrative, indicating that the presence of God, the reign of God, was not geographically restricted. Shekinah had in fact become sabbath. Frank Crüsemann makes a similar point from his perspective on Torah:

> [Post the exile] Israel had to move beyond the foundation of previous law-functioning cult, ownership of the land, effective freedom. Independent of all presuppositions Israel was here subordinated to the divine command in the overall area of creation. We see the change in the fact that first position is given to the creation of the world instead of an altar of law.[345]

Ironically the building of the second temple subverted this insight. Sabbath does not feature as strongly as might be expected in post-exilic literature. When sabbath emerges in the Greek and especially the Roman period, it does so not as a celebration of God's hallowing of creation, but as a mark of minority identity—'Jewishness'. This distinctiveness is achieved through the development of specific and demanding halakah.[346]

In contrast with increased focus upon sabbath halakah, the early Christian community came to understand that in Jesus the reign of God over all creation was present, he was indeed *shekinah*, 'in him all the fullness of God was pleased to dwell' (Col. 1:19). While he lived his earthly life that presence was restricted. Following his death, resurrection and ascension his presence knew no restriction (lo I am with you always to the end of the age, Matt. 28:20). The resurrected Jesus embodied the fulfilment of sabbath.

Sabbath as the Jewish community had come to understand and celebrate it was abandoned. On the first day of the week the Christian community celebrated the resurrected Christ as the one who remained present with them, the one in whom sabbath had been fulfilled. This is the subject of Chapter 4.

In summary, I am arguing that God's presence (*shekinah*) or reign, in Israelite history, begins with the tribal people (tent) and becomes settled in Jerusalem (temple) for approximately 500 years. Focus on Jerusalem is destroyed by the exile and a sense of God's presence is re-positioned within creation itself (sabbath), thus God remains present with his people in Babylon or anywhere else that they have been exiled. Following the return, God's presence in sabbath is reclaimed as specifically 'Jewish' through detailed halakah in the Greek and Roman period. Regular sabbath keeping becomes part of Jewish minority identity. The presence and universal reign of God is enacted afresh in the incarnation; Jesus becomes the fulfilment of sabbath, the foundation is laid for 'the kingdom of God', nothing less than a new creation.

I now turn to an examination of sabbath practice as legislated in the Pentateuch. These requirements prescribe care for the environment and limitation upon human economic activity in order that intergenerational harmony and flourishing might be secured.

The Pentateuch and Sabbath Practice

Apart from the seventh day narrative in Gen. 2:1-4, the Pentateuch contains sabbath stipulations which do not reveal a detailed description of worship, one day in seven, but focus on the sabbatical year and the year of Jubilee. These laws and requirements have the cherishing of community life as their objective. It will be shown that, through these provisions, sabbath celebrates reciprocity. In so doing, sabbath responds to a reality at the heart of creation. 'Community is a more fundamental ontological reality than biology.'[347] These sabbatical provisions are:

1. The Sabbatical Year:

Six years you shall sow your field, and six years you shall prune your vineyard, and gather in their yield: but in the seventh year there shall be a sabbath of complete rest for the land, a sabbath for the Lord: you shall not sow your field or prune your vineyard (Lev. 25:3-4).

Every seventh year you shall grant remission of debts. And this is the manner of remission; every creditor shall remit the claim that is held against a neighbour who is a member of the community because the Lord's remission has been proclaimed (Deut. 15:1).

For six years you shall sow your land and gather its yield; but the seventh year you shall let it rest and lie fallow, so that the poor of your people may eat; and what they leave the wild animals may eat. You shall do the same with your vineyard and olive orchard. Six days you shall do your work, but on the seventh you shall rest so that your ox and donkey may have relief, and your home born slave and resident alien may be refreshed (Exod. 23:10-12).

If a member of your community, whether a Hebrew man or Hebrew woman is sold to you and works for you for six years, in the seventh year you shall set that person free. And when you send a male slave out from you a free person, you shall not send him out empty handed. Provide liberally out of your flock your threshing floor and your wine press, thus giving to him some of the bounty with which the Lord your God has blessed you (Deut. 15:12-14).

2. The Year of Jubilee:

Reference to *jubilee* occurs 21 times in the Old Testament, but its description is restricted to Leviticus Chapters 25 and 27 and Numbers Chapter 36.

In this year of jubilee you shall return, everyone of you to your property. When you make a slave of your neighbour or buy from your neighbour, you shall not cheat one another. When you buy from your neighbour you shall pay only for the number of years since the jubilee; the seller shall charge you only for the remaining crop years. If the years are more you shall increase the price, and if the years are fewer you shall diminish the price; for it is a certain number of harvests that are being sold to you (Lev. 25:13-16).

And when the jubilee of the Israelites comes then their inheritance shall be added to the inheritance of the tribe into which they have married and their inheritance shall be taken from the inheritance of our ancestral tribe (Num. 36:4).

The spirit of the Lord God is upon me, because the Lord has anointed me; he has sent me to bring good news to the oppressed, to bind up the broken hearted, to proclaim liberty to the captives, and release to the prisoners; to proclaim the year of the Lord's favour ... (Isa. 61:1-2).

The following observations can be drawn from the sabbatical provisions:

1. They apply to the land as much as to all living things that depend upon it. Indeed as we have already noted, the Chronicler seems to infer that the Sabbath provision is primarily for the health and well-being of the land (2 Chron. 36:21). If that provision is not recognised then the land will, without reference to humanity, demand its sabbaths be paid in full. 'In other words there is interconnectedness between human behaviour and the well-being of the rest of creation.'[348]

2. They apply to the vegetation upon which living things rely for food. While the land and the vegetation are separate, the health of the land is observed through the flourishing or demise of its vegetation. The health of the land is especially referenced through a sufficient supply of water, a supply that is clearly under threat in times of drought.

3. They apply to both wild and domestic animals. Following the flood, God covenants with all living things that come out of the ark (Gen. 9:8-17). The world that humans enjoy, according to the Old Testament provision of Sabbath, is to be enjoyed in the company of all other living things.

The animals are given to humans for company (Gen. 2:18-20), however, they also have claims that exist independently of humanity and humanity's needs, because God has covenanted with them.

4. They apply to land ownership and its release. According to the sabbath provision, land is not available for sale or ownership. The only right that can be bought or sold is the right to harvest the fruits of the land for a period not exceeding 50 years, a right that is relinquished if during that time the weekly, annual and sabbatical year principles are not observed. This provision is graphically played out in the narrative concerning Ahab and Naboth (see page 99), a narrative in which Jezebel is a central player. 'Practices of release (jubilee) promoted social and economic stability (cohesion). On the one hand they prevented debtors from becoming too weak on the other hand they prevented creditors from becoming too strong.'[349]

5. They apply to slaves and their release. The sabbath provision addresses one of the most inhumane and unjust impositions that humans can perpetrate on one another—slavery: the making of one human being a slave to another's economic and social advantage. The provision is made more poignant in light of Israel's Egyptian experience: they had become slaves in a period of intense privation and dependency. Privation can visit any individual or community at any time. The sabbath provision ensures that this disadvantage, involuntarily imposed, or effected through negligence, is not to be permanent, least of all passed to succeeding generations. Chapter 6 explores how individuals and communities (including the non-human creation), have become 'slaves' of an economic system that

demands minimum cost in production and maximum profit in distribution. This exploration asks how sabbath principles might be enacted in the 21st century to bring release while maintaining health and well-being to the human and non-human creation alike.

6.   They recognise that some are not able to realise economic freedom and remain dependent. In this case, protection and security must be offered by the community, perhaps through a benevolent individual (Deut. 15:17).[350] This point is explored in Chapters 6 and 7. Some peoples and some parts of the non-human creation may be forever under human care. It seems likely that because of human invasive activity, the protection of species diversity may, in some circumstances, be forever dependent on human benevolence.

7.   They appeal to human generosity of spirit because human life is only possible through the grace and generosity of God. (Deut. 15:12-14). Sabbath, and the sabbath provision, referenced through the number seven, is frequently a reference to health, wholeness and abundance. This referencing comes to a climax in the Book of Revelation, when Heaven's abundance is accentuated through the use of the number seven, (seven stars, seven candlesticks, seven seals, etc.). Through the constant use of 'seven' heaven can be described as the final fulfilment of sabbath. In the Old Testament narrative, this abundance is celebrated in iconic narratives such as Jacob's marriage to Laban's daughters, Leah and Rachel (Gen. 29:15-35): although Laban confesses that in his culture a generous response to such abundance does not apply. It is also there in the account of the healing of Naaman, at the behest of Elisha, in the waters of Jordan (2 Kings 5:1-14).

8. They address the problem of debt. 'As in the jubilee and
    as in the Lord's Prayer, debt is seen as the paradigmatic
    social evil.'[351] Sabbath provisions appear to indicate that
    community life cannot sustain long term debt. Forgiveness
    or remitting of debt is therefore essential for social cohesion.
    Between human beings, the sabbath provision is concerned
    not simply with the poverty caused by debt, but with the
    power that the wealthy wield over those who are indebted
    to them. In later chapters I examine the widespread use and
    encouragement of debt as a means of generating wealth
    and sustaining artificial growth in contemporary society.
    However, the sabbath provision does not simply deal with
    debt between human beings, it is also concerned with
    the debt that arises between human beings and the rest
    of creation. As argued in Chapter 1, this debt is growing
    exponentially and the principle of reciprocity warns that it
    cannot be sustained indefinitely without correction.

The yearly, seven-yearly and fifty-yearly sabbath provisions were
designed to safeguard the community, inclusive of the non-human creation,
against inequity and need. Inequity suffered by any part of the community
was deemed to threaten the health and well-being of the whole community.

> Moses takes the 'seven' of the sabbath and makes it into an economic
> mandate for seven years. It is an extraordinary provision that Frank
> Crüsemann calls 'the first social safety net.'[352]

The provisions make a clear assumption that individual human beings
and individual parts of the creation gain their health and well-being from
their relationship with the whole. Threat to any part is a threat to the whole.
These provisions stand in stark contrast to the assumptions of contemporary
economic behaviour in which the flourishing of an individual at the expense
of the well-being of the whole is tolerated. Chapter 4 will argue that

these cyclical provisions were not abandoned by the early Christian community. On the contrary they were assumed to be the permanent way of life of the followers of Jesus. Chapters 6 and 7 assesses how these values can be sustained in the contemporary Christian world.

It is now time to turn in detailed examination of the theology that lies behind the prescription of Sabbath in the creation narrative.

Genesis 2:1-4a: an exegesis

The central message of Genesis 2:1-4a, the rest of God, is enhanced through a chiastic like structure:

1. Thus the <u>heavens</u> and the <u>earth</u> were <u>finished</u> (2:1a)
2. and on the <u>seventh</u> day God <u>finished</u> the work he had done (2:2a)
3. and he <u>rested</u> on the <u>seventh</u> day from all the work that he had done (2:2b)
4. so God <u>blessed</u> the seventh day and <u>hallowed</u> it (2:3a)
5. because on it God <u>rested</u> from all the work that he had done (2:3b)
6. These are the generations of <u>heaven</u> and <u>earth</u> when they were created. (2:4)

In verse 2a *'finishing'* is linked to *'resting'*. In 2b *'resting'* is related to a *seven* day cycle, and in verse 3 *'blessing'* and *'hallowing'* is said to be the outcome of *'resting'*. By providing this poetic rhythm to the passage by virtue of its replicating echo, 'P' is making clear what he considers to be the heart of the blessing and hallowing that God is giving to creation; it is the 'rest' of God.

Rest

The basic meaning of rest (*šabaṭ*), is 'to cease', 'come to an end.'[353] It is never 'rest' from work; rather it infers that what was intended has been secured. Its use is not 'end' in the chronological sense, but in the sense of completion or fulfilment. Karl Barth expresses a similar view, but goes further to connect the completion of creation to what will follow in the course of history: 'The completion of God's creation as the work of rest on the seventh day enables the covenant of which creation is the external basis.'[354] The *Theological Dictionary of the Old Testament*[355] suggests the word, when associated with *sabbat* (Sabbath), has a specialised meaning of 'celebrate'. Westerman argues: 'It is a gift to humankind, a gift that regulates human existence inasmuch as the command to rule the remainder of one's work is limited by what is implied in the sanctification and blessing of the seventh day.'[356] Jürgen Moltmann focusses on this ethical dimension:

> In his rest on the Sabbath the Creator God achieves his goal, and human beings who celebrate the sabbath perceive nature as God's sabbath and allow the world to be God's creation. They heed their own status and the value of all other creatures.[357]

While the noun *sabbat*, does not occur in the text and it cannot therefore be argued that this is an 'inauguration of the Sabbath',[358] nevertheless Fishbane acknowledges: 'Its [the text's] importance may well stem from an historical need to legitimate the Sabbath day and a seven day week by locating them at the primordial time in the creation of the world.'[359]

Fishbane goes on to argue that the 'rest' of God marks a progression from the activity of God to the activity of humanity in relation to creation.[360] Fishbane's position, which infers hierarchy, God—humanity—creation, is difficult to sustain. The weight of biblical reference places humanity as a partner with the rest of creation, not above or apart from the rest of creation.[361] While an inference that responsibility for care is delegated has wide acceptance, the nature of that delegation is predicated on an understanding of the servant nature of the sovereign God. (This is explored in some detail in Chapter 7). In Israelite history prior to the exile the sovereignty of God finds tangible expression through tabernacle and temple. In the account of the making of the tabernacle there is a rare reference to *ruach elohim* (wind or spirit of God), echoing Gen. 1:2, which is said to fall upon Bezalel who is commissioned to fashion the ark, the tabernacle and the mercy seat (Exod. 31:1ff). Such reference seems to lend credence to Barker's thesis that the Tabernacle and Temple are images of the sovereign God over creation and that worship in both places is worship of the creator.[362] Brueggemann makes the same point: 'The shape of the temple is not an accidental architectural detail. It is a replica of an imagined social order.'[363]

Whether or not the text marks the transition of care from God, who remains sovereign, to humanity which must act as surrogate, the virtue of the text is that it indicates how care is to be exercised. 'Rest' is the foundational element. The Exodus Decalogue (Exod. 20:8-10) argues that the Sabbath is grounded in the 'rest' of God and that this rest is to be extended to all living things, for whom humanity has a responsibility of care:

> Remember the Sabbath day and keep it holy. Six days you shall labour and do all your work. But the seventh is a Sabbath to the Lord your God: you shall not do any work—you, your son or your daughter, your male or female slaves, your livestock or the alien resident in your towns (Exod. 20:8-10).

'Rest' is therefore not simply cessation of work, but a commentary upon the kind of life that is served by work. A life well lived is the reason for work. Work's *raison d'être* is service of the community which sustains every individual: community that is inclusive of the non-human creation. Rest restores the balance put at risk by self focussed exploitation. The need for rest is a characteristic of creation in the same way that it is characteristic of God.[364] '*In returning and rest you will be saved, in quietness and trust shall be your strength*' (Isa. 30:15).

In a collection of essays, John Polkinghorne[365] and his fellow essayists argue that God's rest is best understood as the *kenosis* of God, a fundamental and necessary characteristic of God's love.[366] They argue that self emptying or self-limitation is the fundamental characteristic of the God revealed in scripture and especially in the incarnate word of God, Jesus. Humanity, made in the image of God, is to manifest this same characteristic in the care of creation and in so doing to discover the harmony that is its fulfilment.[367] To ignore this characteristic, they argue, is to face the inevitability of conflict. At the commencement of the 21st century conflict shows no sign of waning. Mid-way through the 20th century Westerman, noting the extent of human conflict, drew the conclusion that this tragic reality:

> [Conflict] indicates the limitations of our understanding of creation.
> God created human beings in such a way that it was not necessary for
> them to stand in mortal opposition to one another so as to sustain
> themselves with food. Our experience of God's world, and this was
> also of P's, is that mortal opposition is utterly unavoidable.[368]

If increased conflict is to be avoided in a century of depleting resources and continued population expansion, creation sabbath, or rest, needs urgent rediscovery.[369] 'Unless one learns to relish the taste of sabbath while still in this world, unless one is initiated in the appreciation of eternal life, one will be unable to enjoy the taste of eternity in the world to come.'[370] While Heschel is arguing from his Jewish perspective, his point is invaluable: time and eternity are a continuum. Sabbath's 'rest' sustains life; it is also the source of its ultimate fulfilment.

Finished

'Finished', kala, appears 200 times in the Old Testament.[371] Here its meaning is directly related to sabat. While it is often used in the negative, in this case its meaning appears positive: 'The verdict is that good wins out: the first act of God is complete in the harmonious working together of all that God has created. When the word of God is complete, then it is fulfilled.'[372] In this sense, while creation is finished, it can also be understood as open to its future. 'It is an act that is complete and yet in its continuity it is without limit.'[373] There is paradox here. Each generation appreciates creation afresh, yet its essential integrity remains the same. Scientific hypotheses, (e.g. Einstein's theory of relativity or Newton's laws of motion), are possible within a universe of predictability and inner integrity.

Whatever God intended creation to be, it has now become. We can say therefore that creation sabbath is a celebration of integrity or completeness.

Genesis 2:1: 'thus the heavens and the earth were finished' looks back to Genesis 1:1: 'In the beginning when God created the heavens and the earth.' In the six 'days' of creative activity the various spatial and temporal aspects of the creator's activity are named and in the case of the sun, moon and humans the reason for their creation and their relationship to the rest of creation have been specified. On this seventh day, which unlike the other six has no reference to morning or evening,[374] the completeness of the creator's work is announced. Heidel translates: 'and on the seventh day God declared his work finished.'[375] The absence of a reference to morning and evening is almost certainly not simply a scribal error, but an indication that this is not to be understood as a 'day' in whatever way the other six are to be understood. This is not a day that follows the others, but through the announcement of God's rest, it celebrates and embraces them. Westermann makes this point when he argues: 'The meaning is clear, everything that exists in heaven and in earth is here, even what is not expressly mentioned in Genesis 1 is included here.'[376] The multitude or diversity of God's creation is integral to our understanding of its abundance. The embracing of all creation in this way prepares us for the blessing and hallowing which is to follow, for the blessing and hallowing is to be inclusive of all that this day embraces.

The repetition of Gen. 2:1, 'God **finished the work** that he had done', appears to have become a literary form. It is used in other contexts to encourage the reader to understand that an activity is complete in that it replicates God's activity in creation. The completion of the tabernacle is a primary example: 'Moses finished the work' (Exod. 40:33). As already noted, Barker argues that the commission to build the Tabernacle, and later the Temple, was in fact a commission to replicate, in tangible form, the sovereignty of God over creation; for the tabernacle was the place over which the *shekinah* of God dwelt.

Notwithstanding the harmony and wholeness intended in 'God finished his work', can the words also imply that God, having set creation in motion, no longer has involvement with it? 'Rest' or 'settling' implies the opposite. Having 'finished' creation, God remains present to it. 'Since God was on the seventh day in the position of one who had already finished his work; consequently he refrained from work on the seventh day.'[377] The emphasis is not so much cessation, understood as absence, but rest,[378] a positive state of being in and with the creation. 'Rest' is the character through which the reign of God is to be understood.

The importance to contemporary life of creation being 'finished' is to be rediscovered in its balance or wholeness. There is an inner integrity to creation as a whole that we barely understand. Modern science warns of the consequences to be incurred through large scale interference with this balance. The biblical narrative indicates the importance of human cooperation with this inner integrity for in the end, the land will demand the complete return of its sabbaths, if this balance is lost.

Seventh

Verse 2a is more than a repetition of verse 1, it references back to the beginning of creation in Gen. 1:3-5. Just as creation commenced on day one, it has completion on day seven. As to how seven emerged to be the number signifying wholeness or completion there can be no certainty. That in this narrative the number is being given 'creation status' is clear.

'Seven' may well have its origins in signifying the meeting of 'heaven and earth'. 'Three is the smallest plural number and so represents minimum unity with plurality.'[379] It is the number that represents the Divine. 'Four, understood through the four cardinal points of the compass, expresses wholeness or completion.'[380] Seven, as a number representing perfection, is perhaps therefore derived from the addition of three and four, whereas the number 12, the representative number, is perhaps derived from three times four.

It is assumed that observation of the lunar phases led to the hebdomadal (weekly) division of the month,[381] and yet lunar months do not have whole numbers of days.[382] An early reference to seven-day periods in cuneiform (23rd century BC) is a reference within the context of religious festivals and not the lunar calendar.[383] Seven plays a very significant role in both the Old and New Testaments as the following examples testify. The festivals of Passover and Tabernacles are seven-day festivals. The New Year, the Day of Atonement and Tabernacles all occur in the seventh month. Jubilee is celebrated in the year following seven times seven years. Sacrifices and ornaments for the cult are often counted in sevens. Revelations such as Joseph's interpretation of Pharaoh's dream (Gen. 41:1ff) unfold in a pattern of seven full and seven lean years. Heaven, in the Book of Revelation, is referenced through the constant use of the number seven.

While the references are almost limitless, nevertheless as an introduction to the whole of scripture this reference has a very particular purpose.[384] 'In the overall structure of the priestly document the subject of sabbath has a very remarkable function. It brackets the entire pre-Sinai portion and then leads directly into the centre of the Sinai law. By means of the seven days of creation the structure of Genesis 1 rests upon the sabbath structure of the week.'[385] Through this text 'P' establishes the hebdomadal cycle at the heart of creation and relates its observation to the experience of blessing and hallowing. 'P' would have us understand that Creation Sabbath is not simply the observing of one day in seven but a means of entry into the blessing that God intends for all life through creation. Thus Creation Sabbath celebrates creation's rhythm, rhythm that 'cannot be abrogated or legislated by human beings.'[386]

The significance of seven, be it weekly or in a much longer cycle, is not the number itself but the reality that rhythms carry limits that cannot be abrogated, that must be respected.

Blessing and Hallowing

The creation narrative has already recorded two blessings:

1. The fifth day: '*God blessed them saying 'Be fruitful and multiply and fill the waters in the seas and let birds multiply on earth*" (Gen. 1:22).

2. The sixth day: '*God blessed them and God said to them be fruitful and multiply ...*' (Gen. 1:28).

While the other two blessings were for specific species within creation, the blessing of the seventh day is a blessing upon creation in its entirety: 'Special attention is given to the seventh day, it is holy and blessed precisely as the conclusion to the work of the previous six days and can only be understood in relation to them.'[387]

The Hebrew root *b-r-k* (bless) occurs 88 times in Genesis. 'Nothing was more important than securing the blessing of God in one's life and nation.'[388] The word is used frequently in the patriarchal narratives and especially in relation to God's covenantal people. However here it is used in relation to the whole of creation:

> The first thing that God did after creating was to pronounce his blessing over the work of his hands. It is not an empty pronouncement or an expression of wish or goodwill, nor is it a bare command. Rather the blessing of God has content, it actualises and enables.[389]

Blessing gifts creation with life. 'P' makes the source of the blessing clear by the manner in which he precedes and follows the declaration of God's blessing and hallowing with a statement about God's rest. Creation is blessed and hallowed because it is embraced in the 'rest' of God. It is this 'rest' that is central to the possibility of creation's continuity. It is not further activity or effort which will secure the desired outcome of fertility and continuity, but 'rest'. Lest 'rest' be understood as a state of passivity or neutrality, it is countered by the idea of blessing. In its rest, the seventh day gives the Creation Sabbath 'power to stimulate, animate, enrich and give fullness to life.'[390]

For the *adam* to live within the blessing of God is a matter of choice.[391] 'Behold I set before you this day life and death, blessing and cursing— choose life' (Deut. 30:11ff). Blessing declared is not the same as blessing received. We have already noted 'P's apparent understanding that creation is endowed by its creator with primeval harmony, and yet the experience of history is as much hostility as harmony. In that all living things are blessed, they are blessed with the right, indeed the responsibility, for the continuity of their species.[392] However, one of the significant differences between the human and non-human creation is choice. Humans have the choice to live within the intended blessing of God or to live outside it. At the beginning of the 21st century we have at our disposal sufficient scientific knowledge, albeit disputed by some, to know what human actions are going to enable blessing to continue and what actions are going to threaten life's continuity and sustainability. That we are ignoring that information and continue to live recklessly, refusing to observe the rest that creation demands, is unconscionable. What Sabbath rest might look like in our contemporary context is the major focus of Chapters 5, 6 and 7. Each generation, or epoch of time, is presented with its own particular choices for blessing.

The blessing of the seventh day is also a blessing of time.[393] This point is given weight through the Deuteronomic Decalogue (Deut. 5:15) in which the fourth commandment is referenced through the Exodus.

The seventh day is also 'hallowed' or sanctified. Hallowing, or making holy, '*qadosh*', is the outcome of being associated with God. Religious piety popularly assumes that holiness is especially attributed to that which has been set apart, separated from the world. Many events, places, utensils, celebrations and people are described as holy because of a particular relationship with God. However, the Old Testament canon gives to the priestly author in this passage the status of being the one 'who uses the word holy for the first time in the Bible.'[394] The implication of the text is that the whole of creation is 'associated' with God. This point is forcefully made by Barth in his 'dogmatics':

> In the Sabbath God seriously accepted the world and man when he had created them, associating himself with them in the fullest possible sense ... he linked himself with a temporal act with the being and purpose and course of the world, and with the history of man.[395] To the creation itself belongs also this special event of the seventh day, the 'rest' in which the living God both confronted and associated himself with the cosmos and with man in the cosmos, thus leaving himself a place to be his own witness—alongside the witness creation gives to him.[396]

Thus, the usage of the word in the primeval story proclaims that being associated with God is not restricted to the paraphernalia of religious ceremony, but pertains to all that God has made. This challenges us to rethink conventional understanding that holiness is essentially about being set apart, rather than being set in the midst. This rethink is graphically presented by Capon:

> Holy—not a tacky haloed stain glass window but a million volt charge of electricity. The world God creates and sanctifies is a place of terrible goodness and terrible holiness. In all its beauty and all its roughness, in all its lives and deaths, and in all its matter—down to the most miniscule, it is a place no more tame than God is.[397]

Holiness emanates from God. In a sequence of concentric circles Jacob Milgrom places sabbath in the circle closest to God, thereby suggesting that the whole created order including humanity is made holy through sabbath celebration.[398] In specific reference to Israel, Milgrom notes that in exile, Israel was subject to the monthly Babylonian calendar and that the proclamation of sabbath served to focus the sanctification of time, the context of all temporal activity.[399]

A call to holiness is therefore a call to engagement with creation and with the whole of time. Holiness understood as embrace rather than separation is further explored in Chapter 5.

The Sabbath Principle and Israelite History

The earliest biblical reference to a practice of the Sabbath principle by the Israelite people is their experience of God's providential grace in the wilderness journey (Exod. 16:1-35). In response to the grumbling of the people, grumbling that threatened their identity as free people,[400] God responded by promising to pour down bread from heaven. The promise was actualised in the people's experience of manna,[401] food sufficient for their needs. It was prescribed that the people should gather sufficient each morning and that on the sixth day they should gather twice as much, sufficient to cover the seventh day. If the people gathered more than they needed it was no advantage because it became foul (Exod. 16:20). It was noted that as the people did as they were directed: 'those who gathered much had nothing over and those who gathered little had no shortage' (Exod. 16:17-18). This saying was much later taken up by Paul in his second letter to the Corinthians where, in his exultation that they be generous, he says: 'As it is written, 'The one who had much did not have too much and the one who had little did not have too little'' (2 Cor. 8:15).

The wilderness experience of the providence of God was not simply an experience in a long history of other experiences, but a foundational experience in forming the people's identity. As they looked back, the people were to recite, in creedal form, ownership of the Exodus event, and God's providence in it, as one of their formative experiences (Deut. 26:1-11). Others could identify with Judaism if they could say as a matter of faith: 'A wandering Aramean was my Father, I was a slave and he set me free, he gave me this law, he fed me with manna, he gave me this land.'[402] Trusting in the providence of God was not to be simply a necessity in hard times but a hallmark of the identity of the people of God all the time. As the instructions over the gathering of the manna indicate, restraint was the appropriate response to God's abundance. Failure to accept limitation was judged by biblical historians as well as prophetic writers to be the downfall of the people. The Chronicler concludes the history of the Israelite nation until the exile with these rather astonishing words:

> He [the Chaldean King] took into exile in Babylon those who had escaped from the sword and they became servants to him and to his sons until the establishment of the kingdom of Persia, to fulfil the word of the Lord by the mouth of Jeremiah, until the land had made up for its sabbaths. All the days that it lay desolate it kept sabbath, to fulfil seventy years (2 Chron. 36:20-21).

The Chronicler is referring to Jeremiah's condemnatory words in Chapter 17. In this passage Jeremiah strongly condemns the house of Judah for seeking false security and lacking trust in the providence of God. He describes desire for security in wealth as:

> Like the partridge hatching what it did not lay, so are all who amass wealth unjustly: in mid-life it will leave them, and at their end they will prove to be fools (Jer. 17:9-10).

By way of contrast he asserts:

> Blessed are those who trust in the Lord, whose trust is the Lord. They shall be like a tree planted by water, sending out its roots by the stream. It shall not fear when heat comes, and its leaves shall stay green: in the year of drought it is not anxious, and it does not cease to bear fruit (Jer. 17:7-8).[403]

He then links this inability to refrain, a desire for constant gratification, to the ignoring of sabbath (Jer. 17:19-27). The ignoring of sabbath is therefore attributed with terrible consequences. The implication is not simply personal; it flows into the community, it affects 'common good', it involved the loss of Jerusalem itself. 'If you do not listen to me, to keep the sabbath day holy, and to carry in no burden through the gates of Jerusalem on the sabbath day, then I will kindle a fire in its gates; it shall devour the places of Jerusalem and shall not be quenched' (Jer. 17:27). 'The covenant between God and his land consists in the Sabbath year of the earth. For the sake of this covenant Israel comes into the land and because of failure to observe the sabbath of the land is deported out of the Lord's land so that the land is given its due.'[404]

Jeremiah and the Chronicler are not concerned with the 'sabbath day' in a liturgical sense. They are concerned with the practice of restraint which enables justice and equity to be the hallmark of human transaction, thus enabling a harmonious and peaceful society. The implication of both their writings is that restraint will not ultimately be denied. If limits are ignored, if no boundaries are acknowledged, then that which has been coerced out of the natural order, out of the land, will be claimed back. Balance and equilibrium must be restored. The relevance of this passage to the current environmental debate is obvious. Accumulative environmental debt will one day enforce 'seventy years of sabbaths'.[405] The reference in 2 Chronicles to 'seventy years' implies that sufficient time and rest will be involuntary imposed, to make up for that which has been unreasonably exploited.

The Ahab and Naboth narrative, set within the context of the decline of the State of Israel, illustrates a similar point (1 Kings 21:1-16). Ahab, the King of Israel (c 874-853), a disciple of the Ba'al (*owner*) religion, enjoyed substantial holdings. Neighbouring these holdings was the small garden property of Naboth. Ahab made what he considered to be a reasonable offer for Naboth's land. What he failed to understand was Naboth's, or the Yahwist's understanding of land. It was not freehold. It was not available for sale. Naboth did not consider himself the owner of his land and was therefore not in a position to sell it. His land was his heritage to steward during his life time and to pass on to his children in his death. The sabbath principle expressed through jubilee was that if such land were lost through negligence, ill fortune, or theft from the more powerful, it was to be returned in the year of jubilee (Lev. 25:8-55), for no one, or no family could remain disinherited in the presence of the God who provides for all.[406]

Set within the context of Ahab and his successors' acquisitive culture, the Elijah and Elisha narratives paint a very different picture. They rekindle the desert narrative of feeding by manna as illustrated in the stories of the widow of Zarephath and the jar of oil (1 Kings 17:8-16); Elisha and the widow's oil (2 Kings 4:1-7); and Elisha feeds one hundred men (2 Kings 4:42-44). All these narratives remind the people that faith and trust, not acquisition, are their source of abundance and well-being. Through faith even a very small amount can become enough. In both the Elijah and the Elisha narratives there is an oblique reference to the sabbath principle of abundance though the use of the numeral 'seven'. In the midst of the debilitating drought Ahab is told by Elijah to go and look for a cloud seven times, on the seventh occasion the cloud appears (1 Kings 18:41ff). Elisha brings a child back to life who sneezes seven times (2 Kings 4:35) and Naaman the leper and commander of the army of the king of Aram is told to wash seven times in the Jordan to heal his leprosy (2 Kings 5:10ff). Elijah, described as the iconic prophet of the Old Testament, the one who appears beside Jesus on the Mount of Transfiguration (Mark 9:2-8), is perceived to be the one who calls the people back to the desert faith, faith based on the providence and grace of God.

Amos, the eighth century prophet most associated with justice and righteousness declares:

> Hear this, you that trample on the needy, and bring to ruin the poor of the land, saying, 'when will the new moon be over so that we may sell grain; and the sabbath so that we may offer wheat for sale'? We will make the ephah small and the shekel great, and practice deceit with false balances, buying the poor for silver and the needy for a pair of sandals, and selling the sweepings of the wheat (Amos 8:4-6).

Amos is concerned about what he perceives to be a disjunction between cultic observance and daily life. He warns the people not to seek the 'day of the Lord', which he describes as a dark and frightening day because of the consequences of the people's injustice and greed. (Amos 5:18-24). While sabbath is not given particular attention, he groups all religious observance together as unacceptable and an inappropriate method of appeasing the consequences of greedy practice.

> I hate I despise your festivals ... but let justice roll down like waters and righteousness like an ever-flowing stream. (Amos 5:21-24).

As Richard Bauckham argues:

> Sabbatical institutions: the weekly sabbath, the sabbatical year, every seven years and the jubilee year (the sabbath of sabbaths), every fifty years ... are not just about good farming practice, but about keeping the economic drive in human life within its place and not letting it dominate the whole of life.[407]

In the final days of the Kingdom of Judah, Jeremiah made a desperate plea to the leadership to demonstrate commitment to Yahweh through the implementation of the Sabbatical year (Jer. 34:8-22). In the face of imminent danger from the Babylonians the leadership was extracting as much economic advantage as they could to shore up their position through the use of (Hebrew) slaves. Wealth could be increased if labour charges did not have to be paid.[408] Jeremiah's point was that security would not be found in economic advantage, but in justice and equity. He declared that rather than building security they were contributing to their own downfall. Jeremiah wanted the Israelite leadership to implement the provisions of the Sabbatical year and free the slaves. As Brueggemann describes it:

> Moses intends that none in the community of the emancipated should be landless, or placeless, or homeless in a covenantal society. Covenantal times are organized in order to commit the economically advantaged to a common future with the economically marginalised.[409]

Under pressure from the prophet, King Zedekiah released the slaves (Jer. 34:10). Soon after however he reversed the decision and made the people slaves again (Jer. 34:11). In response to this double action Jeremiah condemned Zedekiah. He reminded Zedekiah and the secular and religious leadership that they were themselves slaves in Egypt, set free by God. In response to this divine generosity they must not keep anyone in perpetual slavery and that Hebrew slaves in particular were to be set free every seven years.

Despite the fact that the leadership would not implement the provisions of the sabbatical year, Jeremiah prophesied that the blessings of the sabbatical year would not be denied to the natural order. The bodies of those in leadership, he prophesied, would become food for the wild animals and the birds (Jer. 34:20); thus fulfilling one of the objectives of the year, to provide for wild life that might otherwise be squeezed out of the food chain by the activity of human beings.

The concept of blessing through limited acquisition seems to be one of the continuing blind spots of humankind through the centuries into the modern era. The following statement from the Church of England in 2005 is illustrative:

> Humankind is easily ensnared in the culture of ownership. Even if it is understood intellectually that the world is God's, and the human role of stewardship means only to have stewardship under him, people can still be caught by the desire for possessions, which is by its nature voracious. ... In the midst of this the Christian is called to stop: completely, properly for a period of time. Not just to pause for a breath before carrying on consuming, but to take a deep dive into God's peace.[410]

The Provisions of the Sabbatical year testify to the obligations inherent in our being dependent beings. Our dependence places restrictions which we might try to ignore, but the consequences of our having done so accumulate. The Old Testament references cited above have underlined a fundamental reality: not to meet the obligations inherent in dependency upon the land, the natural order and other human beings has consequences in accumulated debt. Debt undermines social cohesion—common good. We are bound by the obligations inherent in relationships.

Jesus and Genesis 2:1-4

Sabbath and its fulfilment in Jesus is the subject of Chapter 4, however before leaving this chapter, 'Sabbath and the Universal Reign of God' I want to briefly allude to connections that will be made more fully later.

Genesis 2:1-4 has been seen to be not simply a recording of the last day in a sequence of seven but the embrace of all that has preceded it; it is indeed the 'crown of creation'. Is it similarly the 'crown' of a new creation? Paul (2 Cor. 5:17), speaks of a 'new creation' inaugurated by the resurrection. New Testament writers proclaim that since the 'creation of the world', Rom. 1:20, 8:19, 8:22, Heb. 9:26, 4:3, Rev. 11:8, 17:8, there remained another dimension of creation to be experienced, or perhaps to be reclaimed. It is described as being whole, without division:

> For neither circumcision, nor uncircumcision is anything, but a new creation is everything. (Gal. 6:15).

> In the new creation there is no longer Greek or Jew, circumcised and uncircumcised, barbarian, Scythian, slave and free: but Christ is all in all. (Col. 3:11).

In his recording of Jesus' words from the cross, 'It is finished' (John 19:30), John connects Jesus' death (and resurrection) with Genesis 2.1. John is the Gospel writer (John 1:3) who most specifically links the incarnation to the activity of God in creation. It appears that in his account of the crucifixion he is intending the reader to understand that in Jesus's death and resurrection a new creation is being inaugurated. The first creation is 'complete' through God's rest, God's presence; the new creation is complete through the presence or resting of the resurrected Christ.

This theme is taken up somewhat enigmatically by the writer to the Hebrews (Heb. 4:1-11). He places Psalm 95:11 'They shall not enter my rest' in juxtaposition with Genesis 2:2. 'For in one place it speaks about the seventh day as follows: and God rested on the seventh day from all his works.'[411] The idea of God (in Jesus) 'resting' appears to be contradicted in the exchange between Jesus and the Pharisees in relation to 'doing good' on the sabbath where, in part of his response, Jesus says: 'My Father is still working and I also am working.' (John 5:17). On the face of it the words seem to contradict 'God finished the work that he had done.' (Gen. 2:2).[412] Canon W.H. Vanstone argues that the primary 'work' of God is the refreshment of rest: rest being not an absence of work, let alone of presence, but an opportunity for renewal.[413] The dispute occurred over the curing of the crippled man at the pool of Bethzatha on the Sabbath Day.[414] The writer to the Hebrews is arguing to his Jewish Christian audience that the 'rest' that God intends is not negated by the disobedience of the wilderness because 'rest' is a promise inherent in creation itself. Behind his argument lies the inference that effort or work aimed at individual security or rest is illusory: 'In this transient world there is no ultimate security, no final achievement, no objective fulfilment.'[415] Brueggemann argues: 'The Sabbath in Gen. 2:1-4a (is) a liturgical cessation of all productivity so that the creatures in imitation of God may be at peaceable rest.'[416]

The Hebrews' passage helpfully reaffirms that sabbath rest is both a life principle and a destiny to which we travel. Inasmuch as our *end is in our beginning*,[417] commitment to this principle now becomes even more urgent. 'Sabbath observance is what we work towards as our most important and most encompassing goal.'[418] Wirzba's insight is taken up in Chapter 6 where, it is argued, the destiny to which we travel should shape present priorities.

Conclusions

The experience of God's presence in the wilderness (pillar and cloud) was known as 'shekinah'. Following the settlement and the establishment of monarchy the presence, the reign, the 'shekinah' of God found a permanent home in the temple. The fall of Jerusalem and destruction of the temple, presented a crisis of belief. How and in what way was God's sovereignty to be known? In the midst of this crisis sabbath was given a place within the primeval creation narrative, and came to express, without restriction of time or place, the universal reign of God.

Readers of the canon of scripture are to understand that sabbath reveals the enduring and universal character of God through God's engagement with creation. Sabbath is far more than the ritual or cultic prescription of one day in seven. Sabbath's significance lies in its capacity to reveal how God and God's reign is to be understood and encountered within both the created order and within human history. This sovereignty is to be understood through the manner in which God 'rests' with creation.

God's 'rest' is illumined through 'blessing' and 'hallowing'. Blessing is the enabling of life to flourish. Hallowing is the endowing of all creation with value. Thus God's universal reign, through the window of sabbath is to be understood as God endowing life with a capacity to flourish, bestowing upon it the value of connectedness to the divine being. 'Rest' brings blessing and sanctification, the gift of abundance, diversity and continuity.[419] Elizabeth Barrett Browning captures something of this spirit in her *Aurora Leigh*: 'Earth's crammed with heaven, And Every Bush afire with God: But only He who sees takes off his shoes, the rest will sit around and pluck blackberries.'[420] The failure of the human enterprise to understand and live within the sovereignty of God as understood in sabbath characterises the present generation as much as it does all previous generations.

For the Christian community, knowing the presence or 'rest' of God has its foundations in the Old Testament narrative, but this knowing takes human flesh in the person of Jesus. As a consequence what sabbath means as an expression of God's rest and presence is necessarily reinterpreted in light both of Jesus' life and teaching and the early Church's understanding. It is to this context we now turn.

CHAPTER 4

JESUS: 'LORD OF THE SABBATH'

*The actuality of the life of Jesus Christ declares the completely
universal concern of God over the restrictive and partial concerns of
men, not least men of religion.*[421]

Introduction: Bridging the Old and New Testaments

Chapter 3 examined how sabbath became expressive of the universal
reign of God and how the human vocation in the Old Testament is fulfilled
in the keeping of sabbath. This chapter explores how the universal reign
of God and the human vocation are fulfilled in Jesus and therefore how
Jesus is the fulfilment of sabbath. Reading scripture in the light of Christ
is the Christian hermeneutic. 'The New Testament writers assume the
Old Testament as given.'[422] The biblical narrative is not simply climaxed in
Christ, it is to be read in the light of Christ.

The early Christian community was born out of synagogue
communities in the 1st century. Sabbath practice, an expression of Jewish self
understanding and identity, had become a cultic, institutional requirement
within these communities. Because sabbath was understood to be a gift
to the Jewish community alone, its keeping by the fledgling Christian
community, as it grew away from the synagogue communities, was bound
to pose questions of reinterpretation, or abandonment.

The questioning of sabbath would have been accelerated because conflict between Jesus and the Pharisees often had a sabbath focus. While the religious authorities wanted to engage (entrap) Jesus over religious law keeping, *hālākā*,[423] Jesus would not be so confined. The Gospel writers use these conflicts to take Jesus and his message beyond the cultural and religious boundaries of Judaism. The casuistry[424] found in sabbath regulation together with voluminous and detailed halakah appear to have been the reason for this conflict.[425] Specific implications to be drawn from this conflict are dealt with later in this chapter. However, it is helpful to note at the outset that a boundary-less[426] humanity appears to be the implication of Jesus' emphasis that the life-giving abundance of sabbath should be accessed by all. Jesus' inclusive stand was an unacceptable threat to a religious institution which assumed a proprietary right to define sabbath, rather than be defined by it. If sabbath is redefined by Jesus for the sake of the 'cosmos,'[427] not simply humanity, let alone a small group of humanity, then sabbath can truly be understood as encompassing 'common good'.

Sabbath and its ongoing life in the Christian era have long been debated. Did Jesus 'do away' with sabbath and its celebration on the seventh day, or was it transferred to *The Lord's Day*, the day of resurrection on the first day of the week? This debate is pursued in numerous volumes such as *The Lord of the Sabbath*[428] and in Henry Sturcke's substantive research, *Encountering the Rest of God: How Jesus came to Personify the Sabbath.*[429]

Sturcke's very detailed analysis of the origins and practice of sabbath is particularly interesting because of his starting point and his conclusion. His approach came out of two decades of membership within a sabbatarian church. His conclusion was that 'the function performed by Sabbath in the faith of the Jewish people at the time of Jesus became, for Christians, fulfilled in Jesus.'[430] His reason for this conclusion was that in Jesus the 'boundary between the sacred and profane had been transcended.'[431] The boundary had been transcended in the proclamation of the 'kingdom', the 'new creation'.

Sabbath: The Universal Reign of God

Chapter 3 examined the relationship between shekinah and sabbath in the Old Testament, particularly in light of the loss of Jerusalem and the temple. This chapter argues that shekinah and sabbath are fulfilled in Jesus, indeed that the theological proposition and ethical mandate inherent in sabbath undergirds Jesus' proclamation of the 'Kingdom of God'. Further, because the 'Kingdom of God' is central to the Gospel and therefore at the heart of the Church's mission, Chapters 5, 6 and 7 argue that the ethical implications of sabbath must shape contemporary Church mission. Fulfilled in Jesus, not only is sabbath the divine intention in creation's beginning, but it is also the divine intention in creation's ending, its τελός (fulfilment).

In *A Marginal Jew*, Meier observes the space between opposing poles of sabbath acceptance and understanding, even within a Jewish framework. On the one hand: 'The rabbis stressed that the wonderful gift of sabbath was not given indiscriminately to all human beings, but only to the chosen people.'[432] While on the other hand:

> Aristobulus (Jewish Philosopher and Interpreter of the law 2nd century BC) explains sabbath as rest and sees it as a sevenfold order embedded in nature, and tries to show that Greek pagan poets such as Homer and Hesiod held the seventh day holy, thus giving the sabbath a universal status.[433]

It is not clear what Aristobulus means by 'the sevenfold order embedded in nature', but it seems he is aligning sabbath with wisdom (Prov. 9:1) and in doing so giving sabbath universal application. This example of 'universal application' is at least in part what the Church means by its catholicity, 'that which is true everywhere and for all people'.

This chapter then is not simply bridging sabbath between the two Testaments but is arguing the case that the Church's comparatively weak position in the public square, specifically in relation to the environmental crisis, does not do justice to its biblical foundations. Chapter 1 observed that the Church's contemporary mission remains influenced by the Enlightenment. 'A second response [of Church and Theology to the Enlightenment] consisted in the privatisation of religion. It could carve out for itself a small domain in public life and for the rest remain a personal matter and leave the public square naked.'[434]

The Enlightenment laid emphasis upon the individual. A thorough re-reading of Sabbath mutuality in the light of Jesus adds weight to the argument that 'individualism' receives no comfort in scripture, that creation and redemption are about blessing and sanctification of an individual through their membership of creation in its entirety. 'The biblical meta-narrative is about the relationship between God, human beings and the non-human creation.'[435] This chapter then lays a foundation from the New Testament for a full hearted response to the environmental crisis based upon a Christian sabbath theology.

Sabbath: Creation and Redemption

Central to both the Old and the New Testament is the account of the covenantal relationship of God with the world, and specifically with humanity. Creation is the 'external prerequisite for covenant,'[436] the necessary arena of God's engagement in the course of history. Christ is the climax of covenant; therefore 'reread[ing] the Old Testament in the light of Christ'[437], should focus redemption in the light of creation.

Until relatively recently, however, the Church's emphasis on redemption in Christ has not exhibited a creation focus.[438] The unintended impression has been salvation 'out of' this world rather than salvation 'within' the world. There has been little focus upon the relationship redeemed humanity might or should have within the community of creation. A focus on redemption alone can lead to an outcome that appears to support the notion that Christianity is concerned only for the salvation of 'souls' without reference to the context in which those lives are lived, the community of people with whom they live, and the non-human creation which supports them. As

Joseph Sittler succinctly states: 'A doctrine of redemption is meaningful only when it swings within the larger orbit of a doctrine of creation.'[439]

Emphasis on redemption without a balancing focus on creation has meant that a study of the New Testament as a source of understanding the relationship between humanity and the created order has been relatively unexplored or developed. That it is now being explored is in large part due to a context in which the growing environmental crisis must inevitably shape the mission of the contemporary church. As Walter Brueggemann has observed:

> A remarkable turn has happened in the theological interpretation of the Old Testament. In the first part of the 20th century theological interpretation was dominated by 'God's Mighty Deeds in History'. ... It was relatively easy to find a warrant for 'history against nature' ... it was not until the 1970's that reference to creation as a primal theme of theology in the Christian Old Testament was to develop.[440]

This new found focus is not only overdue, it enables well known scriptures to be refreshingly revisited. Old Testament psalmody,[441] assumes that the created order is not simply an act of God's creativity but that it is also a revelation of God who rests in creation. The prologue of John's Gospel (John 1:1-14), the introduction to the Epistle to the Hebrews (Heb. 1:1-4), and the Hymn to the Universe in Colossians (Col. 1:15-20) proclaim that the God revealed 'in the face of Jesus Christ' (2 Cor. 4:6) is the God of creation. A restored focus on Jesus as the preexisting one, the one through whom all things hold together, positions redemption in the context of creation, placing the $\tau\epsilon\lambda\dot{o}\varsigma$ (end) in the context of the $\dot{\alpha}\rho\chi\eta$ (beginning). Redemption, focussed through creation, as demonstrated in the Book of Revelation, develops an eschatology that links human destiny within the destiny of the whole created order. The window I have chosen into this rediscovery of creation through these and other passages is sabbath.

One of the reasons given for non-involvement by Christians in the environmental debate is the assertion that the material world is passing away. If Jesus' messiahship, the kingdom he heralds, is in fact a redeeming of the whole created order, it becomes clear that the Christian community cannot dismiss as irrelevant that which is important in the final purposes of God.

Sabbath in the Gospels

The Old Testament depicts sabbath as the crown of creation; the New Testament depicts Jesus as the source of the new creation. 'What does the word 'sabbath' mean? According to some it is the name of the Holy One.'[442] In a metaphorical if not a literal sense this chapter implies that 'sabbath' is an appropriate name for Jesus. Whether this depiction arises from an accurate portrayal of what Jesus actually said and did or whether it is imputed from the early Christian community is an important area of research. An example of this tension between the sayings of Jesus and the theological reflection of the early Christian community can be seen in scholarly work over the statement: 'The Sabbath was made for humankind not humankind for the sabbath; so the Son of man is lord even of the sabbath' (Mark 2:2728). John Meier argues: 'This Galilean cycle of dispute stories is an intricate piece of literary art and artifice, written by a Christian theologian to advance his overall vision of Jesus as the hidden yet authoritative messiah, Son of Man and Son of God.'[443]

However, this research is not the subject of this book. It is assumed that the appropriate authority for theological reflection and the appropriate authority for the Church's missional activity is scripture in its canonical form, which includes both historical statements from Jesus and the theological reflections of the early Church. These reflections led the early Christian community to embrace the wisdom of God as the incarnate word of God, to adopt the promises and longings of Hebrew scripture in the messiahship of Christ, and to celebrate the longed for sabbath rest as actualised in Jesus.

I am examining the relationship between Jesus and Sabbath under five headings:

Jesus, Lord of the Sabbath

Sabbath, Jesus and Jubilee

Sabbath Rest and Jesus

Sabbath and the Kingdom of God

Sabbath, Wisdom, and the Cosmic Christ

Together they argue that sabbath is personified in Jesus, that Jesus was not 're-inventing sabbath', but restoring its true identity. They argue that Jesus' proclamation of the 'Kingdom of God' should be understood as sabbath's fulfilment. The arguments have their sequel in the chapters that follow in that if in Jesus sabbath is fulfilled then the provisions of sabbath must be central to the Church's mission and individually to the vocation of all Christian people.

Jesus, Lord of the Sabbath

The context of the statement, 'Lord of the Sabbath', found in all three synoptic gospels, is the gathering of the grains of wheat on the sabbath day. In all three gospels the account is immediately followed by the sabbath controversy found in the narrative of the healing of the man with the withered hand. This section examines the pericope containing 'The Son of Man is Lord of the Sabbath' (Matt. 12:8, Mark 2:28, Luke 6.5); together with the sabbath controversy which follows. The two extra miracles in Luke that continue the controversy and the two in John's gospel that follow the same theme are also examined.

Gathering Grains of Wheat on the Sabbath Day (Mark 2:23-28. Matthew 12:1-8. Luke 6:15)

The story is essentially the same in each account and will be treated as such, although Mark's account, presumably the original, will be the one upon which the reflections are made. There are differences. Matthew for example puts three Old Testament references in the mouth of Jesus to justify the action of his disciples.

1.   The reference to the shewbread and the priests at Nob (which the other synoptic Gospel writers also record).
2.   A reference to law which allowed priests special sabbath privileges.
3.   A reference to Hosea 6:6. 'For I desire steadfast love and not sacrifice, the knowledge of God rather than burnt offerings'.

The extra references in Matthew's account are not surprising given his consistent emphasis that Jesus is the fulfiller of Hebrew scripture. Lohse says of the Hosea reference: 'Matthew uses the statement that the Son of Man is Lord of the Sabbath to argue his disciples are released from the absolute obligations of the sabbath commandment; their supreme command is that they exercise mercy.'[444]

Both Luke and Matthew exclude Mark's erroneous dating: 'when Abiathar was high priest' (Mark 2:26) and both exclude Mark's initial summary: 'Sabbath was made for humankind and not humankind for the sabbath' (Mark 2:27). As noted, the key statement 'The Son of Man is Lord even of the Sabbath', is common to all three accounts.

Two possible reasons present themselves for the inclusion of this pericope in the synoptic Gospel accounts. Either they are there to justify sabbath practice in the early church, or they are there for a Christological reason, that is to say to argue that God in creation and God in Christ are one and the same and that the cosmic fulfilment of creation, through sabbath, is now a reality in Christ. Meier argues that what is essential to this pericope is the placing of humanity and sabbath together, both within creation's beginning, and in its intended destiny. The text suggests that Christ, who has taken human flesh, is also the embodiment of sabbath: he is sabbath's alpha and its omega:

> The Marcan Jesus is alluding to the creation story in Genesis. ...
> Jesus' argument is not so much anthropological or humanitarian as
> it is an expression of creation theology, within the context of end
> time. Both human beings and the sabbath placed in this context are
> seen in their proper perspective and in their proper relationship to
> each other.[445]

The setting, plucking ears of corn, seems initially to be an argument about the legality of this action regardless of whether it occurred on the sabbath day or not. The narrative alludes to Deut. 23:25 where the law states that if you are walking through a property that is not your own you may pick grain (or grapes) and eat them, but you may not collect them to take away. The dispute seems therefore initially a question of the intent of the disciples.

The parallel that Jesus draws with the historical account of the feeding of David's men with the shewbread (1 Sam. 21:1-9), is strange in at least two respects.

1. The history as it is recorded in the Gospel is wrong. The account did not occur in the time of Abiathar but of Ahimelech. It occurred at Nob while Saul was still alive and not after David assumed kingship In Jerusalem. Presumably the mistake is made because of the close association between David, Abiathar and Jerusalem, and because the Gospel writer wishes to connect Jesus with David and Jerusalem, thus authenticating Jesus' messianic credentials.

2. It is hard to understand any parallel between the picking of corn and the eating of shewbread. Jesus' disciples are doing something that may or may not have been legal any day, let alone on the sabbath day; David and his men eat that which in the Holiness Code is not ordinarily sanctioned for them to eat.

The saying: 'The sabbath was made for humankind, not humankind for the sabbath' (Mark 2:27), recorded in Mark alone, is open to at least two interpretations:

The saying either affirms human freedom to set aside the sabbath
law without any qualifications, or we have a saying that values the
sabbath as God's provision at creation, but as a benefit for 'man', the
human creature, with no prescribed or proscribed guidelines for
sabbath conduct.[446]

The latter possibility is not entirely inconsistent with Jewish belief.
Sabbath was understood to be God's primary gift to the chosen people.
'At the beginning of time there was a longing, a longing of sabbath for
man.'[447] This interpretation, that sabbath is a gift from the 'dawn of time',
a gift not simply for the Jewish people, but for the whole of humanity
within the community of creation, a gift that edifies and empowers
human life is the argument I am making This interpretation does not
allow for the abandonment of sabbath, but promotes its rediscovery; its
extraction from the legal requirements of disengagement to a celebration
of engagement with God and the whole created order. Notwithstanding
the fact that the saying is only found in Mark, John Meier argues for its
authenticity on the grounds of its chiastic structure:

> The striking parallelism and chiasm in the short, dense logion of
> Mark 2:27 favours the authenticity of the saying:

> The sabbath
> for man
> was made
> and not man
> for the sabbath.[448]

The link made by the consecutive particle ὥστε (so) between verses
27 (above) and 28 ('the Son of Man is lord even of the sabbath') appears
to make a play on the relationship between 'man' and 'Son of Man', a 'play
which would have been much clearer in Aramaic and somewhat lost in
Greek.'[449] The expression 'Son of Man' can be a generic expression for
'man' but its use here is much more likely to be the title Jesus preferred for
himself; in other words he is saying, while sabbath is a gift for humanity,

its origins are not human, 'I am Lord of the Sabbath'. Indeed Meier goes so far as to say:

> Mark 2:28 is the only Son of Man saying related to a specific question of Jewish *hálákâ*. ... The closest comparable pronouncement anywhere in the Gospels to the 'I am' saying is St John's Gospel.[450]

Putting verses 27 and 28 together then provides a very powerful statement. Sabbath is a gift from God to humanity, a gift that has been with humanity since creation, but this gift is now to be understood afresh in Jesus, his life, his teaching, but above all in his death and resurrection through which a new creation dawns.

Eduard Schweizer, in his commentary on this affirmation in both Mark and Matthew, is anxious to make the point that a link is being made on the one hand between creation and humanity's beginning, and on the other between Jesus and humanity's destiny; and that Sabbath is the factor to be found in both:

> The Creation story in Genesis leads up to Sabbath, which even there was probably understood as a symbol of the world to come, which would be 'all Sabbath'.[451]

> It is the presence of the Son of Man that makes freedom possible, because in him God's will for man has been realised, namely God's full and complete giving. Therefore as Lord of the Sabbath, Jesus gives the Sabbath back to man to be a help ... not a burden.[452]

This pericope cannot on its own make an argument for the place of sabbath in the ongoing life of the Christian community, but together with all the other references so far cited it underscores the significance of sabbath in the ongoing life and destiny of humanity within the created order. It especially makes clear that God's engagement with creation and humanity within creation is focussed afresh in Jesus who not only heralds the reign of God, but inaugurates that reign by becoming the sabbath rest so long yearned for. 'Come to me, all you that are weary and are carrying heavy burdens, and I will give you rest' (Mtt. 11:28).

We now turn to the sabbath miracle controversies, the only context in the Gospels involving sabbath controversy between Jesus and the religious authorities. They are dealt with in some detail because they specifically address sabbath practice. They were probably used by the early Church to justify their abandonment of prevailing Jewish practice. The early Christian community came to believe that Jesus fulfilled sabbath, and that in following him they were practicing sabbath.

These accounts are:

Matt. 12:9-14	The man with the withered hand (Mark 3:1-6 and Luke 6:6-11)
Luke 13:10-17	The crippled woman
Luke 14:1-6	The man with dropsy
John 5:1-18	The man at the pool of Bethzatha
John 9:1-33	The man born blind

The man with the withered hand (Matt. 12:9-14, Mark 3:1-6, Luke, 6:6-11)

The three synoptic accounts of the healing of the man with the withered hand follow immediately after the account of the picking of the grains of corn on the sabbath Day. There are minor differences in the wording of each account for example:

> In Mark 3:4 Jesus addresses the question, 'Is it licit on the sabbath day to do good or to do evil, to save life or to kill'? In the Matthean version of the same story the unnamed opponents make the dispute overt, rather than covert, by taking offence at the beginning of the narrative. They ask Jesus 'Is it licit to heal on the sabbath.'[453]

However, the thrust of the narrative remains the same in all three Gospels. The question of the Pharisees to Jesus is; 'is it right to cure on the Sabbath Day?' The question of Jesus to the Pharisees is around 'saving life and doing good'. Jesus responds to the Pharisees' question by healing the man, the Pharisees do not respond to Jesus question but go away 'and filled with fury they discuss with one another what they might do to Jesus' (Luke 6:11). The focus of these accounts is not the man with the withered hand, but controversy about sabbath. Clearly the man with the withered hand was not strictly in a life threatening situation. 'According to a generally accepted Halakah it was permissible to help a sick man on the Sabbath only when there was imminent danger of death.'[454]

The intended focus of the pericope from Jesus' perspective centres on: 'is it lawful to do good or do harm on the sabbath, to save life or to destroy it?' (Luke 6:9). 'Doing good for Jesus' opponents meant keeping the sabbath.'[455] Doing good for Jesus meant saving life. The intended focus of the pericope from the perspective of the early Christian community appears to be vindication in that they have separated themselves from the Jewish tradition involving the seventh day. 'The end of the Sabbath conflict makes it plain that for the Christian community the Sabbath commandment had already been set aside definitively by the end of the 1st century.'[456]

The development of the early Church from being a child of Judaism to being an autonomous movement was reasonably rapid, not least because of growth within the Gentile world. As autonomy became inevitable, separation from contemporary Jewish Halakah provisions imbedded in the Jewish notion of holiness as separation naturally followed. Keeping the seventh day provision was discontinued and although worship on the first day of the week became the norm, the provisions that had prevailed on the seventh day were not transferred. This change can in part be explained by the growing change in the Christian community from an understanding of holiness as separation to holiness as engagement. Separation infers that 'good' is to be corralled to self, or the culture with which self identifies; engagement infers that 'good' is to be found and experienced through the other—in common. Brueggemann makes this point: 'The move from holiness as separation to holiness as relational engagement is a characteristic one in the early Church. However it is not simple or uncontested.'[457]

Brueggemann goes on to note that in the contemporary period, when Christianity struggles for relevance and influence in the wider world there has been a reverse movement, an inward withdrawal rather than an outward engagement.[458] The third section explores the outcome of this reversal in a secular culture which enables/encourages separation. A largely unregulated market increasingly commoditises and privatises every aspect of human life. As a consequence, little initiative is left either in secular culture, or in the Church, for transformative energy which might lead to an honouring, let alone growth, of 'common good'.

Now, returning to Jesus' concern, as focussed in the synoptic accounts of the man with the withered hand. This appears not to be a focus on what is appropriate on the seventh day, but what is always appropriate, everyday: a focus on sabbath as intended in the Genesis narrative, a focus on blessing and sanctification within the whole created order. 'To the degree that he [Jesus] brings wholeness to this crippled man by restoring his hand and his relationship with God, he brings to reality God's promised intent at creation.'[459] As noted in Chapter 2, God's intention in creation is described in the attestation of 'good', 'And God saw that it was good' (Gen. 1:25); and in reference to the whole of creation[460] 'And God saw everything that he had made, and indeed it was very good' (Gen. 1:31).

Bonhoeffer argues that 'good' as spoken in the creation narrative does not refer to a particular action, but to 'the reality of God which shows itself everywhere to be the ultimate reality.'[461] As argued in Chapter 3 this reality is climaxed in God's 'resting', God's engagement with creation. The ultimate reality to which Bonhoeffer refers is the active life giving presence of God. If 'good' is not an individual action, but is the life that exists in and emanates from God, then for humanity to 'do good' is not to perform any particular action, but to live a life that is conformity with that 'ultimate reality'. Bonhoeffer makes the case that in responding to the reality that is God, the response is not made as an individual human person but in company with 'an indivisible whole'. 'With respect to its origin this indivisible whole is called 'creation', with respect to its goal it is called the 'Kingdom of God'.'[462] A life lived with such conformity and lived in the context of community will, at the very least, act for the enhancement of life and avoid activity which is life denying.

The pericope relating to the man with the withered hand is therefore seen to be far more than a controversy over sabbath, in the sense of 'one sacred day in seven', but is a Christological claim that in Jesus the 'ultimate reality' has taken flesh, creation's sabbath is actualised, common good is celebrated. Further, in Jesus, creation's goal, the eternal sabbath,[463] the 'Kingdom of God', is at hand.

The crippled woman (Luke 13:10-17)

It comes as somewhat of a surprise to find extra accounts of controversy over sabbath keeping in Luke's Gospel, given that sabbath was 'no longer a concern'[464] in the community to whom he was writing. 'The question must be faced as to why he [Luke] tells us more about Sabbath conflicts of Jesus than the other evangelists. For him and his community the sabbath was no longer an urgent problem.'[465] Therefore, presumably Luke's motivation in including these narratives went beyond validating a position taken in a dispute about how the seventh day was to be observed. 'He felt there was something deeper behind this practice on the part of Jesus.'[466]

In keeping with many of the Lukan narratives, this account involves a woman. It is the only miracle associated with the sabbath dispute in any of the Gospels where this is the case. Given that a woman would not have been worshipping in the synagogue with men the miracle must have occurred after his teaching had concluded, when the synagogue service had ended. Unlike the account of the healing of the man with the withered hand, where the man is incidental to the story, in this case the woman is central to the narrative. A link is made between the woman, the covenant with all descendants of Abraham (male and female), and with a breaking of the reign of evil, the restoration of good. These links are contrasted with the 'hypocrisy' of the Pharisees.

Luke's focus on the woman, a focus that grants her the same right to wholeness that a man enjoys, links the reader back to the first creation narrative in which men and women are both created in the image of God, and forward into the new creation where there is no division between male and female, Jew or Greek, slave or free. Through his reference to Abraham, Luke makes the point that the manner in which Jesus understands and celebrates sabbath is not a liberal invention, but the way in which all children of Abraham should be celebrating sabbath, for in celebrating this way, the reign of God (in contrast with the reign of Satan) is established. 'The roots of Sabbath lie in creation itself, but a creation that is meant to serve the good of a humanity created by God in the beginning and now restored by him in the last days.'[467]

The man with dropsy (Luke 14:1-6)

The context of this miracle is a meal. Jesus was invited to the home of a leader of the Pharisees for one of the significant meals of the week, the midday Sabbath meal. We know from other accounts of meals, the feeding of the five thousand, the parable of those invited to a wedding feast and the account of the Last Supper, that meals have an eschatological overtone. Meals are not simply an occasion for the feeding of an individual but they are a family/community celebration. Meals are to be celebrated by all who are present, strangers, servants, foreigners and in this case the disadvantaged. In the context of a meal none can be excluded, equity is to be practised. Jesus asks whether any will refrain from rescuing a child or an animal on the sabbath. The question is met with silence.

Both the extra Lukan narratives emphasise that Sabbath, a celebration of the new creation, was not a 'new liberalism' but a fulfilment of the creation sabbath, a life giving celebration of the presence of God, in and through which none were to be excluded on the basis of gender or disability, but all were to experience together the abundance of God's goodness.

The man at the Pool of Bethzatha (John 5:1-18)

John at first recounts the miracle without any reference to the Sabbath (John 5:1-9a). From verse 9b-18 John then uses the miracle as an opportunity to further assert the divinity of Christ. The passage is not about the sabbath controversy per se, as observed in previous miracle accounts, but about the personhood of Jesus, that he 'made himself equal with God' (John 5:18), as demonstrated through his statement about sabbath.

The saying: 'My Father is still working and I am working' (John 5:17) is somewhat enigmatic. On face value, as noted in Chapter 3, it appears to contradict Gen. 2:1-2 'Thus the heavens and the earth were finished and all their multitude. And on the seventh day God finished the work that he had done and rested on the seventh day from all the work he had done'. How is this contradiction to be resolved? Some attempts include:

1. 'God's physical activity has concluded but his moral activity has not.

2. Sabbath activity does not prohibit work in one's house on the sabbath day. God's homestead is the upper and lower worlds.'[468]

These and similar explanations are less than satisfactory.

Lohse argues that the problem is not the claim that God continues to work, but that Jesus is equating himself with God:

> Rabbis argued that God's work continues even on the Sabbath and that he is uninterruptedly active as Sustainer and Judge of the world. Jesus stresses the constancy of divine work that is not affected by the sabbath.[469]

Lohse goes on to pose the question: 'What was Jesus abolishing and what was he restoring?'[470] It is my argument that Jesus was loosening the bonds of casuistry that bound sabbath to a particular day and restoring the place of sabbath at the foundation of creation.

As noted in Chapter 3, the Genesis creation account, climaxing in *sabat*, is not history describing a past moment: it is primeval narrative that illuminates every moment in history. Creation continues when a seed falls to the ground and dies, producing new life. Creation continues with every new generation. And so also God's presence to, or resting in, creation is a continuing pattern of divine engagement. Rowan Williams articulates this thought as follows:

> God's interests if we can speak in such terms are bound up with the world's so that there can be no temptation to model one's behaviour on a God utterly without any investment in the life of the creation, as if the best form of life were one which repudiated involvement in or dependency upon the material world.[471]

Thus, God never ceases to create and God never ceases to 'rest', to engage with creation. Sabbath is not a cessation from 'work' but a celebration of all that gives work its meaning and purpose. 'The sabbath as the necessity to rest from work makes sense only for man, who gets fatigued from work and needs a day of rest.'[472] Thus, the narrative confirms the ongoing engagement of God with creation, engagement that in Jesus is committed to redeeming all that has been made. While John does not use the synoptic language of Kingdom, he constantly uses narratives such as this, focussed on the Pool at Bethzatha, to make the link from a particular event to a cosmic reality. 'Particularity is not dissolved in universality but remains as it were the essential focus of universal significance.'[473]

The man born blind (John 9:1-40)

While this is a very significant narrative in John's Gospel it is of only peripheral significance to the Sabbath debate. The only reference to Sabbath in the whole account is in verses 14-17. It is noted that the miracle occurs on the sabbath day, which elicits an adverse observation from some Pharisees. 'This Man is not from God because he does not observe the sabbath', while others say 'How can a man who is a sinner perform such signs' (John 9:16).

Following a long dialogue between Jesus and the man born blind and an interrogation of him by the Pharisees, John concludes the chapter with a reference to spiritual blindness. His main point is that the Pharisees have failed to perceive the true nature of Jesus and in him, the manifestation of God at work in their midst. But it is also reasonable to deduce that the dialogue conveys that the Pharisees, in their blindness, have misunderstood sabbath celebration. That through their legalism, insisting upon restrictive halakah, they have been blinded from an understanding that Sabbath is not about denial but embrace, not about restricting life but celebrating it, not about cessation from work but celebrating the reason for work.

Sabbath, Jesus and Jubilee

The term 'jubilee' has currency as a metaphor for celebration following a significant passage of time—a silver, gold or diamond jubilee. But it also has power as a sociological metaphor, a biblical metaphor which means 'release', freedom from debts, a focus on the liberation of the poor and restoring the rights of the alienated.

> Jubilee has come to function as a powerful metaphor, so that what was sociology now takes on literary rhetorical power well beyond the specific social proposal. ... The metaphor as elusive and evocative social possibility continues to push forward into the life of the community wherever the text is taken seriously.[474]

In the year 2000 the Church used the metaphor to capture the spirit of 2000 years of Christianity and linked it to the Gospel imperative to bring hope through its advocacy for the elimination of international debt incurred by the poorest countries in the world. The metaphor has been given a degree of longevity in as much that it has been carried forward into the millennium development goals[475] which reached their end point in 2015.

Metaphor is important in the development of a narrative that empowers, or perhaps transforms, human behaviour because: 'people characteristically think, speak and learn in pictures, stories and analogies.'[476]

Behind the metaphor, in the biblical narrative, lies a requirement of release to be enacted on a fifty year cycle. While required in the Torah (Lev. 25:8–55), there is little if any historical evidence that it was practised. In the material that follows I argue that Jesus took this Torah requirement from its mandated 50-year cycle and transformed it into a metaphor of release, descriptive of his entire ministry and mission, and by implication, the mission and ministry of the Church. Indeed, Jubilee was to be as much a defining characteristic of Christianity, as weekly sabbath was a defining characteristic of Judaism. This case has to be prosecuted not simply through Jesus' use of the 'jubilee passage' (Isa. 61:1-4), but also through an examination of significant passages attributed to him which could be described as expressing 'jubilee conviction'.

The jubilee passage

Luke records that as Jesus commenced his ministry he was given the scroll of Isaiah to read in the synagogue and chose to read the passage from Isa. 61:1-2. While lections were provided for particular occasions, Luke gives his readers the impressions that this was Jesus' choice: 'he unrolled the scroll and found the place where it was written' (Luke 4:17).

> The Spirit of the Lord is upon me,
> Because he has anointed me
> To bring good news to the poor.
> He has sent me to bring release to the captives
> And recovery of sight to the blind,
> To let the oppressed go free,
> To proclaim the year of the Lord's favour' (Luke 4:18-19).

The 'year of the Lord's favour', the jubilee, is characterised by all that precedes its reference in the text.

The passage is paraphrased again in Matthew and Luke as a response to John the Baptist when he seeks clarification about the ministry of Jesus, more specifically as to whether he is the Messiah, the promised one, or whether they should look for another (Matt. 11:26, Luke 7:18-23). Jesus responds to the questions put by the disciples of John the Baptist by saying 'the blind receive their sight, the lame walk, the lepers are cleansed, the deaf hear, the dead are raised and the poor have the good news brought to them' (Matt. 11:4-5). The paraphrasing in this context appears to confirm the impression that Luke gives, that as Jesus began his ministry he was framing it in the context of jubilee and saw himself as the inaugurator of an era that fulfilled the latent potential of this Old Testament provision. As an examination of Jesus' sayings and the early Church's understanding of them indicates, he was not arguing for the 10 or 50 year provision, but for a jubilee way of life.

The text read by Jesus is clearly Septuagintal.[477] It agrees with the LXX against the Hebrew in reading Κυριόν (Lord) instead of ādōnāy YHWH (Yahweh) and largely follows the Greek text. A significant omission is the exclusion of 'a day of vengeance'. The omission may be significant given that Luke records that the hearers 'all spoke well of him [bore testimony to him] and were amazed at his gracious words' (Luke 4:22). Luke appears to be reinforcing that from the outset these words are the words that the followers of Jesus drew upon in their witness of him and in their sense of identity within the newly formed fledgling Christian community. Luke does not commence his Gospel, as does Mark, with an announcement from Jesus as to his intention 'The time is fulfilled, and the kingdom of God has come near, repent, and believe in the good news' (Mark 1:15). It appears that Luke's Nazareth pericope fills the same role as the Marcan declaration.

Nolland makes the point that the Spirit anointing referred to in the Isaiah reading came upon Jesus at his baptism.

> His anointing signals appointment and empowering to be the Isaianic figure who heralds and brings salvation. The salvation in view is presented with jubilee imagery, but is no call for the implementation of Jubilee legislation.[478]

Nolland's point is important; there is absolutely no evidence that Jesus had in mind the reinstitution of the fifty year cycle. However, given this passage is read at the beginning of Jesus' ministry to announce its character and given a paraphrase is used to answer John the Baptist's question 'Is he the messiah?', it is clear that the words carry 'jubilee connotations'. To discover the kind of jubilee inauguration Jesus had in mind we must look to other scriptures.

> A single discourse, that of Nazareth, is not sufficient to prove that Jesus proclaimed the inauguration of the year of Jubilee. Only a more complete reading of scripture could support or undermine this thesis.[479]

Sharon Ringe makes the same point:

> Since there is no distinctive Greek vocabulary associated with the Jubilee traditions, one must begin the search for those traditions in the Gospels by looking for places where Jubilee texts are actually quoted or closely paraphrased.[480]

The Beatitudes (Matthew 5:1-12, Luke 6:20-23)

Both Gospel writers connected their respective versions of the Beatitudes with Isaiah 61 because of the position allocated to the beatitudes in their narrative, and because of the content of the sayings which in some cases mirror the words of Isaiah 61. Matthew positions the beatitudes after a quote from Isaiah 60 (Matt. 4:15-16), while Luke positions his version of the beatitudes within a chapter that commences with his account of the grain fields sabbath dispute, followed by the choosing of the twelve disciples. In so doing, Luke sets the context of Jesus ministry within the sabbath dispute and, implies the calling of Jesus' followers is to live the sabbath, inclusive of the jubilee ethic. He then outlines the beatitudes (and curses) as a summary of what this reinterpretation means for them. Eduard Schweizer is inclined to believe that the assimilation of the statements to Isaiah 61 is a later influence and not the inclination of Jesus.[481]

However, as argued earlier in this chapter, whether the words are the words of Jesus or whether they have been given an emphasis from the early Christian community, they comprise the text in the canon of scripture, the text upon which contemporary mission and ministry is to be shaped. If the canon of scripture places the ministry of Jesus in the context of jubilee, then Christian mission should also be exercised within this context.

The beatitudes are directed at the disciples to identify what is going to be, for them, the source of their blessing. They will be in the right place when they are on the side of the poor; they will be in the right place when they grieve over injustices suffered by the marginalised and alienated; they will be in the right place when they seek to be peace makers, to live without the prejudice and false divisions that divide humans from one another and which despoil the face of the earth. The blessings fill out the Sabbath blessing of Genesis 2 in which, as argued in Chapter 3, blessing is associated with 'being present to' all that God has made in creation, rather than standing apart or above in a position of superiority or exploitation. The beatitudes also amplify the Lord's 'requirement' in Micah 6:8 'to do justice, and to love kindness [mercy], and to walk humbly with your God'.

Ringe points out: 'The Beatitudes ... and the teachings on banquet etiquette found in Luke 14 are the principle places where the 'poor' are listed with other groups as recipients of the blessings of God's eschatological reign.'[482] Eduard Schweizer describes the Beatitudes as a demonstration of 'God's partiality toward the poor.'[483] Whether this partiality is toward the 'spiritually' or 'materially' poor is not a helpful question. The poor are those who are disempowered. The human poor are those whose humanity has been diminished, no matter what the cause. In the case of the non-human creation, disempowerment results from exploitation and alienation; fracturing of the ecology (house) that enables sustainable life.

The beatitudes then are a mandate for a life of jubilee, lived and expressed within a context where disempowerment is most pressing.

Such jubilee living may be directed to a single person or cause for whom one is given a lifetime responsibility of care. However the global environmental crisis, which the prosperous exacerbate out of their wealth and through which the poor are impacted out of their vulnerability, calls for jubilee living by all. Jubilee living is about freeing those who are enslaved, enslavement caused by a (economic) system over which the enslaved have no control. In this context the recipients of jubilee freedom are:

1. The human poor of the world who are most impacted by the activity of the prosperous.
2. The young and the unborn whose future is being decided by the rich and powerful today.
3. The non-human creation whose diversity, fecundity and sustainability is under threat.

The Lord's Prayer

> 'And forgive us our debts, as we also have forgiven our debtors' (Matt. 6:12).

Debt and how it is dealt with is, as already explored, at the heart of sabbath and jubilee provisions. It is also central to the concerns of Jesus. 'The second and third provisions of Jubilee [remission of debt and release of slaves] are not marginal but central in the teaching of Jesus.'[484] Jesus does not distinguish between financial, material and 'spiritual debt'. That is to say, debt that is colloquially understood as 'sins' or 'trespasses', the 'spiritual debt' we owe to God, is linked to the material debt we owe one another. Yoder argues: 'The verb is αφίηι. Accurately, the word ὀφείλημα of the Greek text signifies precisely a monetary debt, in the most material sense of the term.'[485] Debt causes an obligation to exist between one person and another. Making, or encouraging, others to be indebted is often a means of exercising power. This point is clear in Jesus' parable of the unforgiving servant (Matt. 18:23-35). God's release from the obligations inherent in our failures is such that releasing others should be a response of gratitude; however human beings are reluctant to forego debt because of the power possessed in the act of retaining it. Being concerned for equity and mutuality are ideals without support when they conflict with self interest.

In the time of Jesus it was possible for a person to avoid the cancellation of debt owed to them, which the sabbatical year would have required, by appealing to the court. This procedure was known as *prosboul*, 'Jesus was decidedly an adversary of prosboul.'[486] Using debt as a means of exercising power is not restricted to a small minority. In matters large or small it is a trait common to humanity. There is a need for all human beings to address their own claim against others before addressing perceived injustices from others:

> The poor in the Gospel are thus all those people without presumption of privilege, to whom Jesus' message comes as good news. There are very few to whom the message is totally good news, because most people claim something that sets them over others.[487]

The area of greatest current global indebtedness, largely unrecognised, or perhaps ignored, is ecological debt. This debt has a significant moral component because, as indicated above, it impacts the poor and vulnerable, the young and those yet unborn and the non-human creation whose diversity, fecundity, and ecological sustainability is being steadily diminished.

This debt, caused by exploitation of the world's resources at a rate of approximately 150% annually,[488] is accumulative, and has been described as 'the greatest moral challenge of our time.'[489]

When the Christian community recites the Lord's Prayer it confronts indebtedness. It is the responsibility of each individual and each generation to become aware of and address the debt, spiritual or material, that they have incurred.

> The power of these [Jubilee] images to help us say what it means
> to confess Jesus as the Christ, as well as confront our assumptions
> concerning values and priorities in our daily lives, becomes a vehicle
> by which we read forward or interpret from the biblical tradition
> into our own situation.[490]

The Lord's Prayer is then both an expression of Jesus' jubilatory claims, and a challenge to those who recite it to apply the principle in their context:

> Thus the 'Our Father' is genuinely a jubilary prayer. It means the
> time has come for the faithful people to abolish all the debts which
> bind the poor ones of Israel, for your debts towards God are also
> wiped away.[491]

The Rich Young Ruler (Matt. 19:16-29, Mark 10:17-31, Luke 18:18-30)

This pericope is included along with the beatitudes and the Lord's Prayer as an illustration of Jesus' commitment to jubilee because:

1.   The context of the dialogue is the keeping of the commandments (inclusive of sabbath).

2.   It is recounted in some detail in all three synoptic Gospels.

3.   All three Gospel writers use the dialogue between Jesus and the rich young man (ruler) to identify and herald the new era, the Kingdom of God.

While the details of the narrative vary slightly in each Gospel, the essential narrative remains the same. The young man presents himself as a 'righteous' person on the grounds that he keeps the (ten) commandments. Jesus challenged him about what keeping the commandments really meant in his case; he draws him beyond a mere legalism. In a different context Jesus seeks an answer to the question about law keeping in terms of the Great Commandment (Matt. 22:34-40, Mark 12:28-34, Luke 10:35-38). Here his focus appears to be an interpretation of the tenth commandment. From a Jewish perspective Heschel connects keeping the Sabbath with all other commandments, but especially with the tenth commandment, the commandment that focusses upon covetousness and the desire for possessions.

> In ancient literature, emphasis is expressed through direct repetition (epizeuxis), by repeating a word without any intervening words. ... Of all the Ten Commandments only one is proclaimed twice, the last one: Thou shall not covet, Thou shall not covet. ... The tenth commandment would be futile if it were not for the 'commandment' regarding the sabbath day, to which about a third of the text of the Decalogue is devoted, and which is an epitome of all the other commandments. We must seek to find a relationship between the two 'commandments'.[492]

Heschel's point is that just as the inauguration of the sabbath was not the inauguration of a day in the sequence of seven, but a celebration of creation's completion; so within the Ten Commandments, the sabbath Commandment is positioned between the commandments that relate to God and those that relate to human beings as a summary of both. In the keeping of sabbath, all that is required in relation to God and all that is required in relation to that which God has created is fulfilled.

Jesus tells the young man that keeping the commandments is to be demonstrated through the giving of his possessions to the poor, a challenge Heschel associates with sabbath.

Chapter 7 addresses sabbath as 'kenosis' in the context of human vocation. Emptying is not an end, but a means, enabling empowerment or release—the celebration of jubilee. The disciples remark on the difficulty of this teaching: 'who then can be saved?' (Luke 18:26) Jesus responds 'what is impossible for mortals is possible for God' (Luke 18:27). Keeping sabbath in the sense that Heschel suggests, or in the manner that Jesus requires of the young man is difficult. But humans are not required to keep sabbath with God as if it is a human initiative. God keeps sabbath with the whole creation. Humanity is called to be with God in God's keeping of that cosmic sabbath.

The importance given to this pericope in all three synoptic Gospels reflects the significance attributed by the early Christian community to the proclamation of the coming eon.[493] Here we are to understand that the coming eon, the Kingdom of God, is to be marked not by what is kept for oneself but by what is returned, commitment to 'common good'. The coming kingdom is enabled through living the principles of jubilee. Yoder argues that Jesus was lifting the periodic levelling of jubilee into a defining trait of the 'kingdom', the 'new creation'.

> It would be that the fundamental notion of periodic levelling would have been lifted, as Jesus appropriated it out of the Hebrew heritage, from the level of some practices implemented every seven years or every forty nine years. It would have become in Jesus' teaching a permanently defining trait of the new order.[494]

Evidence of this truth having become so quickly a feature of the early Christian community is the description of that community holding 'all things in common' (Acts 2:44).

Sabbath Rest and Jesus

Chapter 3 argued that sabbath 'rest' celebrates creation's harmony. Understood in this way, Sabbath is not about the casuistry involved in keeping one day in seven holy, but about how the whole of life is to be lived. Judith Wray explains:

> For Jesus rest is not about sabbath-keeping, nor was it (merely) some future reward for faithful action today. For Jesus rest was inextricably linked with one's relationship to the world, to the community and to God.[495]

In the New Testament sabbath rest is dealt with most comprehensively in the Epistle to the Hebrews. In doing so, the context is a systematic argument in which the writer proposes that all provisions of Jewish cultic life, and all expressions of hierarchy in relation to God, are fulfilled, or are to be reinterpreted in Jesus:

1.   Angels, Humanity and access to God (Chapters 1 and 2)
2.   Jesus as 'Son' is superior to Moses as servant (Chapter 3).
3.   Rest (Chapter 4)
4.   Priesthood (Chapter 5).
5.   The Priesthood of Melchizedek (Chapter 7)
6.   Mediator of a New Covenant (Chapters 8 and 9)
7.   Sacrifice (Chapter 10)

In Hebrews 4 the writer argues that the Israelites never entered the 'rest' that had been set before them and therefore its promise remained. While the writer quotes from Genesis 2, the creation context, 'and God rested on the seventh day from all his works' (Heb. 4:4), a text which forms the basis of the fourth commandment in the Exodus Decalogue; the text seems to infer he really has in mind the 'rest' implied in the Deuteronomic Decalogue. It is the Deuteronomic Decalogue, not the Exodus Decalogue, which posits rest in the context of the unfolding history of redemption. This emphasis is underlined by the writer's use of Psalm 95:11 'Thou shalt not enter my rest', inferring that because of disobedience in the wilderness the Hebrews did not enter their promised destination—Canaan.

Failure to secure this rest under Moses is deemed to have been a failure of faith, a failure depicted as murmuring, or complaining in the wilderness. Ironically the feeding of the people with manna, the first reference to sabbath practice recorded in the Hebrew Scriptures, is said to have resulted from this 'murmuring', the people's fear that they would die in the wilderness. It appears clear from the text that the writer to the Hebrews is making a strong connection between Canaan and its intended occupation as the 'Promised Land', and the 'Christian' hope of an eschatological future home. 'The key to understanding how it is that the promise remains open is to see that God's promised rest is not the earthly land of Canaan, but a heavenly reality which God entered on the completion of creation.'[496] As Sturcke puts it: 'To enter into divine rest is an expression of salvation.'[497]

However, it is, perhaps, more accurate to say that this passage is not simply an articulation of salvation, but that it is an articulation of creation and salvation together. A closer examination of the writer's source, Psalm 95, is warranted to examine whether what is meant by 'rest' in one context might carry the same meaning in another. The first half of the psalm (verses 1–7a) is a call to worship the God of Creation. The second half of the psalm (verses 7b–11) is a plea for faith and obedience to the Creator God, and sets such obedience in contrast with the wilderness debacle.

The psalm argues that the stumbling block between the people and their enjoyment of God is behaviour typified in actions at Meribah and Massah which 'mean respectively, 'place of contention' and 'place of testing.''[498] It appears that the psalmist is using the names of these two places as a metaphor for the reason why rest that includes the whole created order has not been actualised. That which is exemplified by 'Meribah' is a stumbling block to rest. Contention is the exulting of self, the opposite of contentment, or rest.

The divine 'rest' or 'sabbath' which is creation's hope has always been in need of redemption. The writer to Hebrews implies that this need of redemption has been met in the dying and rising of Jesus. Paul describes redemption as the removal of all barriers, both amongst human beings (Gal. 3:28-29) and within the whole created order (Col. 1:15-20), heralding the creation of a single community. Hebrews continues the theme of a single community; the 'rest' on offer in Hebrews is not simply to Israelites, but also to Gentiles, a rest which the New Testament calls 'a new creation'.

Thus, the writer to the Hebrews takes 'rest' out of an historical context as the goal or destiny of the journey from Egypt to Canaan and re-positions it as the destiny of a reconstituted humanity, indeed a reconstituted creation. Taylor suggests that the 'rest' to which the psalmist is referring is 'the 'place where I shall rest' or a 'state of peace or rest within me'.[499] Taylor's description puts the focus of rest on individual fulfilment or destiny. Judith Hoch Wray, summing up her research into rest as a theological metaphor in the Epistle to the Hebrews, places the important emphasis on individual fulfilment in a relational context. She suggests: 'Entering into rest becomes a participation, a to-be-maintained participation in the completed cosmic work of God.'[500] The relational or cosmic nature of rest and of God's activity in Christ is further explored later in this chapter.

The re-positioning of rest from an historical context to a position within the cosmic, creative, activity of God is underlined as this passage draws to a conclusion. σαββατισμός (Heb. 4:9) specifically links 'rest' to the narrative of creation. The intentional use of a word that does not otherwise appear in the New Testament is significant. 'There remains for God's people a 'sabbath observance' σαββατισμός. The term used in the place of κατάπαυσις [causing to cease] appears here for the first time in Greek literature.'[501]

In summary, 'rest' that undergirds harmony within creation is a gift to every individual who finds life in Christ, for Christ is the one in whom that rest is finally fulfilled. Contention or conflict, 'murmuring', focus on self rather than contentment within the whole community of creation is a barrier to 'entering that rest'. Rest puts the break upon escalating self interest, enabling space for common good. How humanity responds to the challenge of 'rest' in the context of the environmental crisis, how common good might prevail as a priority within 21st century human vocation is the subject of Part 3.

Sabbath and the Kingdom of God

This section argues that the title of this chapter: *Jesus: Lord of the Sabbath*, and the summary title of Jesus' mission: *The Kingdom of God*, are descriptive of the same intended reality. That is to say, the inauguration of the Kingdom of God heralds the fulfilment of creation sabbath. Richard Bauckham defines the Kingdom of God as 'the renewal of creation.'[502]

Christians align themselves with a longing for 'the kingdom' every time the Lord's Prayer is recited. The prayer asks that the reign of God in 'heaven' be replicated on 'earth'. Bauckham and Tom Wright, writing in very different contexts, see in this petition both a cosmic dimension and an intention by God for the redemption of the created order:

> The cosmic scope of the Kingdom can be clearly seen in the opening three petitions of the Lord's Prayer in Matthew's version.[503]

> We have seen at several points that the normal understanding of 'kingdom' ... is mistaken. ... God longed to re-establish his wise sovereignty over the whole creation which would mean a great act of healing and rescue. He did not want to rescue humans from creation ... he wanted to rescue humans in order that humans might be his rescuing stewards over creation.[504]

> Thy kingdom come: to pray this means seeing the world in binocular vision. See it with the love of the creator for his spectacularly beautiful creation; and see it with the deep grief of the creator for the battered and battle scarred state in which the world now finds itself.[505]

What was the 'normal' expectation of the kingdom that Wright describes as mistaken? There can be little doubt that the early expectations related to an immediate 'second coming' of Christ and the passing away of the current world order. When this did not occur, a rethink of what Jesus meant by the 'kingdom' was inevitable. 'During the first century, events occurred from time to time which raised hopes that it was at hand; but they were always disappointed, as similar hopes have been disappointed many times since.'[506] The dilemma between thinking of a kingdom that is coming, that affords an escape from the world, and making sense of a 'kingdom' within the context of continuing history, remains confronting. Resistance to the notion that environmental responsibility is core to the Church's mission receives comfort from belief that the 'kingdom' is a realm of God's spiritual reign and that 'evangelism' involves a conversion to that realm. This is the 'normal' expectation that Wright, an Anglican Evangelical, describes as mistaken.

Understanding Jesus' teaching on the kingdom requires an understanding of its Old Testament context:

> The term the Kingdom of God, which Jesus uses without explanation has its own background in the Hebrew Bible. It can be found in Isaiah 52:7 which is also the source of the word Gospel and in Daniel Chapter 7, but the biblical book in which the kingship and rule of God is most prominent is the Psalms.[507]

The verse in Isaiah 52.7 reads: 'How beautiful on the mountains are the feet of the messenger who announces peace, who brings good news, who announces salvation, who says to Zion, 'Your God reigns''. The context is Deutero-Isaiah's proclamation of restoration post the exile. In a subsequent Jewish context these words might well be interpreted as reinforcement of specialness, of being set apart, even of entitlement. Read by the early Church, wrestling with their sense of being the new Zion, they were read differently. Here redemption was not understood to set the community apart from the world but as the transformative energy that enabled them to be agents of God's redemption for the world. They understood that 'Zion' was not being redeemed for its own sake but that it might be a source of redemption for the whole of humanity, indeed for the whole of the world. Redemption has become anthropomorphised in today's popularised Christianity, but this is not a conclusion to be drawn from scripture. As Bauckham says: 'The kingship and rule of God in the Psalms, are closely related to creation.'[508]

Further, the early Christian community and indeed any subsequent Christian community does not come to its understanding of the Kingdom of God, only, or even primarily, on the basis of Jesus' teaching, but in the light of his death and resurrection. 'If Christ has not been raised then our proclamation has been in vain and your faith has been in vain' (1 Cor. 15:14). The resurrection is the reconstitution and unifying of physical and spiritual reality, not the freeing of spiritual reality from the physical. Through the resurrection Jesus gathers with him the world of which he became part, into the realm of God. Because of the resurrection nothing can be considered disposable, of no account. The resurrection bestows renewed value upon all physical reality.

Further, on the cross Jesus cried 'it is finished', echoing the words in Genesis 2:1 which heralded the sabbath, the celebration of 'complete' creation. There could be no resurrection without the crucifixion. The crucifixion, the divine self emptying, became the avenue through which the new creation could begin.

> The goal of God's kenosis in the creation and preservation of the world is that future which we describe with the symbols of the kingdom of God and the new creation, or 'world without end'.[509]

The resurrection is thus the event, both in time and beyond it, which brings to fulfilment the promise, inherently present from the beginning of time, that all things that belong to God have a continuing destiny with God. The resurrection is the door to the kingdom; we are not waiting for another door, or another event, the resurrection gifts the whole creation with blessing and sanctification, the resurrection is 'the seventh day', it is creation's sabbath. Heschel's words that reflect sabbath, from his Jewish understanding, can be reinterpreted to proclaim the resurrection as sabbath: 'Every seventh day a miracle comes to pass, the resurrection of the soul of man and of the soul of things.'[510] As Jesus took jubilee out of its seven- and 50-year cycle to be a constant principle of release, so in the resurrection sabbath is taken out of its seven day cycle to be a constant celebration of the 'seventh day'. Resurrection is indeed the new creation, not simply its harbinger.

Thorwald Lorenzen argues that the resurrection does not take the believer out of the world, but demands that this world is taken very seriously. 'The resurrection of Jesus Christ has set a process into motion, a process of liberation, to which every believer is called to contribute.'[511] He goes on to argue that this process of liberation is inclusive of the whole creation which 'longs for liberation from the powers of estrangement' (Rom. 8:18-25). Thus, resurrection is justice and equity for a material world that otherwise is destined to futility. In as much that this justice relies upon the cooperation of humanity, the ethical demands of sabbath are to be fulfilled.

Finally, the book of Revelation wrestles with a world, post the resurrection, in which the 'Lamb' reigns, yet a world which still awaits liberty from conflict and alienation. The final two chapters, 21 and 22, speak of the reconstituted city of Jerusalem and the new creation watered with the 'River of Life'. As this passage reaches its climax, before the final epilogue and benediction, the residents of this new creation are said to be 'marked' with God's name; 'his name will be on their foreheads' (Rev. 22:4). This passage stands in contrast with Chapter 13 where we read 'Then I saw another beast. ... It causes all, both small and great, both rich and poor, both free and slave, to be marked on the right hand or the forehead, so that no one can buy or sell who does not have the mark, that is the name of the beast or the number of its name' (Rev. 13:11-18). In the Hebrew the mark of the beast is *neshet* which can mean the mark left by a serpent bite; it can equally mean the mark caused by 'exorbitant interest on money.'[512]

In this post resurrection world, a world in which we have noted Lorenzen's claim that a process of liberation has begun, the text can be taken to imply that greed is the enemy of resurrection and an opponent of the kingdom of God. Greed, making money at the expense of another, removes God from human interaction. This is the point made by Amos, the 8th century prophet (Amos 5:18-24); it is the point that should be made by 21st century Christian prophets seeking justice in face of the environmental crisis. A market which appears to favour those who are already advantaged at the expense of the non-human creation and at the expense of the human disadvantaged is in opposition to the Kingdom and inconsistent with a sabbath ethic. The serpent's bite, greed, takes from common good for self interested gain. Sabbath and common good, in the context of the environmental crisis, inevitably challenge economic norms of greed and growth.

The Kingdom of God and Sabbath both speak of the reign of God and the manner in which liberty is to be experienced. The narrative of the Garden in Genesis 3 warns humanity of our capacity for delusion. We mistake having for being. Ringe captures it well:

> The structures of economic and social life must embody the people's affirmation of God's sovereignty. In other words, God's reign and humankind's liberation go hand in hand.[513]

Sabbath, Wisdom and the Cosmic Christ (Col. 1:15-20)

Rereading Hebrew Law, History and Prophets in the light of Jesus is productive, but in terms of a renewed understanding of creation, rereading wisdom literature is especially productive. In describing Jesus as the 'Wisdom of God' (1 Cor. 1:30), the New Testament looks back to wisdom's personification of creation imagery as a reference point for its understanding of him as the 'pre-existent' one. As Edwards states:

> The early Christian community identified Jesus with Sophia, thus identifying Jesus with Sophia's care for the *oikos*, the household of living creatures. It was this identification between Jesus and Sophia that was to be the bridge whereby the community which believed that God had raised up Jesus of Nazareth came to see this Jesus as the pre-existent one.[514]

Edwards' point is powerful. The book of Proverbs, in speaking of wisdom says: 'The Lord created me at the beginning of his work, the first of his acts long ago. Ages ago I was set up, at the first, before the beginning of the earth' (Prov. 8:22-23), and: 'Wisdom has built her house, she has hewn her seven pillars' (Prov. 9:1). These two passages imply that the whole created order is to be identified as a single house, held together not so much by its mechanical structure, but by the wisdom inherent in its relationality. The Christian community identified Jesus as the one in and through whom relationships within the universe hold together, the one at the centre of the single house. We are not given the identity of the seven pillars, we can only note the sabbath allusion through this septet.

The writings of Wendell Berry draw attention to humanity's contemporary reduction of wisdom's seven pillars to one, the 'economy'. The etymology of economy (and ecology) links both words to *oikos* (house). Berry notes the serious implications inherent in contemporary politics when 'economy' (how human house rules are constructed), is given ubiquitous priority over ecology (the timeless wisdom of mutuality and interdependence sustaining the house).[515] A sabbath focus reverses the hierarchy in favour of wisdom's mutuality, the priority of common good. This is explored more fully in Chapter 6.

The identification of Jesus with creation is especially clear in the Johannine writings and most notably in the Gospel prologue where he is described as the pre-existing one, the one through whom creation comes into being. Strangely though, Jesus is identified as 'Word' not 'Wisdom'. 'If we ask why the hymn of the prologue chose to speak of 'Word' rather than 'Wisdom' the fact that in Greek the former is masculine while the latter is feminine must be considered. Moreover the relation of Word to the apostolic kerygma must be considered.'[516]

Central to the kerygma, the 'proclamation', was the assertion that Jesus, the Word, is God: 'in him the fullness of God was pleased to dwell' (Col. 1:19). The kerygma confirms that *shekinah*, the indwelling of God in the Old Testament becomes the Incarnate Word of the New Testament. 'In the idea of Shekinah—God indwelling—we find the Old Testament presupposition for the idea of Christ's kenosis, and its Jewish equivalent.'[517] Whereas tent and temple celebrate the *shekinah* (presence) of God amongst the Hebrew people, sabbath and the incarnation celebrate *shekinah*, the indwelling of God, within the totality of the created order.

This celebration within the whole created order is particularly expressed in the 'Hymn to the Universe' (Col. 1:15-20). It contains no overt reference to sabbath; however in this ancient hymn can be found the clearest New Testament articulation of what sabbath had come to mean.

The hymn appears to have its origins in Hellenistic Judaism and not to have been written by Paul.[518] There are various reasons for believing this to be the case. In the 'undisputed' Pauline letters the eschatology points to belief that the world is 'passing away'. (Rom. 13:11-14, 1 Cor. 7:31, 1 Cor. 15:23-24, 1 Thess. 2:19, 2 Thess. 2:1). Vicki Balabanski argues that in the undisputed letters of Paul 'Christ is seen messianically, shaped by the Danielic vision of the subjugation of powers and kingdoms.'[519] In other words, Paul speaks with some urgency about the end, for he understood it would happen soon. An additional argument that this is not Paul's work is demonstrated from the vocabulary. Words such as ἀρχή (beginning), are not used elsewhere in Paul's writings to refer to Christ; and εἰκών (image) is used only one other time in 2 Cor. 4:4.

In this hymn, the indivisibility of the entire universe is its theme; creation and redemption are linked together and embrace the whole cosmos. 'Creation and reconciliation, cosmology and soteriology are dealt with in order to praise Christ as the Lord of the cosmos, who is head of the body and whose reign encompasses all things.'[520]

The hymn commences with two powerful statements.

First, that Jesus is the εἰκών (image) of God. When we see Jesus we see God. The hymn goes on to link creation and redemption, 'through him God was pleased to reconcile to himself all things, whether on earth or in heaven, by making peace through the blood of his cross' (Col. 1:20), the implication being that Jesus 'icons' God in both creation and redemption. However this imaging is not simply of Jesus, but of the crucified Jesus. 'Jesus' sacrificial and shameful death illuminates more than anything else, his significance for the whole creation.'[521] God resides in creation as the emptying one, the one whose love is poured out so that which is 'not God' might be nourished and sustained. Christ is not the cosmos, but it is through Christ that the whole cosmos comes together. 'These verses [Hymn to the Universe in Colossians] sing out their triumphant music between two huge and steady poles—'Christ' and 'All things.'"[522]

The second statement is that Jesus is the 'the firstborn of all creation' (Col. 1:15). Jesus is being equated with wisdom, the one through whom and for whom everything exists. Wisdom is the 'first born' of creation. 'The Lord created me at the beginning of his work, the first of his acts long ago' (Prov. 8:22). Nothing exists beyond the reach of Wisdom. 'For wisdom is more mobile than any motion; because of her pureness she pervades and penetrates all things. ... Although she is but one she can do all things ... in every generation she passes into holy souls and makes them friends of God and prophets; for God loves nothing so much as the person who lives with wisdom' (Wis. 7:22-30). The all pervasive, all connecting attributes of wisdom, which in this hymn are being attributed to Jesus, are persuasively articulated by Kathleen O'Connor:

> At the centre of the Wisdom Literature stands a beautiful and alluring woman. She is lady wisdom, or, as I prefer to call her, the Wisdom Woman. The primary mode of being of the Wisdom Woman is relational. In all the texts where she appears, the most important aspect of her existence is her relationships. Her connections extend to every part of reality. She is closely joined to the created world; she is an intimate friend of God; she delighted in the company of human beings. No aspect of reality is closed off from her. She exists in it as if it were a tapestry of connected threads, patterned into an intricate whole of which she is the centre.[523]

The Christian confession appropriates this view of Wisdom's role as the agent of creation and transfers it to Christ in order to express the universal validity of the Christ-event.

These two statements, 'Jesus is the icon of God' and 'he is the first born' (the wisdom of God) take the reader into a cosmology, a cosmic Christology. Colossians does not stand alone as the purveyor of such a broad Christological view. John commences his Gospel with the same imagery (John 1:1-14) as does the writer to the Hebrews (Heb. 1:1-4). However such breadth of understanding is not regularly part of contemporary Christian language, at least not of Protestant language. Balabanski makes this point:

> It is this very cosmic Christology which is largely foreign to Western Christianity and to Protestant theology most particularly. Jesus is proclaimed as 'Lord', 'Saviour', 'Friend', but not as the one through whom and for whom the whole world was created.[524]

Recovering this cosmology must be an essential corrective to a prevailing dualism of matter and spirit that in turn informs an eschatology in which the material world appears to have no part. Balabanski again:

> It is almost a truism to say that the duality of matter and spirit lies at the heart of Western thought, and that the Christian faith is shaped and determined by such fundamental, binary opposition. In Colossians, however, we have a Christology which allows us to see something different. All things in Heaven and on Earth are shown to be connected via Christ.[525]

In verse 18 the Church is implicated in this cosmology. 'He is the head of the Body, the Church: he is the beginning, the first born from the dead, so that he may come to have the first place in everything'. The verse is usually taken to be a gloss in that it does not appear to fit appropriately into the flow of the hymn. If it was part of the original, it is reasonable to assume it would have been part of the final strophe which focusses on redemption. However, it is where it is in what is now the canon of scripture and the link is clearly made between the Church as a universal body and the cosmos itself. 'Men are members of this world-encompassing body which binds all things together.'[526] The hymn gives the impression that Jesus' role within the whole cosmos takes shape from his place within the Church. 'The author of the letter gives this cosmological train of thought a new direction by designating the Church as the place where, in the present, Christ exercises his rule over the cosmos.'[527] This is a powerful, and neglected, paradigm from which the Church could re-conceive its mission in and to the world. Indeed, from this paradigm one can draw the conclusion that the Church does not have a mission at all, it is Christ who has the mission; this mission is to and with the whole cosmos.

Christ's mission to and with the whole world is for its harmony and wholeness, its re-imagining and redeeming, its blessing and hallowing. This is a vision of sabbath fulfilled. If the mission belongs in the first instance to Christ, the Church can only be a willing partner/facilitator of that which belongs to Christ. The Mission of Christ places the caring and redeeming of the whole created order at the heart of the life of the Church, it is its reason for existence, its catholicity. 'Colossians will not allow us to contain our theology of redemption within the narrower (although profoundly important) orbit of human sin and forgiveness.'[528]

The final stanza of the hymn commences: 'For in him all the πλήρωμά (fullness) of God was pleased to dwell' (Col. 1:19). The concept, 'pleroma', was a significant part of the Gnostic debate in the second century.[529] 'Pleroma' referred not simply to all that was not God, but to the uppermost pneumatic world in immediate proximity to God. Hippolytus, one of the early patristic fathers, argues:

> The goal of the work of redemption is that all things which are of pneumatic origin be reassembled in the pleroma 'in order that the Pleroma be formed into an aggregate according to a perfect number.'[530]

Creation began when 'the Spirit of God moved over the face of the waters' (Gen. 1:2). The pneumatic world is therefore all that has emanated from God, all that is 'in heaven and on earth'. In the Gnostic debate the work of Christ was to 'catch up' creation into that sphere which is in closest proximity to God. Presumably Hippolytus' perfect number is the number of both creation's beginning and its destiny, the sabbath number—seven.

Having said all of that, in this hymn 'pleroma' (fullness) is not a reference to that which is 'not God' but to God. Jesus is described as being the one in whom the 'fullness of God was pleased to dwell'. Presumably this phraseology is to explain how 'in him (Christ) all things hold together' (Col.1:17). The word 'pleroma', in the Christian tradition, is pregnant with meaning. We are to understand that Christ who, because he is the 'fullness of God' is able to bring creation to its fullness, to all that is implied in a 'heavenly banquet'.

> There could hardly be [in Colossians] a grander image of Christ as the cause, the logic, and the goal of the visible and invisible cosmos. Colossians' cosmology not only affirms the present coherence of the cosmos in Christ but identifies Christ *ontologically* in the cosmos.[531]

On its own, the 'Hymn to the Universe' in Colossians might perhaps be considered an aberration. But it is not on its own. Rightly or wrongly it is attributed to Paul. As already noted, John, the other great New Testament theologian, commences his writings with a similar prologue. The anonymous writer to the Hebrews does the same in his opening remarks.

> When these [New Testament] hymns are considered together a pattern emerges of one who was with God in the beginning, was an agent in creation, became truly human, died on the cross, rose from the dead, is exalted above all powers and is the source of universal reconciliation.[532]

Together these texts set the mission of Jesus in the widest possible context: the harmony, reconciliation and completion of the whole created order. It is to this mission that the followers of Jesus must also be committed. In a world where competitive advantage is cherished, to prosecute this mission is to be somewhat subversive. As the crucified and risen Jesus subverted the power struggles and violence of the first century world, indeed of all worlds, so his 21st century followers are called to stand against the greed and exploitation, even violence that threatens the environmental harmony of the 21st century world. Divine redemption, prosecuted through the emptying demanded by the cross, marks the character of the intended new creation. Thomas Berry speaks well of the dilemma that while harmony and wholeness is creation's goal, competitiveness leading to violence has been history's experience:

> The universe, earth, life and consciousness are all violent processes. The basic terms in cosmology, geology, biology and anthropology all carry a heavy charge of tension and violence. Neither the universe as a whole nor any part of the universe is especially powerful. ... Life emerges and advances by the struggle of species for more complete life expression. Humans have made their way amongst the harshness of the natural world and have imposed their violence on the natural world. ... Amongst themselves humans have experienced unending conflict.[533]

In the 'Hymn to the Universe' creation's primeval dream of harmony and wholeness is transported across history's pages of violence and conflict to a sabbath destiny in and through which all things are reconciled. Everyone and everything is destined to be included in the pleroma of God, finding their blessing and fulfilment in the company of a single house, sharing in and contributing to, 'common good'. If this is the mission of Christ it must be the mission of the church, its reason for existence, its catholicity.

Conclusions

The early Christian community came to understand Jesus as the embodiment of sabbath. Sunday is not a Christian version of the Jewish sabbath but a celebration of Jesus who through his death and resurrection has inaugurated a new creation—sabbath fulfilled.

Sabbath is fulfilled in Jesus:

1. Jesus establishes his ministry within a Jubilee context. He commences his ministry by choosing to read Isaiah 61 and when asked by John's disciples if he is 'the one' replies with jubilee references. By making forgiveness (of debt) a hallmark of the new community Jesus embraces the practice of jubilee, commitment to a community in which the experience of 'good' is common to all.

2. The Kingdom of God, its proclamation and inauguration, and the fulfilment of Sabbath are metaphors for the same divinely intended destiny. This destiny is an inclusive, boundary less, 'new creation', the renewal and redemption of the whole created order. Contemporary focus on the individual cannot be read out of the New Testament but is read into it. Building this new community is the mission of Jesus, it must therefore be the mission of the Church.

3. Sabbath rest, the presence of God, *shekinah*, is experienced anew through the incarnation. God dwells afresh with the world: Jesus is the promised rest, the *shekinah* of God. Encountering Jesus, in whom heaven and earth meet, is to encounter sabbath, the 'commandment' that enables God's love and goodness to be available to, and embraced by, humanity. This encounter, reflected in the narrative of the rich young ruler, gives sabbath keeping a clear economic focus.

4. Jesus is identified as pre-existent Wisdom, the personified presence at the birth of creation. Spirit and matter are one in him. A dualism between spirit and matter has been read into the New Testament, is not supported by it and needs to be challenged wherever it appears in Christian piety and practice.

5. The new creation is inaugurated through the death and

resurrection of Jesus. Having 'emptied' himself on the cross, Jesus, mimicking God's words at creation, cried: 'it is finished'. Embracing creation within redemption, Jesus fulfils sabbath and demonstrates that kenosis is the foundational element of both. Understanding that the desire to have everything is to potentially lose everything, and that kenosis is life enhancing rather than life diminishing, is the subject of the final section.

These two chapters have examined sabbath 'from creation to Christ' and in doing so have found that sabbath illumines both the manner of God's engagement with the created order (fulfilled in Christ) and the cosmic destiny to which creation, inclusive of humanity, is called. In the process implications are drawn as to the role or vocation of humanity as a participant in that destiny. It is to a specific articulation of those implications within what might be called 'the human vocation' that we now turn.

PART 3
SABBATH AND THE HUMAN VOCATION

God longed to re-establish his wise sovereignty over the whole creation. He did not want to rescue humans from creation any more than he wanted to rescue Israel from the Gentiles. He wanted to rescue Israel that in order that Israel might be a light to the Gentiles and he wanted to rescue humans in order that humans might be his rescuing stewards over creation.[534]

The first part of this book laid out the theological and pragmatic contexts of the environmental crisis. It then went on to examine, from the Lambeth Conference material, a methodological approach used by the Anglican Church in response to social issues; an approach that could be applied in response to the environmental crisis. This examination unveiled three principles that had been consistently applied over the more than 140 years of the conferences: recourse to scripture, the prioritising of common good over self interest and consistency with a Christian understanding of the human vocation. This examination argued that the Church's catholic identity is as much demonstrated in applying these principles as it is through its teaching and order.

The second part, *Unfolding Sabbath from Creation to Christ*, focussed on the first principle, recourse to scripture, through the window of sabbath. This focus demonstrated that 'good' or 'blessing' was not a gift to an individual but the shared experience of the community, inclusive of creation. Individuals in the biblical narrative are not blessed for themselves, but that they might be a blessing to others. Crucially, the vocation to be a blessing in the biblical narrative is not restricted to contemporary life, but is inclusive of responsibility for the well-being of generations to follow.

This, the third section examines how 21st century human vocation might be both informed and enhanced through an application of the sabbath ethic. Human vocation is lived out in the ordinariness of life, but is shaped and honed by crisis and changed circumstance. War and global depression were the great shapers of human life in the early 20th century, bestowing an indelible sense of duty upon those formed in this period. Multi-culturalism, technology and global trade have shaped and redrawn human boundaries in the latter part of the 20th century. In this context commercial and individual competition has emerged as a foundational ingredient to human flourishing.

Finitude of resources, inequity, and the environmental crisis will shape humanity in the 21st century. In this context, it will be argued that humanity must nurture cooperation as humanity's more noble character if it hopes to flourish in this context and not be consumed by it.

Chapter 5, drawing upon the sabbath insights of hallowing and blessing, argues that humanity must urgently move from an independent mindset to one of interdependence, and in doing so consciously prioritise community over self interest. Community is understood to include immediate family and associates, but extends beyond regions and national boundaries to be globally inclusive. This inclusivity must embrace all humanity within the ecological communities without which human life is impossible.

Chapter 6 argues that common good expressed through sabbath demands an intergenerational responsibility, that human vocation requires each generation to live with the next generation in mind. This is argued theologically as implicit in the eschatological expectation of sabbath fulfilment. It is also argued as a moral necessity that flows from the impact that the current generation's life style is having upon future generations.

Chapter 7 argues that contemporary human vocation necessitates living within limit. Limits are established through moral codes. They also emerge from the necessity of contextual circumstance. This chapter argues that *kenosis* (emptying), the revealed character of God in creation as well as redemption, is to be imitated by humanity. Limitation is commonly resisted as an unnecessary and unwanted impediment to human development; however, it is argued, *kenosis* should be understood as a source of fulfilment, not diminishment. The chapter applies this insight to the limits that must be directed to individual consumption and to the size of the global human population.

Chapter 5

The Human Vocation: and Interdependence

Bearing the image of God is a calling to represent God's interests and to reflect God's character and thus to participate in God's action to bring shalom to the earth.[535]

Sabbath is not simply a theological proposition but that its ethical implications shape a framework upon which community life can be safely forged. Barth declares: 'Into the totality of creation and therefore of the created world there is built as it were, this special thing—the gracious address of the seventh day in which the high God wills to coexist with it, and will actually do so.'[536] Barth's 'special thing' is the presence, or resting of God, an invitation for all creation to enter and share the same space. Moltmann, building on the earlier arguments of Barth, argues for ethical parameters that enable the sharing of this space to be life-giving: 'biblical creation ethics is essentially sabbath ethics, for the Sabbath is the law of creation.'[537]

For the Christian, doctrine must flow over into ethical behaviour. What we believe should have a profound influence upon the way we live. 'If theology is more (though never less) than thinking clearly and speaking rightly about God—if it involves attaining wisdom (*sapientia*) as well as knowledge (*scientia*)—then it concerns how we act, how we live, how we order our individual and collective lives.'[538] Indeed, a test of how seriously

Christian belief is held could well be measured by the manner in which a said belief affects the way life is lived. Michael Northcott, an Anglican priest/scientist argues that Sabbath commitment has universal moral implications. 'Sabbath laws sanctified time and space, and indicated that work and making are moral as well as material activities, governed by transcendent principles as well as by biological laws and relationships.'[539] Because sabbath belief informs our understanding of the nature of God, and the practical implications that flow from it inform 'the human vocation', sabbath is central to Christian self-understanding.

Sabbath as presented in Genesis 2:1-4 penetrates this human self understanding in two ways. Firstly through the concept of hallowing: how life is to be valued, who and what is to be afforded respect. Secondly through an understanding of blessing: how life is blessed and how blessing is received or denied.

Sabbath Rest and Hallowing

In his 'The Idea of the Holy'[540] Rudolf Otto famously proposed the origin of religion as an experience of the numinous which he described as 'mysterium tremendum et fascinans.'[541] For Otto the 'holy' was isolated from a sense of moral awareness or obligation, 'hallowing' described that which was totally other, apart. Otto's view, retained in piety which emphasises separation as a source of divine approval, is not supported by the idea of the 'holy' which appears in the Bible for the first time in Genesis 2:1–4. Here the idea of the 'holy' is associated with God's rest, God's presence, God's engagement with creation. Through God's presence, all that is not God is sanctified, given value. 'Value' is intrinsic; it does not derive from usefulness to humanity. Value is to be enjoyed not through exploitation, but through the appreciation of being a companion part of the created order in which God rests.

Being a companion to, and with, the rest of creation implies ethical responsibility. Barth's view of Sabbath is that nothing exists outside its ethical mandate:

If we link the significance of the holy day in salvation history and its eschatological significance, and if we remember that in both instances we are concerned with its relationship to the particularity of God's omnipotent grace, we shall understand at once, and not without certain awe, the radical importance, the almost monstrous range of the Sabbath commandment.[542]

This 'monstrous range' is implied through Genesis 2's primeval setting. That is to say, sabbath is set in the context of a narrative that seeks not simply to throw light on the origin of things, but to undergird meaning and purpose in every time and in every place. In the sabbath narrative, what is hallowed, claimed by God, is not just the emerging material world of creation, but history itself. Through the sanctification of time, all spaces and all creatures in their particularity are hallowed—'claimed by God'. Barth again:

> This time it is the new thing ... something takes place which had not happened even in God's utterances in Gen 1. ... If the New Testament is correct in its exposition of the Old, then the history attested by the latter was the week at the close of which the Sabbath dawned as the announcement of a new era and a new calculation of time. It dawned because God, who in time past spoke in sundry times and in divers manners, ... has in these last days spoken to us by his Son. Hence the Sabbath too came in the full sense by the word of God.[543]

It is no coincidence that the first creation saga and announcement of the rest of God is immediately followed by a narrative that speaks of God, 'walking in the cool of the evening' (Gen. 3:8). 'It is a fact that there is an inner connection between the sabbath rest of God recounted in the first saga and the history of the Garden of Eden which is in the second form.'[544] God's walking is an encounter with the *adam*,[545] the one drawn from the dust of the earth and yet made as God's counterpoint to commune with God. 'It is in the co-existence of God and man on the one hand and man's independent existence on the other, that the real and yet not discordant counterpart in God himself finds creaturely form and is revealed to the creature.'[546]

The primeval narrative flows from the proclamation of sabbath, 'creation's crown', to a narrative that tells of humanity's desire to usurp that crown. Humanity is crowned with supreme value in the embrace of sabbath, the inter-connectedness of life shared in communion with God and the whole created order. However, history tells us that humanity (singularly and in plural) is not satisfied with interdependence, but seeks self dominance. This 'usurping' is referred to as the 'fall'. This classical Christian doctrine assumes a moment in time when humanity lost innocence, when a life of perfect harmony or sanctity through the presence of God was lost. However, the whole narrative (Genesis 1—Genesis 11) is primeval; that is to say, it does not change at one point from being primeval to another point which can be considered an historical account. 'The biblical saga knows nothing of an original ideal man either in Gen. 1 or Gen. 2, or elsewhere. ... What man does not possess he cannot bequeath or forfeit.'[547] There is no 'time' of bliss when death and pain were unknown and after which they had become an unavoidable reality. As Claus Westermann argues, the text does not support a moment in history when humanity 'fell':

> The whole course of the event from the moment that the man was put into the garden up to his expulsion from it is primeval i.e. on the other side of historical experience. ... The question behind the narrative is not 'how did death come into the world', but why is a person who is created by God limited by death, suffering, toil and sin.[548]

Our choice is between a life of mutuality shared with other human beings in the company of the whole created order, under the sovereignty of God, or a life of competitive independence—separation. While our destiny is a shared life, our history illustrates a lack of the necessary confidence in that mutuality. We seek independence, falsely believing that life is best secured through self-interest, ignoring the reciprocity required in belonging. Self limitation that enables engagement, even intimacy, is resisted. Like many aspects of human life this situation is a contradiction. All humans seek fulfilment in the intimacy of loving relationships. No meaningful relationship is possible without the limitations inherent in this choice. Refusal to accept limitation is therefore destructive of self because: 'love is a relationship which is itself limited and defined by the object.'[549]

In every generation humanity has shared the struggle between a longing for mutuality, peace, shalom, and a desire for control, independence and competitive advantage. The contemporary age is no different to any other, except in one significant matter. The size of the global population together with the rate of consumption and the technological capacity to exploit means that ignoring sabbath ethics leaves humanity open to the possibility of devastation unknown in any other era. 'The sabbath is an order of peace for everyone. ... It is impossible to celebrate it and enjoy it ... at the cost of other people.'[550]

A biblical narrative that honours creation has not been universally welcomed, perhaps not even understood even within the Christian community.[551] Human history and the current environmental crisis record a hostile struggle against respect for creation's integrity. Creation has been considered a resource at the disposal of humanity, to be conquered and dominated by the strongest. As creation's resources become the property of self-interest they are no longer available to serve common good. Physical infrastructure is allowed to dominate over the prior importance of social infrastructure. 'Persons living in a system of anxiety and fear—and consequently of greed—have no time or energy for the common good.'[552]

The presence of God confronts humanity with choice. This choice has become stark and immediate through the environmental crisis: 'the point is that God's world is so made that human actions have their effects, that sinfulness has repercussions well beyond the person concerned.'[553] Or as Norman Wirzba puts it 'The issue is whether we can learn to see, and then welcome, the divine presence wherever we are.'[554]

Hallowing as Engagement

Hallowing (holiness), how it is understood or conferred, has been of intense interest to people of faith in every generation. 'The issue of *holiness as separation and holiness as unanxious engagement*, with somewhat different nuance, is powerfully present in the life of the early Church.'[555] The early Church grew out of the synagogue community in which holiness practiced through separation was justified on grounds that God's people were called to be separated from others. The Christian community rejected this position accepting no differentiation between Jew or Gentile, bond or free, male or female (Gal. 3:28). 21st century Christianity is called to consider this inclusiveness beyond the confines of the human family.

Human inclusivity grasped and practised by the early Christian community was an outcome of a renewed understanding of the nature of God revealed in Jesus. This renewed understanding was not 'new'; it was a rediscovery of the truth that God's embrace knows no boundary. Through *sabat* God engages with and hallows creation in its entirety, inclusive of humanity. Although made in God's image, humans do not exist in isolation from the rest of creation. Humanity's membership in and with the whole of creation is expressed well by Moltmann:

> There is a fellowship of creation and the human being is a member of it. ... We see too that—both in creation and redemption—the human being is not isolated, nor is seen in confrontation with the world. He is viewed as belonging within the enduring cohesion of the whole creation. ... Finally all will be created anew to become the dwelling place of God and the banqueting hall of the eternal sabbath.[556]

Thus, in contrast with much contemporary piety, hallowing should not be interpreted as authenticating withdrawal from the world but as engagement with it. A newly baptised person is not baptised to a life of separation from the world, least of all separation from the wider human family, but of engagement with it. Those who come to the Eucharist are fed with the 'food of tomorrow,'[557] the food that links the contemporary pilgrim with the food of the kingdom in which past and future also participate. Eucharistic attendees are not simply individuals who come to be fed, but participants of a shared loaf and cup, graced for the shared work of transformation in the world of which they are part. They are sent into the world and go 'with courage in the power of your Spirit.'[558]

However, an argument for sanctification or hallowing through engagement, rather than separation, runs counter to popular piety which comforts Christian non-engagement in the public square. This is especially true of the environmental debate with its inherent challenge to an economic status quo. Sabbath gives no comfort to the idea that a person can seek self interested economic advantage and at the same time seek divine approval or sanctity. Berry makes a crushing critique of an inwardly focussed sanctity:

> Despite its protest to the contrary, modern Christianity has become willy-nilly the religion of the state and of the economic status quo. Because it has so exclusively dedicated itself to incanting anaemic souls into heaven, it has been made the tool of much earthly villainy.[559]

As noted in the account of scholarly debate over sabbath's origins in Chapter 2, sabbath 'almost certainly had its origins in an agrarian context, in the human desire to benefit from nature's bounty and avoid the adverse consequences of nature's fickleness.'[560] Because of their dependence on natural cycles over which they had no control, the agrarian community appears to have developed rituals of restraint from activity which was deemed to erode nature's gift of bounty and fruitfulness. The Jewish festival of Unleavened Bread also appears to have had its origins in these rituals. Sabbath therefore has its origins in celebration or engagement with that which was deemed to be universally life giving. As sabbath gradually became 'the mark of being Jewish' it lost its focus on the sanctity of the whole of creation to be replaced by prescribed acts of withdrawal that focussed individual piety and identity. A minority people's need for identity, for particularity, even for exclusivity in the face of a majority culture, accelerated the process of an inwardly focussed sanctity and an identity defined through separation. This is well illustrated in the writings of Haggai, one of the last prophetic books of the Hebrew Scriptures:

> If one carries consecrated meat in the fold of one's garment and touches bread or stew or wine or oil or any kind of food, does it become holy? The priests answered 'no'. Then Haggai said, if one who is unclean by contact with a dead body touches any of these, does it become unclean? The priests answered 'yes, it becomes unclean' (Haggai 2:12-13).

Separation became a feature of Jewish faith and practice. According to Jonathan Sacks separation disabled the Jewish community from being agents of transformation in the world they shared with others.[561] In contrast, refusal to accept separation brought Jesus into conflict with religious authorities who considered such separation to be a core element of the Law of Moses. Jesus was accused of eating with tax collectors and sinners. He touched and was touched by lepers, the possessed, women in menstruation, and the dead. He was not made unclean but they were made whole.

The challenge faced by an embryonic Christianity to engage beyond previously conceived boundaries of sanctity is amply illustrated in the narrative of Peter's dream (Acts 10: 9-16). Peter, the titular leader of the fledging Christian community, had to confront the logical consequences of belief in a single world over which Jesus, the Lamb, reigned, against the particularities of his Jewish foundations. Wrestling with the question of engagement with the Gentile world was not easy. He had been conditioned to believe that identity as the children of God was secured through separation, not only from those who were not, but also from those who had no right to be accepted as equals. This wrestling reached a climax in his dream in which animals he believed to be unclean were let down in a net for him to eat. He was affronted and said he could not eat that which was unclean. His indignation was punctured by the voice of God: 'What God has made clean, you must not call profane' (Acts 10:15). While the context of this dream was Peter's wrestle with the reach of divine redemptive love within the context of the whole human race, our wrestle extends to the manner in which that redemptive love touches the whole created order.[562] Sadly, recent history indicates this journey of enlightenment is far from complete. The idea of holiness through separation has remained the cause of contemporary alienation and suffering.

Apartheid in South Africa, and the segregation of black people in America, had Christian underpinnings. In both cases there was an assumption that the perceived superiority of one group would be tarnished by what was deemed to be the inferiority of the other group. 'Ethnic cleansing' in many parts of the world has received religious sanctity and approval as witnessed by the involvement of Christian leadership in the 1994 atrocities in Rwanda.

These atrocities are all the more heinous in light of Jesus' teaching about 'neighbour'. Clearly Jesus intended 'neighbour' to be inclusive of all humanity; I am arguing that the idea of neighbour should extend to all creation. A refusal to accept environmental responsibility, on the grounds that humans are 'apart from' creation and therefore not in a neighbourly relationship with it receives support from wide sections of Christian adherence.[563] Brueggemann helpfully underlines neighbourliness, or an attitude of neighbourliness, as an antidote to apathetic disregard of the other: 'defilements are not material contaminations, but they are distortions of neighbourliness.'[564]

Hallowing sought through separation is marked by what is opposed, rather than with what is embraced. The attractiveness of a theology of hallowing based upon separation is that it is perceived as being a way of strengthening membership. Such is human nature that we appear more easily to unite against an enemy (perceived or imaginary) than we seem able to unite around a common cause for good.[565] Such is the nature of modern politics that political parties seem to solidify their political identity, and by implication their membership, by opposing the initiative of their political foes whether that initiative be in the best interest of the people they represent or not.[566] Because of the global nature of the environmental crisis it is necessary to gain bi-partisan political support for major reform. Such support seems most unlikely in the contemporary political climate.

If we are to understand the whole created order as hallowed by the presence of God, then just as Moses was commanded to remove his shoes before the presence of God in the burning bush, the appropriate mindset of people of faith to the total environment should be humility, gentleness and respect, for this is not terra nullius. The non-human creation is not simply a material entity that is separate to God or to humanity; we are part of it for we are in relationship with God who rests within it.

Sanctity or holiness through engagement rather than separation is therefore a foundational theological proposition for the Christian community. Failure to understand this, as already noted, has led to some of the darker moments in the Church's history, but equally it has been behind a lack of commitment to engage fully with the non-human creation. To live the ethical requirements of sabbath is to engage, to engage fully and equitably with human and non-human creation alike, it is to contribute to the community of all living things.

Sabbath Rest and Blessing

Blessing is associated with a yearning for well-being, peace, harmony, wholeness. While this yearning is inevitably shaped by individual desire, the biblical narrative gives no comfort to a notion that individuals are blessed outside their relationship with the community(ies) to which they belong. Humanity's blessing is dependent upon its relationship with the non-human creation.

The Septuagint renders 'blessing' as εὐλογια (good word).[567] 'The term may refer to the spoken word, the words themselves, and to their effect.'[568] The Bible often renders the recipients of blessing as 'blessed' or 'happy'. Blessing is more than an expression of hope. It is generally understood to be efficacious, to be a source of goodness or grace. Its opposite is a curse, which in many cultures is understood to be the utterance of words that are irreversibly imposed, ultimately issuing in an evil outcome. The Genesis 2 account of the seventh day is a claim that in sabbath rest there is blessing for the whole created order. How are we to understand that blessing; how does it become effective?

As noted in the exegesis, the chiastic like structure of the seventh day account emphasises that the 'rest' of God enables creation to be 'finished'. It is complete. Blessing derives first and foremost from being part of a completed creation in which God rests. Blessing is not first and foremost dependent upon human activity. Bauckham notes: 'The order [of creation] is already established before the creation of humans. It does not need humans to put it in order.'[569] It is the height of hubris to assume that through human effort we can add to creation or that creation's blessing is only available to us through our own effort, that the more we exploit the more we shall be blessed.

Walter Brueggemann makes the same point. He argues that creation is imbued with the extravagant abundance of God and that the excessive, perhaps obsessive, human desire for exploitation and consumption does not arise from knowledge of that abundance but from a fear of scarcity. Blessing can be understood as the consequence that arises from the knowledge of abundance.[570] In this sense blessing is akin to contentment, which, as was argued in Chapter 4, is more accurately descriptive of a desired Christian virtue than 'happiness'. Further, Brueggemann asserts that what we call human sinfulness is a refusal to accept the limits which enable abundance:

[sinners] are those who refuse to receive life in creation on terms of generous extravagance, no doubt in order to practice a hoarding autonomy in denial that creation is indeed governed and held by its creator. Creation has within it the sovereign seriousness of God, who will not tolerate the violation of the terms of creation, which are terms of gift, dependence and extravagance.[571]

In Chapter 2 I referred to John Vincent Taylor and his *Enough is Enough*[572]. He commenced his first chapter with a quotation from Charles Dodgson's *Alice's Adventures in Wonderland*:[573]

'I wish you wouldn't squeeze so', said the dormouse who was sitting next to her.' I can hardly breathe'. 'I can't help it,' said Alice very meekly: 'I'm growing'. 'You've no right to grow here said the dormouse'. 'Don't talk nonsense,' said Alice more boldly: 'you know you are growing too.' 'Yes, but I grow at a reasonable pace,' said the dormouse: 'not in that ridiculous fashion.'[574]

Dodgson may or may not have had growth stimulated by the industrial revolution in mind; however, it is now true that growth is the ubiquitous mantra of modern economic systems.[575] (It will be argued in Chapter 7 that humanity has to live with the assumption that such growth is now no longer possible).[576] Western culture has come to measure blessing as 'more'. Taylor started his book with the Lewis Carroll reference to alert us to the reality that we have misunderstood blessing in Western culture. That it is not related to 'more' but to 'enough'; that abundance should not be understood as a quantitative measurement but as a qualitative experience of contentment lived in the context of a life-giving community.

Vocation within Community

The community of creation, crowned by sabbath, is described in the first creation narrative, (Gen. 1:1–2:4), as three habitats: the water, the sky, and the earth. The narrative then describes how each habitat is filled with the life that God intends (days 4-6). The spaces, together with that which fills them, become living communities. Every species, all of life, shares an interdependent existence. There is no life outside this interdependence.

> The Torah of Moses develops what is nearly a mantra of social revolution, widow, orphan, alien, the marginalised and vulnerable now valued, noticed, protected, entitled. Outside of this stringent costly provision there is nothing but Pharoah, nothing but anxiety, scarcity, and eventually new waves of bondage.[577]

The health and vitality of the land, the plants, the animals and humans are inseparable and interdependent. God is as concerned for the land as for the forms of life that depend upon it. In this context, what is the role or vocation of humanity?

A number of biblical images have currency:

Dominion. While the biblical narrative implies that the human habitat is the earth, *adam* (human) from *the adamah* (earth), it is a fact of contemporary life that human aspirational activity is all pervasive. Humans treat all three habitats as commodities to be exploited rather than as a home to be protected. By bridging all three habitats through our ubiquitous activity, humans have imposed a single human world (the anthropocene) upon the single organic system of creation. Humans display a cavalier approach when exploiting a desired resource, showing no apparent understanding of the complexity that is being disrupted and the life giving balances that are being put at risk. While humanity now speaks of a global world our actions do not reflect this assertion; we behave tribally:

We human beings are vitally important as part of Gaia. ... Like it or not we are now its heart and mind, but to continue to improve in this role we have to ensure our survival as a civilised species and not revert into a cluster of warring tribes that was a stage in our evolutionary history.[578]

Given the extent of contemporary human capacity and technology it is tempting to give theological justification to human exploitation (dominion) in all three habitats on the basis of Gen. 1:27.

Richard Bauckham argues differently:

> When we see it [dominion] in the context of all other aspects of
> what it means for humans to be part of the interdependent network
> of relationships in the community of creation, when we realise our
> distinctive power is rooted in a more fundamental dependence on
> the rest of creation, then we can see that dominion has its place
> within a wider pattern of reciprocity.[579]

The exercise of 'dominion' is at the root of the current crisis. While
sabbath's blessing and hallowing is bestowed on the whole of creation,
human experience of that blessing is won or lost as responsibility to act
in accord with sabbath provisions is honoured or ignored. 'Deuteronomy
makes it very clear that abandonment of God's will and God's ways, and
a failure to live justly will result in God's curse—a curse which extends to
the cities and the fields and to the fruit of the ground, and in which the
climate too is affected with fiery heat and drought and rain becoming dust
(Deut. 28:20ff).'[580] The community to which humanity belongs, and upon
which it is dependent, is the whole created order in which God rests.

Shepherd. Fishbane[581] amongst others argues that *dominion* does not
have to be understood malignly but can be understood benignly, that is
to say that humanity is commissioned with the task of caring for creation
through control over it.

> Human dominion is a power bestowed by God and must serve to
> maintain God's order. Human rule must have positive consequences
> for the ruled; in ruling, humans must preserve their humanity and
> remain humane. Therefore human dominion can be understood
> only as an action for which humans are accountable to God.[582]

Teilhard De Chardin,[583] argues that the evolution of humanity is
essential to the evolution of creation and that it is the role of humans in
every generation to respond to the needs of the created order. Richard
Middleton makes the same point.[584] He argues the royal motif and its
further clarification in shepherd imagery is a consistent scriptural response

to the needs of humanity for order. It should therefore not surprise us that similar imagery is transferred to creation and its needs for similar protection. He argues that in his resting on the seventh day God delegates the administration of creation to humanity on his behalf.

Delegate is the metaphor preferred by Bonhoeffer.

> The father acts as a deputy for the children ... he is not an isolated individual, he combines in himself the selves of a number of other human beings. ... This reality shatters the fiction that the subject, the performer, of all ethical conduct is the individual. Not the individual in isolation but the responsible man is the subject, the agent, with whom ethical reflection must concern itself.[585]

Desmond Tutu makes a similar point when he says: 'My humanity is inextricably bound up in [others]. We belong in a bundle of life. We say a person is a person through other people. It is not: 'I think therefore I am'. It says rather: 'I am human because I belong.'[586] Bonhoeffer argues that acting as deputy is not restricted to specific relationships but is a feature of being a human: 'even the solitary lives as a deputy, and indeed quite especially so, for his life is lived in deputyship for man as man, for mankind as a whole.'[587] This understanding does not sit well with my argument that far from delegating responsibility, by resting in creation God continues to grace creation through his presence.

Steward. The most frequently used title to describe the human role is 'steward'. While 'steward' is not a word the biblical narrative uses, it is a reasonable interpretation of *shmr*, keeper (Gen. 2:15). The verb shmr (keep) is perhaps more accurately translated 'the protection of another's welfare.'[588] This verb can be linked to the idea of stewardship, the caring for that which is not one's own, that which must be passed on to another. The verb does not survive the 'fall' and is absent from the narrative of the driving out of *adam* from the garden. However it reappears in the narrative of Cain and Abel. In the 'real world', outside the Garden of Eden, Cain still has the responsibility to 'work in reverence to' the ground and he brings his offering, the fruits of such tilling. However he quickly learns that this is not his only responsibility. In reply to the question 'where is your brother Abel', we hear the response: 'Am I my brother's keeper'. In light of Genesis 2:15 the response is more shocking than it might first appear. Cain responds with the word 'shmr'. The reader of the text is left with no alternative other than to realise that guarding that which belongs to another remains the human responsibility. This caring is equally in the arena of human and of non-human activity. Caring for that which belongs to another arises out of the knowledge that we human beings are created in relationship with God and with all that God has made. The steward metaphor gains considerable impetus in the New Testament, especially from the parables of Jesus.

While the idea of stewardship is, and will remain appealing, it is not without difficulty in the light of 'sabbath'. If stewardship infers that humanity is somehow above or apart from creation, with a mandate to care for that which does not include itself, the practice of stewardship can fall into the trap of caring from the perspective of humanity, caring from the point of view of creation's usefulness to human activity. As Bauckham argues from the story of Cain and Abel 'Their [human] taking possession of the earth has actually filled the earth with violence. Instead of an appropriately limited use of the earth's resources, humans have over exploited the earth with the result that they engage in violent competition amongst themselves, they deprive wild animals of their food, and both humans and wild animals revert to meat eating.'[589]

Baukham's critique of the human vocation towards creation being described in anthropocentric terms is referenced again in Chapter 6.

Priesthood of Creation. As the people of Israel reach Sinai they hear these words from God through the mouth of Moses: 'If you obey my voice and keep my covenant, you shall be my treasured possession out of all the peoples. Indeed the whole earth is mine, but you shall be for me a priestly kingdom and a holy nation' (Exod. 19:5-6).

This text cannot be construed as a basis to undergird the general vocation of humanity. It is a specific affirmation of the role of the Israelite people whose blessing and particularity is not to be construed for their sake alone, but that they might be a conduit of blessing to all peoples. However, Christians, who accept the covenantal provisions of the Old Testament as authoritative, should see in this text an imperative to accept care of the 'whole earth' as core business. Philip Sherrard argues the case:

> Because it is only through man fulfilling his role as mediator between God and the world that the world itself can fulfil its destiny and be transfigured in the light and presence of God. It is in this sense that man, when he is truly human, is also and above all a priest.[590]

A clear call to a priestly role in creation for the whole of humanity is present in the theological writings of George Herbert (1593-1633), poet/priest, influential to the formation of Anglicanism:

> Of all the creatures both in sea and land
> Only to man hast thou made known thy ways
> And put the pen alone into his hand
> And made him secretary of thy praise. (Providence 11:5-9)

> Man is the world's high priest, he doth present
> The sacrifice for all, while they below
> Unto thy service mutter an assent. (Providence 11:13-15)[591]

In more recent times a call to human priesthood is also clear in the writings of John Zizioulas, a widely respected Orthodox theologian:

> The Christian regards the human being as the only possible link between God and creation, a link that can either bring nature in communion with God and thus sanctify it; or condemn it to the state of a thing, the meaning and purpose of which are exhausted with the satisfaction of man.[592]

Moltmann agrees: 'In his [human] praise he acts as a representative of the whole creation. His thanksgiving, as it were, looses the dumb tongue of creation. It is here that the priestly dimension of his designation is to be found'. He goes on to add: 'This is not meant anthropocentrically; for in the community of creation 'everything that has breath' praises the Lord.'[593]

But can they be right? If God rests in creation why is there need for mediation? Perhaps the problem is not with the idea of priesthood, but in describing priesthood as 'mediation'—the vocation of the go-between. God does not require a go-between. Perhaps priesthood should be understood not in terms of mediation, but in terms of guardianship. A priest could therefore be understood as the guardian and enabler of the space where God rests, the space in which earth recuperates. Within this interpretation the priest guards the space in which debts are forgiven and slaves set free: the space which encourages a mindset of abundance: the space in which creation's cycles of rest and refreshment are honoured. The psalter, and Psalm 148 in particular, indicate that all parts of creation, including humanity, are equally called to praise God and need no mediator to act on their behalf. If the space is guarded, if creation is 'let be', all creation naturally praises God. The sun moon and stars; the whales and dolphins; the snow clad hills; fruiting trees, wild and domestic animals; creeping things and flying birds; and finally all peoples, young and old, rulers and common folk, all exist to praise God.

Whatever biblical metaphors are relied upon to describe the human vocation in relation to creation, care must be taken, for idleness in this regard can justify Toynbee's critical analysis:

> Some of the major maladies of the present world—for instance the recklessly extravagant consumption of nature's irreplaceable treasures and the pollution of those of them that man has not already devoured—can be traced back in the last analysis to a religious cause, this cause is the rise of monotheism.[594]

Sabbath requires an understanding that the earth cannot be owned; that our right to harvest its food, cannot impinge upon the rights of the non-human creation.

> A theology of dominion or stewardship fails to accentuate that we belong to the earth more than it belongs to us, that we are more dependent upon it than it is on us, that we are of the earth, not living on the earth.[595]

Overlaying the metaphor of ruler, steward, delegate, or keeper, sabbath insists that no matter which metaphor is utilised, the overarching human responsibility is to safeguard equity and mutuality within community, recognising that the primary community is creation itself.

Bauckham argues that whatever view we hold about the divinely intended human role, its starting point must be an understanding that we are part of creation.

> Exceptional though we may be in various ways, our exceptionality is embedded in the community of creation to which we belong and would be impossible without it. We are not aliens imposing ourselves on, or intruders ourselves within, the community of creation, but naturally members of it.[596]

The process of evolution has enabled life to adapt to changing conditions over millennia. Humanity now finds itself in a position of not simply adapting to changing conditions which have come about through some external cause, but to conditions that are changing as a result of human activity. In this context the consideration of human vocation cannot simply begin from the perspective of human relationship to an externality over which humans may or may not consider responsibility or care; but must begin from the consideration of a community to which humans belong. In this sense vocation is less about role and more about 'being', a consideration of who or what we think we are. It is in consideration of this question that the future harmony and sustainability of life depends.

Conclusions

There is indeed more to Sabbath than simply a break from regular routines.[597]

1. **Sabbath's ethical mandate shapes human vocation.** Human vocation arises from self understanding. Sabbath frames this self understanding by establishing the conditions for human living. These conditions are to be in 'cooperation with' rather than in 'competition with'. Sabbath's 'monstrous range' is a rhythm or order which undergirds the well-being of all life including the land itself, from the beginning to the end of time. Entering into the order or discipline of sabbath is the human vocation.

2. **Sabbath shaped vocation serves community.** To live 'in cooperation with' is to build community, both human and non-human. The criticism of White, Toynbee, and others that monotheism, and Christianity in particular, are the primary causes of over-exploitation is countered by a sabbath requirement for mutuality. The problem is not Christianity, but the failure of the Church to understand and apply that which is at the heart of faith. Ignoring the sabbath principle has resulted in the crisis now faced by the whole created order, inclusive of humanity, a crisis of self interest at the expense of common good.

3. **Sabbath shaped vocation is served by community.** Blessing or contentment, the desired goal of all human living, is derived from relationships, from belonging. In this context limits to self interested exploitative activity is enhancement not diminishment. Blessing is bestowed upon creation in its entirety. Individuals experience blessing as an outcome of

participation in the well-being of the whole. Accepting limits is, arguably, the greatest challenge facing western culture, requiring changed economic expectations for the greater good.

4.   **Sabbath shaped vocation builds common good.** Many metaphors are in currency as a way of describing a human vocation in relation to the created order. While most metaphors, particularly that of 'steward', carry biblical currency and authority, all are in danger of being understood from the perspective of humanity rather than creation. Any metaphor for the human vocation must be understood and interpreted as facilitating the good of the whole created order, inclusive of the good of all human beings.

CHAPTER 6

THE HUMAN VOCATION: LIVING WITH THE FUTURE IN MIND

God has placed us at a new beginning. We are here for the future. Our role is crucial ... God permits us in some way to be co-creators with him in his continuing act of creation.[598]

Chapter 5 has examined community as the sabbath context in which human vocation is to be nourished and fulfilled. It was argued that sabbath assumes non-human creation to be the primary community which humanity shares. This chapter argues that future generations need also to be considered part of this community, their needs and rights being taken into consideration as contemporary choices are made. Human beings have in the past felt responsibility for future generations of their tribe or family. What is now different is that this sense of responsibility must extend globally to include those who in the past would have fallen outside the parameters of familial or national responsibility.

The impact of the present on the future is a theme in which theology and science, faith and philosophy can find convergence. The implication of scientific research discussed in Chapter 1 is that the status quo is no longer viable; we cannot simply live with this generation's aspirations in mind. While the nuclear threat of the 1950's and 1960's was an obvious and existential threat to humanity as a whole, including future generations, the perniciousness of the environmental threat lies in its capacity to be ignored because it appears not to be immediate. What makes this threat different to the nuclear threat is that it is being exacerbated by a generation that could choose to act differently, but chooses not to. The effect of global warming is permitted by political leaders who fail to pass urgently needed regulation, and perpetrated, knowingly or unknowingly, by humans in all walks of life.[599] Its most serious consequences are predicted to fall upon those who have not created the problem and who may have few options to mitigate the outcome. That is what makes the present crisis qualitatively different to any that has gone before. 'One great philosopher, Hans Jonas, has argued that we need a whole new ethic for the future, since never before has a human generation held in its hands the prosperity or ruin of the generations to come.'[600]

Living with the future in mind is a theological imperative for Christians for whom the present is shaped by eschatological hope. Chapter 4 explored the eschatological relationship between sabbath and Jesus' proclamation of the Kingdom of God. The 'Kingdom of God', the now but not yet expression of the reign of God, is shaped by God's intention in creating and God's purpose in creation's destiny.

Eschatology has been popularly understood in the context of linear time—'the last things', seemingly a concern not for things on earth, but for things in 'heaven'. This eschatological application has been instrumental in diverting Christian commitment away from the problems of the present world. John Passmore[601] doubts that Christian theology can ever reshape itself in an ecologically helpful manner without ceasing to be Christian. He argues that Christianity's traditional longing for another world is too ingrained and pervasive in its theology.

This parodying of Christianity as 'other worldly', cannot be exclusively blamed upon an aggressive secularism. Passmore is right: a misunderstood eschatology is a significant contributor. Convincing church membership of the necessity of Christianity's essential role in transforming human society is a mammoth task. It was C.H. Dodd who famously encouraged the Christian community to realise the future is already present: 'The Church prays, 'Thy kingdom come'; 'Come Lord Jesus'. As it prays it remembers that the Lord did come and with him came the Kingdom of God.'[602] Dodd's 'realised eschatology'[603] has since been reworked, but the essence of what he argued remains. 'Good works' do not earn one a place in 'heaven', but they are an outcome of belief in the redeeming of all things. Rowan Williams has recently drawn attention to the shortcomings inherent in the concept of linear time as the only way of understanding its meaning. 'If there is no single 'linear' story of God's liberative action ... there is no movement to a last end, a millennium—only a confidence that within the divine matrix nothing is ultimately lost.'[604]

As argued in Chapter 5, the sabbath ethic speaks to the right of all creation for liberty, not simply human liberty, not simply liberty for other creatures, but liberty for the land itself. Such a broad sense of liberty is not found in popular Christian, let alone public, awareness. However, the theological promotion of liberty in the writings of Gustavo Gutiérrez and Desmond Tutu, is well known. Although written in the context of human liberty from oppression, their writings throw light on the broader concern for creation's liberty. In both cases it might be assumed that the movement for liberation from current human despair calls primarily upon an ethic of human inclusiveness,—'neighbourliness'.[605] It does, but that is not all.

Gutiérrez argues 'the driving force of salvific history is radically orientated towards the future. Eschatology is thus not just one more element of Christianity but the very key to understanding the Christian faith.'[606] What he meant by this, in terms of Christian living, can be illustrated by his statement: '[It must be remembered that] through the struggle against misery, injustice and exploitation the goal is the creation of a new humanity.'[607] His liberation theology was set in the context of God's intention for the whole created order.

Desmond Tutu's perspective from the pain and alienation of apartheid is also helpful. While his words reflect human from human alienation, the principle of which he speaks applies also to the non-human creation.[608] He speaks of *ubuntu*[609] as 'the very essence of being human.'[610] It means my humanity is inextricably bound up with yours. He says 'when we want to give high praise to someone [for their common humanity] we say they have ubuntu.'[611] He goes on: 'we belong in a bundle of life ... what dehumanises you inexorably dehumanises me.'[612] 'We have to accept that what we do, we do for generations past present and yet to come.'[613] He speaks of those who care for and about the total, intergenerational, community of life as having *ubuntu*.

Ubuntu, given currency within the whole created order, could be understood as God's intention in a new creation, the redemption and transformation of the whole created order, the forgiveness of debt, sabbath fulfilled. Ubuntu carries a communal ethic, the rejection of individual advantage at the expense of interconnected responsibility. Within this ethic an individual is said to be well if the community to which she/he belongs is flourishing. Kapya Kaoma argues that corruption which appears rife across the continent of Africa, corruption which has had serious ecological consequences, has come about through the loss of ubuntu and the growing dominance of individual competitiveness which has undermined traditional values and culture.[614]

Gutiérrez and Tutu thus approach reconciliation, health and well-being, from the perspective of intergenerational connectedness. This must also be the case in response to the environmental crisis. Hans Schwarz, in his overview of theology's recent developments comes to a similar conclusion about connectedness and the future:

The Church cannot confine itself to serving individuals and acting as a conservative force, as society might expect it to. The task and mission of the church is determined by its own peculiar horizon—the coming peace and the coming freedom of all humanity. This means 'the realization of the eschatological hope of justice, the humanizing of man, the socializing of humanity, peace for all creation.'[615]

This connectedness is at the heart of sabbath which celebrates the whole (heaven and earth) and the relationship, in God, that exists between them. 'Earth', the material world inclusive of humanity, exists within 'time', therefore the blessing, hallowing, and redeeming activities of creation and redemption embodied in sabbath include the blessing, hallowing and redeeming of past present and future. The past, present and future are a continuum. This is articulated well by Barth:

> What is now? What is present? It is the time between the times. And this strictly speaking is not time at all, no duration, no series of moments but only the boundary between the past and the future, a boundary that is never stationary, but always shifts further ahead. It is the moment we can never prevail upon to stay for always it has already gone or not yet come.[616]

The present has been enabled or deleteriously infected by the past. 'The ethical isolation of the individual is a fictitious notion ... it fails to understand the historicity of human existence.'[617] Our present is framed equally by the actions of the past, and by the opportunities and obligations inherent in living with the future in mind. For the Christian community, the future is not simply the next chapter of time, it is destiny revealed in the purposes of God. The biblically revealed future informs present responsibility and commitment. This destiny is a new creation in which all that God has purposed is redeemed. 'While human salvation is spiritual in nature and providential work is orientated to the material creation, both human and non-human creation will live in eternity through the triune God's ongoing work.'[618] Christians are called to live in the present with this future in mind; more than that, to trust in the ultimate purposes of God, even when privation and alienation appear to prevail. To live this way is to live in hope.

In this chapter I am developing themes found in earlier chapters and relating them to 'human vocation' within the context of the environmental crisis. These themes, well known in that they are regularly exposited from the biblical narrative have ,in my view, been insufficiently applied by the contemporary Church to its mission within an environmentally challenged world.

1. **Living hopefully under the reign of God.** In the absence of temple, sabbath emerged as an expression of the universal reign of God. 'Sabbath fulfilled', and Jesus' proclamation of the 'Kingdom of God', speak of the same reality, the harmony of living in peace with God and with all that belongs to God.

2. **Living generously in the presence of God.** Responding to the presence of God, *shekinah*, is the source of creation's blessing.

3. **Living together in the house of God.** Sabbath bears witness that the world is where God rests, it is the house of God. The earth must matter to humanity because it matters to God. All creation shares the companionship of this house. Mutuality in this house shapes the human vocation.

Living Hopefully under the Reign of God

The proclamation that individual parts of creation are 'good' and that creation as a whole is 'very good' is reason for confidence that, because God reigns: 'all will be well, all manner of things will be well.'[619] Julian of Norwich was articulating the truth that each fleeting moment needs to be understood within the context of a much broader continuum; to live in hope is to integrate the past and present within the future.

'To be human is to live in hope. It is intrinsic to the human condition.'[620] Despair felt by the scientific community specialising in environmental science, is not caused by the crisis itself, but by an ineffectual political response, regionally, nationally and internationally. This despair is shared by a significant percentage of the wider population.[621] A Christian response to the environmental crisis therefore cannot simply be reduced to the mechanics of energy conservation and climate change mitigation, it must counter despair and a sense of helplessness; it must be founded on hope. Arguably the most thorough development of a *theology of hope* has come from Jürgen Moltmann[622] whose theology 'combined the theological influence of Barth with the thought of the Marxist philosopher Ernst Bloch.'[623]

> Bloch used the category of hope (*hoffnung*) to construct a form of atheistic philosophy. ... Man is a being who by his very nature is not closed or complete, he does not have an 'essence' that is already there or complete. He is open to the future into which he is moving and in which his identity is yet to be discovered realised and affirmed. Bloch believed that this openness to the future was the real human meaning of the Bible's speech about God.[624]

Being open to the future is to imagine the emergence of the harmony and wholeness of the biblical narrative and invest in it corporate and personal action and influence. 'Bloch showed that hope is a universal characteristic of humanity';[625] that 'true genesis is not at the beginning but at the end.'[626] If Bloch is correct, in that 'hope' is an essential component to a healthy and fulfilled human life, at least in part, this explains why environmental science is denied by many. For some in the farming community, for example, acceptance of the science carries a loss of hope; it is interpreted as meaning that what is currently practised cannot continue. The wisdom that needs to be absorbed is that hope lies in changed practice. Hope is the energy to accept and transform the present in light of the future.[627]

Moltmann forged his theology through the desperate inhumanity of World War II, including but not exclusively the *shoah* (holocaust).

Equally, his theology emerged through the period of cynicism that prevailed during the period of the Cold War when neither communism nor materialistic capitalism, seemed to provide a way forward to a future worthy of hope. In this vacuum Moltmann set out to define the present by the Christian end of history, the reign of God.

In the context of the environmental crisis a similar narrative is needed to lift the global community out of an economic life that appears to be shaped, not by hope of a sustainable future, but by short term economic opportunism. The priority of profit has swamped other concerns or values. Within this world view there is little if any incentive to adopt policies that safeguard long term ecological health and well-being if those policies are perceived to curtail short term, self-interested, profit. The narrative is all important. Rather than resisting changed behaviour for fear of economic loss, the narrative of increased quality of life and the benefits of human collaboration through change, needs to prevail.

Despite globally driven economic strategies to increase consumerism, Hugh Mackay's[628] recent research affirms that material wealth does not easily, if at all, translate into human meaning and contentment. In other words, it is fair to ask why humanity seems so inexorably driven on a course of individual economic materialism that does not easily, or necessarily, translate into qualities that really matter. It is in relatedness that human satisfaction and contentment resides.

The current context has few similarities to the world in which Moltmann's theology was developed, and yet humanity's longing for meaning remains constant. Belief that this world is 'tuned' for life, that imbalances can be restored, that in 'reclaiming its sabbaths' the land's harmony and equity can be shared by all living things, and that liberation from poverty, slavery and debt are built into God's desire for human and non-human life, is a hope worthy of human cooperation and commitment. Added to this, a view that sentient human life can and should contribute to an evolving, sustainable, and harmonious world, should be sufficient motivation for humanity to work together for this 'common good'. If this motivation cannot be achieved out of a spirit of altruism, it should be achieved out of the knowledge that it is in the interest of the 'self' to do so.

From where will such a narrative of 'common good', with power to capture mainstream imagination, emerge? Bridging the 'disconnect' between contemporary religious life and secular society appears increasingly difficult.[629] However, 'hope' is a point of human connection and articulated with integrity could be a connecting point between Christianity and a materialistic, secular culture.

Moltmann warns that the Church's capacity to engage the secular world in a narrative of hope, rooted in a conviction of a shared future, has been severely reduced because it has:

> lost the character of *cultus publicus*[630] to which it had been accustomed ... it became something in religious form that it never was and from the theological standpoint of the New Testament it never can be—*cultus privatus*.[631]

Moltmann was keen to point out that this movement away from a faith engaged with the totality of life, the reign of God, towards a faith focussed 'out of the world' is not an outcome of the reformation, although the trend may have been exacerbated, but an outcome of the identification of Christianity with the state, an outcome of the period we know of as Christendom.[632] While the contemporary decline, perhaps even 'death' of Christendom in the West carries a loss of status it does not necessarily mean a loss of influence, indeed this period could be grasped by the Church as an opportunity for focussed re-engagement with the whole of life.

As noted in the introductory chapter, Lesslie Newbigin has also been very critical of the contemporary Church's inward focus and emphasises that this was not the character of Christianity when suffering under persecution in its fledgling years.

> The Church could have escaped persecution by the Roman Empire
> if it had been content to be treated as *cultus privatus*—one of the
> many forms of personal religion. But it was not ... The Christian
> mission is thus to act out in the whole life of the whole world the
> confession that Jesus is Lord of all.[633]

The whole of life is the theatre of the reign of God. In this space there is no place for a privatised religion, certainly not one that seeks salvation 'out of this world'. Sabbath regained; faith in, and commitment to, the God whose creating and redeeming presence transforms and renews creation, can re-engage the Church with the world, and in the engagement, hope, with the power to transform, can be shared.

The whole of life must integrate past present and future. The pattern of daily living experienced by past generations naturally integrated present and future. The future was seen as a continuation of the present. The expectations and hopes of the next generation were mirrored in the lives of the present generation. By way of contrast, the present era is marked more by dissimilarity between the present and the future. Change has been and continues to be so rapid that coping with incremental change is difficult enough without imagining a future half a century away. In these circumstances it is not surprising that public discourse focusses more on what are perceived to be immediate problems, rather than a vision for a sustainable (hard to conceive) future. And yet, as has been argued, future choices are being shaped, and perhaps more seriously limited, by present choices, choices made without the future in mind.

Part 2 explored a sabbath narrative through which God's purpose in creating, and God's intention in creation's destiny, folds the past and present into the future. 'Made in the image of God' (Gen. 1:27), human collaboration with God in this purpose and intention could therefore be understood as the human vocation. This collaboration must also mean collaboration with one another in the human family, indeed with the whole of the non-human world.

If, as Mackay argues, collaboration is a greater guarantee of well-being than individual material prosperity, limiting present opportunity for material acquisition for the sake of an equitable and sustainable future not only undergirds that future, it also contributes to human well-being and contentment in the present.

Collaborating with one another, 'discovering what God is doing and doing that', is what John Crossan names as 'collaborative eschatology'. 'It is not that we are waiting for God, it is that God is waiting for us.'[634] Clearly 'collaborative eschatology' is not the only word to be said about eschatology,[635] but the motivation of 'working' with God for the redemption of the world should be highly motivating to the Christian community. Crossan continues: 'To see the presence of the kingdom of God, said Jesus, come, see how we live, and then live likewise.'[636]

Tom Wright found this motivation when writing *Surprised by Hope*:

> What I understand Crossan intended is this. Because the early Christians believed that 'resurrection' had begun with Jesus, and would be completed in the great final resurrection on the last day, they believed that God had called them to work with him, in the power of the spirit, to implement the achievement of Jesus and thereby to anticipate the final resurrection in personal and political life, in mission and holiness.[637]

While he does not use the term 'collaborative eschatology' Moltmann articulates the same idea. 'The proclaimed word is directed towards that which in every respect lies ahead of it. ... It provides no final revelation, but calls us to a path whose goal it shows in terms of promise, and whose goal can be attained only by obediently following the promise.'[638]

The promise, the sabbath reign of God, integrates past, present and future in a renewed creation. Such a promise has the power to ignite transformative living in light of the future; a human vocation cannot be conceived to be less than this.

Living Generously in the Presence of God

As already explored, the biblical account of sabbath is a narrative of the indwelling of God (*shekinah*) through which creation and human history are blessed and sanctified. Chapter 3 explored God's indwelling both in creation and with God's people in salvation history (tent and temple). Chapter 4 argued that both creation and human history (creation and redemption) are unified in the 'Word made Flesh', the coming of God amongst us.

While western, protestant, Christianity has until recent times tended not to emphasis this dual understanding of God's presence in creation and redemption, this understanding has always had deep roots within Orthodox Christianity as contemporarily articulated by Metropolitan John of Pergamon: 'Christianity regards the world as sacred because it stands in relationship with God.'[639]

However, contemporary theologians such as Moltmann,[640] Conradie,[641] and Bauckham[642] now speak of *shekinah* in connection with creation without needing to argue the case, such has been its widening acceptance within creation theology in recent decades. 'The indwelling of God is perhaps, as Moltmann suggests, 'the inner secret, of creation.'[643] It is the starting point for his *Doctrine of Creation:*

> If the creative God himself dwells in his creation, then he is making it his home, 'on earth as it is in heaven'. All created beings then find in nearness to him the inexhaustible well-spring of their life, and for their part find rest and home in God.[644]

The West shares with the East indebtedness to the early Fathers of the Church. Sigurd Bergmann argues that this sense of divine indwelling, ultimately fulfilled in the *eschaton,* but a currently lived reality, has been integral to the teaching of the early fathers of the Church and especially of Gregory of Nazianzus:

> As the human body and thereby all created bodily life has been drawn closer to the Creator through Christ, the Spirit vivifies the world from the inside by making herself a home in and with creation.

... The mystery of creation and salvation goes on in a process of making-oneself-at-home on earth. ... The *inhabitation* continues the redemptive *incarnation*. The Spirit now corresponds to nature within the redemptive process.[645]

'The 'indwelling', the shekinah, is the goal of all the creating, preserving, liberating and redeeming in history ... if the goal of creation, the covenant, and the kingdom of God, is his indwelling, this must be the goal of the way the world is treated and ruled by his image, the human being.'[646]

It is only when the world is treated in this way that humans learn to enjoy harmony, the blessing that is otherwise buried under a cycle of competitive violence. The human and non-human world is to be equally treated with the dignity and respect that indwelling affords—herein lies blessing.

When Moltmann and other theologians engage the Christian community with ethics that flow from a concept of God's indwelling in creation, from where can a theological critique of this position emerge? The answer is probably to be found in debate over 'panentheism'.[647] 'Panentheism seeks to avoid either isolating God from the world as traditional theism does, or identifying God with the world as pantheism does.'[648]

In the following chapter I argue with Moltmann and others that in light of the incarnation, kenosis, or God's self-emptying, is to be understood as a feature of creation as well as redemption; that the nature of God revealed in Jesus is the same nature of God displayed in creation. This position is almost certain to be described as panentheistic, in the sense of unorthodox, by those who contend that God and the nature of God is totally other than creation.[649] I argue the reverse. That it is not possible to read scripture without coming to the conclusion that because the *shekinah* (presence) of God is manifest through divine self-emptying in both creative and redemptive activity, the vocation of the emerging redeemed (and redeeming) community must also be similarly shaped, not simply for its task of redeeming, but for its fulfilment and blessing.

To be truly present is to embrace with dignity and respect the company to which one intends to be present. Embrace is not possible without space being created for the other. Space is created when something is given up or relinquished. In the case of exploiter and exploited or the oppressor and oppressed space can only be created for embrace when the more powerful relinquishes power, position, wealth, or argument, to the one exploited or oppressed.

Embrace[650], has not been an obviously demonstrable mark of a historically divided Christian community. Unable to fully embrace one another, it is hardly surprising that embracing membership of the whole created order has proved so difficult for the Church, a microcosm of the global human family.

The problem is exacerbated for the Church by an innate sense that to be 'holy' is to be 'separated', an Old Testament view explored in Chapter 5, but which still lingers in the contemporary Church. In its lingering a dualism between the spiritual and material worlds is maintained. The New Testament affirms both 'worlds' are united in Jesus, the fulfiller of Sabbath. In his name, engagement is the calling of Christians: sin is isolation.

A market driven, profit seeking, secular world which needs to treat material reality as a commodity to exploit cannot easily accommodate a sense of interconnectedness. Commodities need to be treated as something apart. The innate foolishness of this position is well articulated by Leonardo Boff when he says: '[sin] is the disruption of universal connectedness.'[651] Boff's insistence that from an ecological point of view 'sin' is not so much violence done to creation, but the violence of isolation from it, is shared by Moltmann:

> We can understand sin and slavery as the self imposed isolation of open systems from their own time and possibilities. Sin is isolation. ... While the word sin can only indicate human failure, the concept of fatal self-isolation can lead to a wider understanding of the slavery of the whole creation to futility of which Paul speaks in Romans 8:19ff. ... We can describe salvation as the divine opening of closed systems. ... The man who has alienated himself is liberated and open to his own future.[652]

Human sinfulness is not simply acting with intentional violence to another; the more passive choosing of isolation (independence or individualism), the refusal to acknowledge reciprocity and interdependence, is an equally important insight into the nature of 'sin.' The insight of sabbath is that this truth finds corollary in human dealing with the whole creation. The environmental crisis is not simply the result of intended and demonstrable wanton human acts of exploitation against creation, it is equally an attitude of mind that permits human activity out of the assumption that humanity exists, or has the right to exist, 'apart from' the non-human creation.

To belong is to be blessed. To be connected is to be blessed. To engage with the God who is present in creation is to be a participant with creation, seeking a harmony and wholeness into which future generations can enter and find blessing. The human vocation is not to be understood only in terms of duty and responsibility but in terms of a connectedness through which God's intended blessing is experienced as a reality. The intergenerational dimension of this connectedness infers disciplined commitment to the 'now but not yet' of God's new creation, the *oikos*[653] (house) of God.

Living Together in the House of God

'Thus the heavens and the earth were finished and all their multitude' (Gen. 2:1). This is how the biblical creation narrative introduces sabat (rest), upon which the celebration of sabbath is premised. The seventh day not only celebrates all that has 'preceded' it, but gathers it as a single community into the dwelling place of God. God and the whole multitude of creation share a single house or home. 'The very purpose of shekinah (indwelling), or the work of the Holy Spirit, is to render the whole creation the very 'house' of God.'[654] A home is the habitation of those who live in relationship. 'I am no thing apart from everything'[655] is Joseph Sittler's anthropological insight. How humanity initiates and shares the 'common good' of relatedness within this single house has been the source of various crises over the centuries, but never before with such a clear environmental focus. As explored in Chapter 2, the commitment of Lambeth Conferences to common good as an essential ethical principle, is founded upon belief in a 'single house'.

Earlier chapters have addressed individualism as antithetical to the biblical narrative. Understanding the cosmos as a single house implies that all life is lived relationally and, as sentient beings, humans must understand and adapt their place in relation to all that occupies the house. McFague, in her examination of human responsibility for environmental degradation, says: '[ecological sin] is the refusal to accept our place.'[656]

That we live in a single house is implied by a number of words in common English usage. Larry Rasmussen helpfully connects 'economy' 'ecology' and 'ecumenics':

> Creation is pictured as a vast public household. The English words, economics, ecumenics and ecology all share the same root and reference. Economics means providing for the household's material and service needs and managing the household well. ... It also has theological expression, 'the divine economy of which one of the marks is shared abundance'. Ecumenics means treating the members of the household as a single family, human and non human together and fostering the unity of that family. 'Ecology' is knowledge of that systematic interdependence upon which the life of the household depends.[657]

'Economy' is most commonly used to refer to the arrangements that need to be made for the financial well-being of citizens within a sovereign state, although it is also used in reference to the 'world economy'. That there is as yet no adequate mechanism to deal with inequity and exploitation in and beyond nation states is one of the reasons why developing a strategy to overcome environmental problems is so difficult.[658] Strategising beyond the arena of sovereign states has become crucial because 'global interdependence points to the fact that interconnections do not stop at national boundaries.'[659]

As already stated, Wendell Berry distinguishes between the 'Big Economy' of human activity, and the 'Great Economy' of the total environment, upon which the big economy depends.[660]

A growing understanding of the cosmos as a single house is shared by science and Christian faith. Chapter 1 recognised the contribution that James Lovelock has made through his use of *Gaia* as a metaphor for the biosphere as a single organism. Views from space have sparked a sense of earth as our only home.[661] Sallie McFague links the whole cosmos in her *ecological theology*: 'No two things are the same ... however the exploding stars and the zebras are related through their common origin and history.'[662] These viewpoints are consistent with and amplify the creation narrative 'crowned' by sabbath, a celebration of every aspect of life gathered in the presence of the creator.

However, is a house automatically a home? Conradie's thesis in *An Ecological Christian Anthropology: At Home on Earth*, is that we have not yet made it our home for we have not yet learned to live in harmony with all who share the same house. 'Human beings are not necessarily at home on earth, at least not yet.'[663] He argues with Charles Murphy that, 'life in communion and solidarity with others is the divine model for all earthly existence.'[664] 'The earth is God's house which we also inhabit and wherein we are invited to find a home for ourselves in fellowship with God and all of God's creatures.'[665] This is the household that sabbath celebrates and to which we journey. 'All things are moving towards the state in which everything intelligible and sensible will be encompassed by God. This movement ... is the essential principle of their nature.'[666] However, accepting the full implication of Conradie's and Elizabeth Theokritoff's sense of movement towards integration is not easy, and certainly not easy in a culture which idealises material independence. To a greater or lesser degree a human home is a walled environment that separates a space of personal comfort and security from the rest of the world. Building this personal environment is a high priority for most human beings. The challenge facing 'developed' populations is that extravagant investment in personal wealth and security may indeed prove counterproductive. Economic investment, at the expense of global sustainability, may increase the sense of fragility that investment in personal wealth was geared to minimise.[667]

Clearly humans live in tension between the destiny to which we are called and the reality of the world in which we live. 'There remains a tension within God's household here on earth between the already of God's acts of restoring *shalom* in the household and the not-yet of the *shalom* which God will ultimately bestow on the whole of creation.'[668] In this tension we are called to live with the future in mind. The Christian community has always been called to live this way, but never with as much urgency as required in our present circumstance.

Can humans be motivated to live with the whole planet in mind? Roger Scruton, in *Green Philosophy*, uses the *oikos* metaphor to support an environmental ethic he calls 'oikophilia' or love of home.[669] His argument from what he confesses to be the conservative or 'right' of politics is that humans can only be motivated to enhance that to which they are immediately attached—their immediate home and those with whom they share it. For him this is the Nation State.[670] He argues strongly against any attempt at regulation beyond the Nation State and refers to such attempts from the 'left' of politics as 'oikophobia'. While his argument that folk should be encouraged to care for that for which they are immediately responsible is to be applauded; nation states have historically shown that their desire to seek advantage over other states is greater than any commitment to environmental responsibility. Human networks and complex systems know no state boundary.

Notwithstanding what I consider to be a serious flaw in his argument, Scruton develops his own thesis for 'living with the future in mind'. He does so by drawing on three ideas he takes from Edmund Burke[671]—'respect for the dead, the little platoon and the voice of tradition.'[672] 'Respect for the dead' refers to gratitude for that which we have inherited from the past. 'The little platoon' refers to his idea that effective action is local collaboration. 'The voice of tradition' means for Scruton the need to pass on inherited value to future generations. While Scruton's 'house' is localised, nevertheless he emphasises that life is to be lived communally and in solidarity with others. One of the outcomes of this solidarity is his conviction that carbon should be taxed at a flat rate, across all products, and paid by producer and consumer alike.[673]

If living in communion and solidarity with others is the defining feature of the single house, 'economy' (house management) must serve this underlying characteristic. As already noted, the Lambeth Conferences did not specifically address the environmental issue until 1968, however they consistently drew upon the notion of a single house as their reference point in addressing social issues, and in so doing called for the triumph of 'common good' over individual self interest. Common good is not served when 'getting' is disproportionately advanced over 'giving'. 'Belonging means giving... society is the home we build together when we bring our several gifts to the common good.'[674] Attention given to the nature of the house we say we believe in will alter the character of the housekeeping. An economy with changed priorities will reposition humanity as a participant in the ongoing life and well-being of the whole created order. Commitment to self-interest is a refusal to contribute to a 'new creation' and it is therefore to stand outside the destiny that God chooses. What 'living with the future in mind' might mean for exponential growth, the dominant feature of 'housekeeping' in the Western market driven economy, is addressed in Chapter 7.

What metaphor best describes the vocation of humanity in *oikos*, a single house? In Chapter 5 various metaphors from the Old Testament were explored, including steward, keeper, and priest. All metaphors are limited in their capacity to convey meaning and are open to being misunderstood. If human vocation is somehow to be linked to 'Imago Dei', Douglas Hall warns that this metaphor, taken from Genesis 1:27, is not to be understood in terms of a function which distinguishes humanity from the rest of creation such as intellect or the capacity for self-reflection, but is to be understood in terms of the capacity for fellowship with God.

> The humanity for which Adam/Eve was intended, the humanity which was incarnate in the Christ is the very humanity into which, through grace, we are being called. It is the new humanity which the writer to the Colossians urges the readers to 'put on.'[675]

Following the logic of Hall it may be best not to rely upon any specific metaphor rather, as he suggests, to imagine humanity clothed as in Col. 3:12-17. Thus, the human vocation is not simply to imitate the God revealed in Jesus, but to be clothed with that nature.

Hall recognises that human calling is always challenged by the human propensity for dominion. 'Only when we expose ourselves to the dangers inherent in some of our widely held beliefs, such as the popular belief concerning human 'dominion', can we entertain correctives.'[676] Richard Bauckham is another who cautions against the use of a metaphor for fear of its misuse.

> It is the exclusive focus on a vertical relationship to the rest of creation—whether it be called rule or dominion or stewardship or even priesthood—that has been one of the ideological driving forces of the modern technological project of dominating nature.[677]

The caution is widely shared, as instanced by Michael Northcott[678] and Ernst Schumacher.[679]

What is the alternative? Is there a single word that describes the human vocation to 'image God'?

That peace and fulfilment might prevail in a home with many occupants each must seek to serve the other. 'Diakonia' (service) is the New Testament's primary description of ministry. In the New Testament it is used of service within the human family. However, given that a 'new creation' is the dominant eschatological theme of the New Testament and that this theme is inclusive of the whole created order, then 'service' towards the whole created order should be the character of an ecological 'living in the household of God'. 'The Church should provide service (*diakonia*) to the world instead of serving its own needs or expansionist interests.'[680] Because of the etymology of 'human', Conradie is drawn to the metaphor of 'humus' to describe human service in relation to creation.[681]

The single house of creation, in Orthodox theology,[682] is seen in microcosm in every human being. When human beings are gathered into the community of the redeemed—the Church – the Church itself can be understood as a microcosm of creation, sacramentally pointing to a redeeming or redeemed new creation. Discovering how to live in a shared environment in a single house is the human vocation.

To conclude this section therefore I wish to ask, does or should the environmental crisis cause a reconsideration of the Church's marks of self identity?

The Marks of the Church Reconsidered

The classical 'marks' of the Church, as Stephen Pickard has reminded us,[683] name the Church's core identity. Whatever the Church is, or has become, it can never be less than the character measured by these marks if it is to be true to its vocation as a witness to Jesus. While the creeds give unalterable authority to the classical marks, their value is enhanced or impeded by the manner in which they are reinterpreted in changing contexts and by emerging challenges. For example, catholicity, shaped in a patriarchal society, is diminished if in succeeding generations it is used as a tool for the exclusion of women.

'One'

Ecclesiastical division has made it hard for the Church to defend the first 'mark', its inherent unity. Organic unity, the ideal of the ecumenical movement through the middle decades of the 20th century, appears to have been abandoned. Unity is no longer sought organically, but cooperatively as partner members of the same faith: 'There is one body and one spirit, just as you were called to the one hope of your calling, one Lord, one faith, one baptism, one God and Father of all, who is above all and through all and in all' (Eph. 4:4-5).

Unity understood in this way demands that Christian adherents not only respect one another out of common allegiance to Christ but that they share in common an understanding and commitment to what it means to be 'holy' 'catholic' and 'apostolic'. It is my argument that just as major movements of the past, such as the emancipation of women, have required a reappraisal, or rather a development, of the ideas inherent in these marks, so the environmental crisis is doing the same. This reappraisal is happening particularly in relation to what is meant by 'holy' and 'catholic'. In the past these marks have had an anthropomorphic focus; they now need to have a bearing upon the totality of the created order and its future. That the focus has been almost exclusively towards humanity has contributed to silence from the Church on what should have been a primary not a secondary matter. This has led Metropolitan John of Pergamon to say: 'Christian theology and the Church should not have remained silent for so long on this matter [environmental degradation].'[684]

'Holy'

As already noted, Christian piety has commonly understood holiness as distinctiveness or separation. But this is not the biblical view; it is not a sacramental view. The sacraments of the Church, particularly the Eucharist, take, break and bless ordinary elements of life, not that they might remain separate, but that they become instruments of blessing to the world from which they have been drawn. 'Holiness' is therefore not about sacredness corralled from the world, but about immersion in the world for its transformation. God in Jesus became immersed in the world for its transformation; we are called to do the same.

Douglas Hall captures this truth in his *Imaging God*: 'Whatever else it may designate, Jesus' 'heaven' encompasses earth—or would do so if only earthlings would stop denigrating their God made habitat and desiring to exchange it for heaven.'[685] A theology of 'indwelling' demands that 'holy' is rethought in two perspectives. First that in Jesus heaven and earth have met, all the ground upon which we walk is 'holy ground'. Second that any 'holiness' to which Christians might aspire is to be sought through engagement not separation; through a desire to be a blessing to fellow humanity, the non-human creation, and the generations to follow. As argued in Chapter 3, the 'seventh day' celebrates the sanctity and blessing brought to creation through God's 'rest' within it. Blessing or sanctity sought by any part of creation is derived through its membership of the whole.

A Church that is 'Holy' is a Church fully engaged with the non-human world for its health and well-being.

'Catholic'

'Catholic', no matter how it is conceived in ecclesiastical affairs, assumes the reality of a single house; explored in here through the metaphor of *oikos*. The Anglican Church has robustly defended its catholic credentials. Every Church that claims 'catholicity' understands itself to share the life of a single but diverse community, a community that seeks to embrace the world that in turn is embraced by God. Communion or fellowship is sought with 'the heavens and earth and all their multitude'. Because we conceive ourselves to be members of this single house: 'Christian engagement concerns the vision of the good—that which defines what we as individuals and societies should seek.'[686]

The biblical narrative compels us to value community as the context in which individuals flourish. A biblical narrative with 'shalom' at its core compels us to prioritise 'common good'. The biblical presentation of sabbath compels us not simply to engage with the environmental crisis, but to live a life of hope, embracing the 'not yet' of a new creation.

Attending to creation's brokenness and alienation has become an overriding ethical issue. It challenges the Church to consider whether its sense of catholicity has been 'catholic enough'.

Being 'catholic' must more overtly embrace a ministry of service which supports the 'integrity of creation'.[687] I make this argument Christologically on the basis of sabbath's fulfilment in Christ, eschatologically on the basis that life must be framed by its destiny, and ethically on the basis that the current environmental crisis places humanity in an unprecedented position of affecting the future, human and non-human. The Church is less than the 'catholicity' it claims for itself if its teaching and its practice do not seek a sustainable, equitable environment in anticipation of the 'new creation' that Christ's death and resurrection established.

'Apostolic'

The reimagining of holiness and catholicity inevitably entails a refocussing of the Christian community's sense of being 'sent'. The world into which Christians are sent as agents of transformation and renewal is not simply the world of humanity, it is the whole created order. Redemption has to be rethought in the context of creation.

Conclusions

The human vocation is to fill the present with confident hope in the universal reign of God. Belief in the destiny to which we travel, a new creation, compels us to live with this future in mind. To live this way is to endow the present with richness, lifting the transient beyond the mundane to a more complete context of potential fulfilment.[688]

The human vocation is to treat all existence with respect and value because God is present to and engaged with it. Human 'sin' is isolation, disengagement, corralling material goods for private gain—a refusal to accept our larger calling.

The human vocation is to live appropriately in a single house of creation. In this house the past and the future give purpose and meaning to the present. What it means to live appropriately in this house should be cause for reflection in every generation and context. An 'appropriate place' infers preparedness to adapt human behaviour rather than expecting the house to adapt to humanity. Humanity is called to value the non-human creation for its own sake, not simply in terms of its value to humanity. Lived in light of the environmental crisis the human vocation embraces the priority of common good beyond individual human aspirations.

The environmental crisis requires the Church to rearticulate its classical marks of identity. The Church can never be less than what it claims for itself through these marks, but a changed context calls for reinterpretation. This should be part of the Church's evolving organic life. The environmental crisis of the 21st century is a significantly changed context. All four marks could be reconsidered, but in particular the environmental crisis challenges the Church to rethink what it means when it says it is 'holy' and 'catholic'.

CHAPTER 7

THE HUMAN VOCATION: LIVING WITHIN LIMITS

Long-term flourishing often requires
short-term sacrifice.[689]

We face a choice between a society where people accept modest sacrifices
for common good, or a more contentious society whose groups selfishly
protect their own benefits.[690]

Chapter 6 acknowledged that an environmental ethic is not dependent upon religious belief. Indeed, scientific research that explores the mutuality of ecological systems implies the necessity of collaborative behaviour to enhance life. However, I am arguing that an environmental ethic is a necessary concomitant of Christian belief, an ethic that demands limits to exploitative ambition in order to serve common good. This ethic has its foundations rooted in the notion of kenosis. In what follows I argue that kenosis, emptying or limiting, is not only expressive of the divine nature but a necessary characteristic of creation and therefore of the human vocation. I make this argument in some detail before illustrating its application in two specific challenges facing 21st century humanity.

Kenosis

While the word kenosis, from the verb κενόω (to empty) (Phil. 2:7), is rarely used in the New Testament, its reference in the self emptying of the cross dominates the New Testament. This section explores how kenosis is as much a character of creation as it is of redemption and consequently that kenosis, in the sense of limitation, is an appropriate and necessary human response to the environmental crisis, indeed that it is a necessary expression of the human vocation.

It is customary when contemplating the idea of kenosis to begin with the revelation of God on the cross. To argue that the character of God manifested in one context—the cross—must also be true in other contexts—creation. Karl Rahner expresses part of this truth when he says: 'We can understand creation and incarnation as two moments and two phases of the one process of God's self-giving and self-expression, although it is an intrinsically differentiated process.'[691] However, the traditional argument goes further, demanding that an understanding of creation has to be considered in light of Christ. Marianne Meye Thompson captures this truth succinctly: 'What happens to Christ in microcosm happens to the whole world in macrocosm.'[692]

Philippians 2:1-11 encapsulates 'what happens to Christ'.

> Though he was in the form of God he did not regard equality with God a thing to be grasped, but emptied himself (kenosis), taking the form of a slave, being born in human likeness. And being found in human form he humbled himself and became obedient to the point of death—even death on a cross ... (Phil. 2:68).

If self-emptying is the best way of describing the activity of God in Jesus, then it must also be a way of describing the activity of God in creation and as a consequence also a way of illuminating the meaning of 'rest', the climax of creation. John Vincent Taylor argues that creating this space demands divine self-limitation or emptying.

Creation entails for God a degree of self limitation and vulnerability[693] ... God makes room for a world of beings that are not God, by inward self withdrawal, abandoning a space within himself and leaving a primordial emptiness and darkness, the non-God.[694]

If 'divine emptying', described in this way, is of the very nature of God, it cannot therefore be attributed simply to a necessity that arises because of the 'fall'. 'The self limiting and suffering of God with regard to the world, the *passio Dei*, is not to be attributed to the fall, the disobedience of humanity as it often has been ... but to the very desire of God to be given away.'[695] This gives added impetus to Paul's statement: 'Since in the wisdom of God the world did not know God through wisdom ... Jews demand signs and Greeks desire wisdom ... but we proclaim Christ Crucified, a stumbling block to Jews and foolishness to Gentiles' (1 Cor. 1:21-23). 'This [1 Cor. 1:22-23] is Paul's most epigrammatic description of the world in which the Gospel is preached, and of the Gospel itself.'[696]

Paul's statement can be read not simply that in Christ God acts in a self-emptying manner, but that this is how God always acts, this is the Wisdom of God. Weil, writing in her *Notebooks,* captures something of the same insight: 'God has created, that is, not that he has produced something outside himself, but that he has withdrawn himself, permitting a part of being to be other than God.'[697]

However could we put the process of kenotic examination in reverse, to begin with creation and in doing so find that the cross confirms the nature of God revealed from the beginning of time? Brunner and Moltmann believe so:

> God does not wish to occupy the whole of space himself but ... wills to make room for other forms of existence. In doing so he limits himself ... The κένωσις which reaches its paradoxical climax on the Cross of Christ begins with the creation of the world.[698]

In their development of kenosis as a feature of creation Brunner and Moltmann are drawing upon the thought and argument of Isaac Luria,[699] who wrestled with the question 'can there be any freedom at all for man if God was supposed to be omnipotent.'[700]

He expressed his ideas through what he called *Zimsum* (contraction and concentration), a withdrawal into oneself. He first developed his idea in relation to *shekinah* the withdrawal of God into himself to the extent that he could dwell in the temple. He extended this thought to creation where as Moltmann says: 'God makes room for his creation by withdrawing his presence.'[701]

Moltmann further developed this argument when he says: 'In the idea of Shekinah God's—'indwelling'—we find the Old Testament presupposition for the Christian idea of kenosis, and its Jewish equivalent.'[702]

In Chapter 3 I proposed that when the exile caused a physical and theological crisis for the Jewish people, *shekinah* did not simply 'go into Babylonian exile with the captured people ... the comrade on the way and the companion in suffering of the homeless Israelites,'[703] but that the idea of shekinah was reshaped into a more universal understanding of God being present not simply to Israelites, but to all humanity, indeed to all creation through sabbath. Matthew Anstey articulates this thought when he describes sabbath rest as the space God creates for shared activity. 'God rests for our sake, to create a shared space, where we can rest together. This is the essential characteristic of Biblical rest, that it is a shared space for all to enter.'[704]

Thus we can say, creation is possible through God's self-limitation, space is created for that which is not God, and yet on the other hand, in sabbath rest God purposes to engage with that which has been graced with its own autonomy. These truths, like the apparently contradictory truths of the divinity and humanity of Christ, are to be held in life-giving tension. God's resting in creation, sabbath rest, is not a denial of the divine self-limitation which enabled creation to exist, but is a celebration of it. Indeed, in faithfulness to humanity's vocation to image the nature of God, the sabbath ethic as described in Chapter 3 catalogues the various limitations that humanity is called to observe to safeguard the harmony and equity of creation.

Before considering specific limitations that humanity must consider in response to the environmental crisis and in commitment to common good, I would first like to explore a little further theological discussion about kenosis.

What 'kenosis' means in an ontological or ethical sense has been debated from the first century until now. Is kenosis a reflection of 'what Jesus did rather than who he was'?[705] Is it a temporary description not linked to the pre-existing Godhead, or is it descriptive of the perichoresis within the persons of the Trinity as suggested by Balthasar?[706] In *Mysterium Paschale* Balthasar argues that the kenotic character of God in redemption reflects the same character of God in creation and vice versa. 'In serving, in washing the feet of his creatures, God reveals himself, even in that which is most intimately divine in him, and manifests his supreme glory.'[707] Here Balthasar is relating to the whole created order (Col. 1:15-20) the character of God reflected in Jesus' self-giving death (Phil. 2:1-11). Divine, self-emptying love, clearly shown in redemption (crucifixion), is the same self-giving love to be found in creation. In this argument Jesus displays 'the self-giving humility which is the essence of divinity.'[708]

Does the idea of kenosis have an application beyond the divine? In applying the idea of 'emptying' to nature Sarah Coakley warns against using the term 'kenosis' in the field of science in a manner that is disconnected from its Christological or Trinitarian roots. To do so she warns is to risk inappropriately conveying ethical or moral baggage.[709]

In her essay, *Kenosis and Subversion*[710] Coakley deals with what might be described as the psychological difficulties of teaching, or expecting, that the character of kenosis be demonstrable in the oppressed, in those who have had 'emptying' forced upon them. Where 'emptying' has been experienced as 'self-diminishing', disempowering, Coakley argues, it cannot be taught as a desirable human characteristic. This is entirely understandable when argued from a feminist or perhaps an indigenous position where 'emptying' has been the constant experience of unwanted domination and coercion.

Coakley's warning is timely in the context of the environmental crisis. It is not appropriate to expect the developing or 'majority' world to make the same adjustments that must be made in the developed world. In the developing world, fertility rates, levels of consumption and technological exploitation can only be addressed in the context of improved education and health, the embedding of women's rights, the general lifting of levels of empowerment and reduction in poverty. This is addressed later in this chapter.

Notwithstanding these difficulties Coakley supports Charles Gore (see below) in arguing for an understanding of kenosis as foundational to both divine and human nature. Her use of a quotation from John Macquarrie expresses it well:

> The self-emptying of Jesus Christ has not only opened up the depth of true humanity, but has made known to us the final reality as likewise self-emptying, self-giving and self-limiting.[711]

God's omnipotence, as revealed in Jesus, is empowerment: a scandal to a world that treasures power not empowerment. Paul describes the cross as a scandal: the scandal of the creator taking the role of servant to his own creation: 'a stumbling block to Jews and foolishness to Greeks' (1 Cor. 1:23). In our 21st century context the scandal is not about a self emptying God. God has become largely irrelevant to a western secular, materialistic culture. No, the scandal is to contemplate with Macquarrie that emptying reveals the potential depth of 'true humanity'.

Notwithstanding Coakley's reservations that kenosis be used cautiously as a scientific descriptor, George Ellis, the emeritus professor of complex systems in the Department of Mathematics and Applied Mathematics at the University of Capetown, South Africa, argues for kenosis as 'a unifying theme for life and cosmology.'[712] He argues that kenosis is the underlying link behind the various physical laws of the universe: 'one can act freely within the confines of these laws, but the laws themselves cannot be altered by any action of humanity.'[713] His argument is that when the unifying theme of the universe is understood and accepted, then kenosis is not a burden but freedom, not sacrifice but fulfilment, for kenosis is the way 'the world operates'. To live this way is not simply a matter of altruism, a matter of wanting to 'do good for others', it is deeper than that. It is a matter of conformity with the governing principles of the universe, of wanting to be where God is, to do what God is doing.[714] Genesis 2:1-4 testifies that sabat (rest) is the governing principle of God's creation. Our argument thus far therefore links rest and kenosis together. God's resting in creation creates the space for that which is not God. As material and living things take up residence in that space they must rest in the manner that God rests, in offering themselves for the good of the other. This is the sabbath call, the desire of God that creation be as it is intended to be.

One of the strongest proponents of kenosis in the Anglican tradition was Bishop Charles Gore the 19/20th century Bishop of Oxford, who caused a storm when appearing to imply that Jesus, in his humanity, was 'emptied of God', that he was restricted to the cultural ideas and norms of his time. It is used here to argue, as Gore later asserted in his Bampton Lectures,[715] that rather than 'reducing' God, kenosis is of the very nature of God.

Gore's theology of kenosis, formed through his reflection and meditation on the beatitudes,[716] has already been touched on in light of his contribution to Lambeth Conferences (Chapter 2). He understood the beatitudes to reflect the divine character, a character to be imitated by the followers of Christ. 'Our Lord demands not conduct merely but character. He says, not 'Blessed is he who does this or that', but 'Blessed is such and such a character.'[717] Applying the beatitudes, Gore's moral theology was formed through a theology of the 'brotherhood of humanity in Christ' and what he saw to be the necessity of the character of kenosis for such fellowship to be a reality. 'There exists what can rightly be called a Christian Socialism, by the very fact that the law of brotherhood is the law of Christ.'[718] Mark Chapman, in his essay *Charles Gore and the crisis of power* writes: 'Gore's question was quite straight forward: how does the doctrine of the Christ—the one who empties himself to be with us—affect the ways in which we relate to one another and to the wider society.'[719] Gore's question is applicable to the combined power humanity now exerts over the natural order, as we have previously observed, what Crutzen calls the age of the anthropocene.

My reason for writing is to contribute to a meaningful conversation that engages Christian Mission purposefully and relevantly within the context of contemporary life. This is a context in which human beings live in increasing conflict with the non-human creation and in competition with one another for the limited resources available in a finite world. If it can be demonstrated, as Ellis has argued, that there is a unifying theme that links everything within the universe and that this theme is celebrated in what the Bible refers to as sabbath ethic, then as George Newlands asserts, this theme can and should be the basis for a confident and robust public theology.

> Christology, more precisely the kenotic, vulnerable, generous Christ who is the incarnation of the self-giving creative responsive love of God, is a basis for pubic theology, which is open to dialogue with all humanity, religious or non-religious. ... Generosity cannot immediately relieve radical suffering, which may repeat violence

suffered in violence inflicted. But it may create the conditions of
the possibility of forgiveness, which may lead to reconciliation and
so to a weakening in the cycle of violence.[720]

Such is human nature that to live sabbath, to live kenotically, is strongly
resisted.[721] The paradox caused through God's creation of space for that
which is not of God is well picked up by John Vincent Taylor and Andrew
Elphinstone:

> Because the Creator, for the achievement of his purpose, has chosen
> to 'make the world by making it make itself' and because it is at
> the level of the human spirit that evil has been established in the
> creative process, its power could be confronted and overcome says
> Elphinstone, 'only when the incarnation had made the uncreated
> love of God an indigenous part of the createdness of humanity.'[722]

Paul Ricoeur also argues the same paradox, that evil emerges out of the
very freedom that God has enabled.

> Reciprocally, an ethical vision of evil is a vision in which freedom is
> revealed in its depths as power to act and power to be: the freedom
> that evil supposes is a freedom capable of digression, deviation,
> subversion, wandering. This mutual 'explanation' of evil by freedom
> and of freedom by evil is the essence of the moral vision of the
> world and of evil.[723]

That which has always been indigenous to creation must become
indigenous to humanity otherwise we remain 'strangers and foreigners on
earth' (Heb. 11:13). It is in Jesus that what is indigenous within creation can
become indigenous to us. Chapter 3 and Chapter 5 drew a link between
the fourth and tenth commandments in the Decalogue. The fourth
commandment is essentially about the manner in which each part of life
contributes to the fulfilment of the whole, the tenth commandment is a
warning that individuals should not seek to possess that which rightly
belongs to another, or seek fulfilment through possessions. Brueggemann
expresses this juxtaposition creatively:

Consumers, are those who, after they 'eat and are satiated' use as a
third verb variously 'exalt self ... self sufficiency self-indulgence, self-
reference'—an ocean of self. Citizens are those who after they 'eat
and are satiated' have as a third verb 'bless, remember', that is they
turn life back to the Giver.[724]

Thus, the predominant ethical issue now facing humankind is how and
to what degree will humanity accept limits to its own desire for domination,
its desire for exploitation; indeed limits to its personal and national
'freedoms'. As argued from the biblical material, accepting limits in a world
of relational responsibility is at the heart of the sabbath ethic. 'In a world
of limits, certain kinds of freedoms are either impossible or immoral. The
freedom to endlessly accumulate material goods is one of them.'[725] 'The real
limits to the earth's carrying capacity preclude both unlimited growth in
human population and an an ever increasing consumption of the world's
resources.'[726]

The ethical challenge has been described as the 'Micah Challenge',[727]
drawing upon the inspiration of Micah 6.8 'What does the Lord require of
you but to do justice and to love kindness and to walk humbly with your
God'. The second injunction, to love kindness is frequently translated 'to
love mercy'. The English word 'mercy' has its origins in the Latin *merces*
meaning pay or wages, being connected to 'merchant' or 'mercantile'.[728] In
the ancient world pay was received at the end of each day. Pay could not
be withheld for it amounted to that which was necessary for that day's
provisions. For our current world to 'have mercy' the world's human poor
and the ecologically poor must receive sufficient for sustainable health and
well being.

Addressing these issues through a mechanism of global politics is
proving difficult, if not impossible, when the issue is considered from
the perspective of 'national interest'. As already noted, there is increasing
incongruity in the idea that national interest can in some way be different

to global or 'common' best interest. Insufficient attention is given to the reality that every nation gains its well-being from its membership of the global family and should feel obligated to attend to the problems that a globally focussed world has created. 'People ... share in a global public good precisely because their nation is part of a global network in which that good is present.'[729] In a global world, 'linking the terms 'national' and 'interest' becomes increasingly incongruous.'[730]

In this anthropocene era the two overriding issues that must be considered within an ethic drawn from the kenotic theological proposition are the size of the human population and the level of human consumption.

Limits to Human Population Expansion

That the human population cannot for ever expand is implicit in recognition that all resources are finite and human environmental impact results from a combination of the size of the population, the rate of consumption of each individual, and the technological capacity to exploit. One factor cannot be addressed in isolation. The situation is made more complex in that population expansion is a particular feature of the developing world while disproportionate rates of consumption and technological exploitation are features of the developed world. Herein lies a moral conundrum. The developing world cannot morally have limitations to the prosperity enjoyed by the developed world imposed upon it. All human beings have the same right to prosperity and well-being. For these reasons a response to the environmental crisis must first be addressed by the developed world's commitment to lift the freedoms and resources of the developing world. This has been the aim of the millennium development goals. It is only through education, the alleviation of poverty, the development of women's rights and freedoms, and an appropriate sharing of technological advancement that peoples in the developing world can become aware that limited family size contributes to both human well-being and environmental sustainability.

Family size is of course not simply a matter of relative wealth or poverty. Kapya Kaoma argues that serious account must be given to the reality that on the continent of Africa a belief that 'children are a sign of divine and ancestral blessings'[731] and are a 'responsibility to ancestors'[732] is widespread and women are therefore resistant to birth control. Nevertheless he also testifies to the reality that an exploding population is causing pollution and land degradation which will ultimately mean that, in the future, Africa will support a smaller population, not a larger one.

Having recognised these difficulties, can the concept of limiting population expansion find congruence, even tacit encouragement, within the biblical narrative?

Over millennia 'natural causes' have limited human population expansion. 'In nature, [population] growth always slams up against non-negotiable constraints sooner or later.'[733] The removal, or reduction, of these natural causes has resulted in a population explosion never before experienced. 'It took all of human history for the population to pass 1 billion. The population has doubled since 1950.'[734] This doubling of population has been achieved through technological intervention, especially the creation of artificial fertilisers[735], enabling a vast expansion in food production. Failure to anticipate this explosion made Thomas Malthus[736] and his predictions, and even those of the Club of Rome,[737] look foolish. Malthus' proposition was that 'population when unchecked increases in a geometrical ratio. Subsistence [resources to meet the necessity of life] increase in an arithmetical ratio ... this implies a strong and constantly operating check on population from the difficulty of subsistence.'[738] Common sense dictates that population cannot endlessly expand; food cannot be produced to feed an endlessly growing population, all material resources are finite. Malthus himself said: 'a careful distinction should be made between an unlimited progress and a progress where the limit is merely undefined.'[739] An ever expanding human population is not just a challenge to future generations, it is also a threat to all other living things.

The stress that humans place on the planet and other species on the planet is closely related to human population growth. Stabilization of atmospheric composition and climate almost surely requires a stabilisation of human population.[740]

Despite the almost unarguable logic of the above statement, the problems caused by human population expansion remain unaddressed. The topic is the silent 'elephant in the room' of public debate. Why is this? 'One of the most oft-quoted and most fervently believed-in dogmas ... is the principle that human ingenuity can overcome all environmental problems.'[741] It is confidence that technology, technology that with hindsight made Malthus seem totally out of touch, will forever prevail. Professor Will Steffen[742] has warned of the serious dangers inherent in this assumption. 'While technology will have to be part of the solution, it cannot be the complete solution. We also need changes in human aspirations, value systems, behaviours and institutions.'[743]

The problem also remains unaddressed because 'the givens of economic growth simply define the necessity of population growth.'[744] Economic growth is the assumed and uncontested underpinning of a free market economy, and because it is, an argument for a stable population is presented as a threat to living standards.

Is the championing of population expansion a necessarily implied tenet of Christian belief? In this respect, has Christianity been an unwitting ally to a market driven economy?

The first creation story, climaxed by sabbath, appears to encourage, almost demand, limitless expansion: 'Be fruitful and multiply, fill the earth and subdue it' (Gen. 1:28). The text and its various interpretations have been examined in Chapter 3. In light of this text, is the proposition that population be limited at odds with biblical narrative? Raising the issue is difficult enough; however, 'only when we expose ourselves to the dangers inherent in some of our widely held beliefs, such as the popular belief concerning human 'dominion', can we entertain correctives.'[745]

Scripture must be read and interpreted in the light of other scripture. Hebrew scripture, as a whole, is concerned with life's continuity, its well-being, equity, justice and diversity. The Patriarchal narratives concern generational succession, while wisdom literature is considered a resource to equip the next generation with the wisdom necessary to cope with life's challenges. Intergenerational ethics implicit in Hebrew scripture teach that each generation has an obligation to secure health and well-being for the next generation. This obligation is not simply to produce progeny, but to gift that progeny with wisdom and knowledge, and, as much as is possible, to free future generations from negative consequences arising from behaviours and decisions of the previous generation. Chapter 3 has examined the sabbatical requirements embedded in the sabbatical and jubilee years which were designed to guard against generational alienation and poverty. Each generation has to live with the next generation in mind.

Thus, rather than supporting, or promoting, the idea of endless population growth, the overriding scriptural principle is that each generation has a responsibility for the well-being and security of the generation that follows. The whole of human history preceding Malthus witnessed a fertility rate sufficient to compete with the threat constantly posed by 'natural causes'. However, since Malthus, the explosion of food technology combined with extraordinary growth in medical science has enabled human beings to overcome many 'natural causes' that had previously proved the feared victors over human longevity and population expansion. In light of these remarkable achievements humanity has so far seemed incapable of philosophical, religious and political debate which might lead to a rethought position on fertility in light of a context where population growth has the potential to threaten the future, rather than guarantee it.

It is of course true that the problem is not simply the size of the human population, but its level of consumption. 'A newborn in the United States requires more than twice as much grain, and ten times as much oil as a child in Brazil and Indonesia—and produces far more pollution.'[746] 'When it comes to human beings, it's the relationship between population size, technology and level of consumption that determines the impact upon the environment.'[747]

Steven Bouma-Prediger provides a good summary:

> Human population growth is a critical factor in assessing the groaning of the earth, Creatures, human and non-human, are imperilled, in some instances simply because there are too many of us humans. But as [Wendell] Berry reminds us, both affluence and technology play crucial roles in determining environmental impact. The question is not simply how many humans the earth can sustain, but at what level of consumption and using what kind of technology?[748]

Sustaining and cherishing life undergirds all biblical ethics. It is anathema to Christian morality to knowingly diminish life or cause its cessation. Scientific knowledge does not simply suggest, but affirms with some certainty, that if humanity does not address the problems associated with the size of its population then it imposes upon future generations severe deprivation at best and at worst a threat to survival. This knowledge presents the Christian community with a very significant ethical challenge. If creation is about continuity, diversity and fecundity then the size of the human population has become a threat to creation's integrity.

Grappling with this dilemma presents three significant challenges to secular politics and Christian missiology:

1. Human sexuality and intimacy must be treasured and respected independently of the need to procreate. The Church must be in the forefront of teaching which encourages family planning, especially in communities and cultures where such planning is not understood, is not accessible, or has been denied.

   In his [Professor John Painter's] view, while human sexuality will continue to find expression in a deep and abiding human love as a basis for community or family, and procreation and the birth of children in the context of a loving relationship remain very important, these need to be within limits that allow other species to flourish.[749]

2. Because fertility rates are at their highest where extreme poverty prevails, the Church must direct both its aid programmes and its lobbying to ensure that extreme poverty and alienation is eliminated, that the health of young children is improved and that the dignity of women is enhanced through education, independence and equality.[750] Justice demands that where human population is exploding because of poverty, fertility be addressed within the context of the causes of poverty, not in isolation. While many areas of unacceptable fertility levels have been reduced, those that remain (like the Gaza Strip) are characterised by extreme poverty, child mortality and lack of respect, education, and freedom of choice for women.

> The United Nations revision of world population projects global population[751] to reach 9.22 billion ... before stabilization and decline. ... This depends urgently on continued fertility decline in developed countries. It assumes that in less developed countries fertility will decrease from 2.75—2.05 children per woman ... and in the least developed countries from 4.63—2.50. ... To achieve this family planning access must be expanded in the poorest countries.[752]

3. Because population growth has become a necessary underpinning of economic growth, the Church in the developed world must intelligently, and by example, challenge an economic system which espouses economic growth as its fundamental principle. Lesslie Newbigin believes this to be the Church's most urgent missionary task:

> [Following the collapse of Marxism] the free market now has nothing to limit its claims ... its destructive potential both for the coherence of human society and the safeguarding of the environment are formidable. ... It has deep roots in the human soul. It can be met and mastered only at the level of religious faith. ... The Churches have hardly begun to recognize that this is their most urgent missionary task during the coming century.[753]

Human well being, and the well being of creation, are in danger of diminishment or fracture if an expanding human population has an economic rather than a relational determinate.

If economic growth is reliant upon population expansion, then it is not only unsustainable in the medium to long term but it is morally indefensible. 'Population growth readily translates to economic growth which is the prime goal of governments. But it is an easy, even lazy way of achieving growth and is potentially very damaging.'[754] Contemporaneously Australia appears unable to support its desired level of economic growth without increasing the population. Whether the population of Australia should be increased to provide a home for needy people throughout the world is one matter, to increase the population for the purpose of artificially delivering an internal economic objective to an already overly prosperous citizenry, on a global scale, is another.

It is an urgent matter that the world community cooperatively develop a sustainable and just economy based upon a static (even reducing) population. If such an economy is more reliant upon relationships than material goods, more reliant upon cooperation than competition,[755] more reliant upon enduring quality than replacement, and more committed to zero waste, then we will be living in a more sabbath like world, a world shaped by the destiny it longs for, a world shaped by the desire for 'common good', a world that fulfils a deeper sense of human vocation.

Limits to Consumption and Environmental Debt

Chapter 4 examined the Old Testament sabbath ethic as mandated in the weekly, annual, seven-yearly, and fifty-year cycles. Chapter 6 noted that, as described in Exod. 16:18 and reinterpreted in 2 Cor. 8:15, the cycles provided for the principle that: 'those who had much did not have too much and those who had little did not have too little'. Faithfully applied, the principles guard against intergenerational poverty, ensure that debt does not become ingrained, and secure 'common good' for all citizens. This sabbath living assumes commitment to community as a source of identity and prosperity, thereby limiting the assumed right of individuals to unrestrained consumption and possession.

By way of contrast, in his *What Money Can't Buy: The Moral Limits of Markets*[756] Michael Sandel argues that since the 1980's there has been an escalation of the influence of markets and a commensurate decrease in the adhesiveness of altruism and trust. Trust has traditionally undergirded and bound society, and protected investment in equity and 'common good'. He notes: 'to a remarkable degree the last few decades have witnessed the remaking of social relations in the image of market relations.'[757] By way of illustration he shows how normal human relationships have been commoditised and made available for sale, from hiring someone to stand in a queue on your behalf, to gaining advantaged access to anything from health to entertainment. In a fair and just society access to basic services should be equally available to all.

This commoditising assumes that everything is reducible to an entity that can be bought or owned without consequence to anyone or anything else. In this thinking, the only measure to judge the value of a commodity is the value it is to the person seeking it. This market character runs directly counter to a growing understanding, in the fields of science and of faith, that value exists in the context of relationship.

The shift in thinking from an understanding of relationship as an accidental connection of substances to the notion that relationship is the very substance of things has been a catalyst in a renewed appreciation of God being all in all. There are no substances existing independently of relationships. It is true of God; it is true of God's creation.[758]

The juxtaposition of these 'trends' lies at the heart of the struggle that exists between a market point of view and a sabbath or 'common good' point of view. The struggle is between a view that there is nothing that cannot or should not be bought or sold and that there are to be no limits, and the sabbath premise that fulfilment and abundance is to be sought within limits through relationships within community, the global human community and the community of creation. It is a struggle between the rights and interests of individuals (or individual nations) and the global rights and interests of intergenerational 'common good', inclusive of the whole biosphere.

The struggle is also between transient, economic, opportunism and the present understood as a bridge between past and future. To reduce everything to a saleable commodity is to reduce all reality to transience. A 'commodity' is an owned or desired entity that exists simply in its contemporary usefulness. When such usefulness has passed then the commodity can be abandoned. To live within a sabbath ethic is to treasure the enduring relationship that exists in and between all things, seeking not usefulness from, but blessing with and for, the other. The commoditising of everything—the reduction of reality to transient usefulness—accelerates the desire to have today that which belongs to tomorrow. Such a desire accelerates both economic and environmental debt. Even more seriously, it is to denude the future: 'to take no account of future life on earth ... is to break the eighth commandment 'thou shalt not steal.'[759]

The sabbath ethic requires that the poor and vulnerable be relieved of the debt that they owe to others; on the other hand, if payment (for a day's work) is owed to them, it is to be immediately met. Because of the enslaving nature of debt, Jesus, the fulfiller of sabbath, teaches that as God forgives debt, humans are to forgive it in one another. An obligation that remains unmet is a burden; it is a reduction of freedom. In the spiritual realm this burden is lifted through an offer of forgiveness, the relief of the burden by the one to whom the debt is owed. This forgiveness restores a future to the one indebted.[760] In a similar manner, in the world of material things the burden remains unless paid out or forgiven. Debt creates a situation of unequal power which cannot be tolerated within the sabbath intention of God.

Environmental debt is an outcome of taking from the future to fulfil the perceived needs of a transient present. Environmental debt ultimately entails a loss of choice, both for the natural environment through loss of diversity and capacity to regenerate, and also for humanity whose global economy is limited by the depletion imposed upon the natural order. Unattended debt experienced by a section of community ultimately undermines the whole community.[761] While the biblical sabbath narrative underscores the interdependence of the whole created order, and sabbath specifically identifies human responsibility to give 'rest to the land', until recent times indebtedness has usually been understood in the context of inter-human relationships alone. There is now an understanding that indebtedness applies equally to the non-human creation, an understanding always reflected in sabbath.

Humanity now carries a growing environmental indebtedness. In human affairs indebtedness is often 'managed' through an expectation that inflation reduces the value of debt in real terms. Environmental debt operates in the opposite direction. Because all material resources are finite, loss is magnified in that what has been used can never be replaced, its loss continues in every succeeding year.[762]

Addressing inter-human indebtedness is a matter of morality and conscience, not law or compulsion. The jubilee programme of 2000 could not be imposed any more than human forgiveness can be forced. However, environmental indebtedness will directly impose itself upon humanity if not addressed. Science tells us that this is the situation we now face; the impacts of environmental indebtedness are already apparent and likely to escalate into the future. The biblical narrative supports scientific research, suggesting that the land upon which humanity and all living things depend will ultimately demand that its 'sabbaths be repaid'.

In a desire to protect 'common good' and mitigate both an increasing environmental debt together with its debilitating consequences, I propose two sabbath ethical principles. While these principles are unapologetically Christian in foundation, their application could find resonance in the wider community which appears to languish without a reasoned basis for environmental ethical action.

The Principle of Today

'Give us today our daily bread' (Matt. 6:11).

'He sets a certain day—'today'' (Heb. 4:7).

'Today', in the Lord's Prayer, and as argued in the fourth chapter of the Epistle to the Hebrews, was discussed in Chapter 4 and the link to sabbath established. Chapter 5 noted that the narrative of manna in the wilderness, and the daily gathering of it, is the quintessential touchstone of this truth. The character of every day is to be neither taking that which belongs to the future, nor living in dependence upon that which has been bequeathed from the past. Stewarding 'today', should honour and not exploit the past while at the same time enhancing and not diminishing the future.

Each new generation must reinterpret biblical and theological insights and their ethical implications within their own lived context; this applies to the principle of 'today'. Christian communities are used to examining biblical principles for the light they shed on human to human relationships, but far less used to examining them in relation to non-human creation, despite the overlay of sabbath principles already enunciated. Post industrial practice, such as the burning of fossil fuels, has not been considered within the appropriate ambit of religious commentary. Because the practice is being scientifically shown to have long term destabilising consequences for life on the planet, commentary is not only appropriate, but necessary.

What makes the consumption of energy by contemporary humanity different to previous generations of humans is that since the industrial revolution we have developed the capacity to harness stored solar energy (fossil fuel) from past millennia as a cheap and relatively accessible means of powering 21st century energy needs. On a monumental scale, we tap into the stored energy of yesterday in order to satisfy the needs of today, while at the same time passing on the negative aspects of this consumption to tomorrow.

To live this way is not in keeping with ethical principles. We are depending upon a finite resource; once used it is not available to other generations. Future generations will not only rely upon renewable energy as finite resources are diminished, they will also have to cope with the effects of additional trapped energy as a result of increased density in greenhouse gases. This situation, caused by a desire for energy with apparent contemptuous disregard for responsibility, will play out in the life cycle of accumulated greenhouse gases, especially carbon dioxide.[763] When fossil fuels are harvested, released carbon increases the greenhouse effect, causing more heat (energy) to be trapped in the atmosphere. Weather patterns change and become more intense.[764] Energy is not 'consumed' it is transferred, recycled.[765] Generating energy without negative consequences is the aim of a sustainable future. Technological advancement indicates that transition to dependence upon renewable energy is now possible.[766] Christian communities should be in the forefront of lobbying for this transition to 'today', and for renewed investment in the research and development of such technology.

On the one hand each individual Christian and each Christian community should seek opportunity to reduce their reliance upon energy that comes from a fossil fuel source. On the other hand the Christian community must join the global endeavour to slow or stop investment from banks and other lenders (including government through subsidies) to the fossil fuel industry, thus speeding up global transition to renewable energy sources.

Moving to an economy based upon the harvesting of current rather than historical sources of energy is known to be manageable and deliverable. What is lacking is the political will to do so.

The Principle of Enough

Contemporary society has developed a mindset intolerant of limits. At one level this is admirable, no mountain is too high to climb, no distance too far to travel, no problem too difficult to solve. However, given the dominance of a materialistic ideology, this mindset is not limited to altruistic ambition: there is no limit to what we can or should consume, no limit to natural resources that can or should be exploited, no limit to acquisitions that individuals can or should alienate from the 'common good',[767] no ethical principle or regulation that should limit the means by which advantage is, or can be leveraged.[768] This mindset, as already argued, is ultimately self defeating, and when applied to the environment is, as Dr David Suzuki has argued, suicidal.[769] It is to live as if somehow the present is disconnected from the past and the future: 'in our actions we are bound by certain limitations from the past and the future that cannot be leaped over.'[770]

Accepting limits to personal aspirations that do not build and sustain community, lies at the heart of Christian praxis. 'That the battle is of an ethical kind means that for Jesus, as for the Christian, it is about renouncing oneself in order to serve others ... the free development of humankind happens not at crosscurrents to, but in line with, the blooming of creation in its yearning for freedom and imperishability.'[771]

'We are preservers because the creation is intrinsically good and we are delivered from the kind of egotism that is able to find goodness only in what is useful to ourselves.'[772]

It has already been argued that the biblical and theological basis for ethical limitation is to be found in 'sabbath'. Every aspect of creation, including humanity, is to experience rest. Rest avoids exploitation, it recognises the need for recuperation, recognition that every aspect of creation must live within limits out of respect for the other. 'To know our place means to recognise and accept the limits which being located implies.'[773] While it is right that human beings constantly test the limits of their intellectual, physical and emotional capacity, it is not appropriate that this right impinge upon others, either other human beings or the non-human creation.

The environmental crisis points unequivocally to the necessity of limits being placed upon human exploitation and consumption. However, while some limits to human behaviour can be, and are, imposed by law, in western culture at least there remains a strong disincentive for further imposed limitation to individual aspiration. This disincentive is based on the grounds that such imposition will impede what is perceived to be the necessity of economic growth, or that it interferes with the personal rights and freedoms of an individual, or that it implies the imposition of a 'nanny state'.

As Walter Brueggemann argues in a short essay, *The Creatures Know*,[774] living within limits, is a matter of 'knowing' not of imposing. He argues that non-human creatures intuitively know their place within the created order and that for human beings there is no excuse. Conradie makes a similar point about the necessity of discovery. 'There are ecological limits, including limits to economic growth on a finite planet. Nevertheless these limits are not simply given, they have to be discovered'. Brueggemann argues that the Old Testament wisdom literature confirms that from the non-human creation, humanity has all the evidence necessary to understand what is important to sustain health wholeness and well-being.

Richard Bauckham argues a priori that humanity must understand its hopes and activities lie within the non-negotiable context of the wider creation to which it owes respect.

> Exceptional though we may be in various ways, our exceptionality is embedded in the community of creation to which we belong and would be impossible without it. We are not aliens imposing ourselves on or intruding ourselves within, the community of creation, but natural members of it.[775]

Chapter 2 recognised the contribution made by John Vincent Taylor to Anglican reflection on ecological debate in his book *Enough is Enough*.[776] Taylor argues that the biblical dream, the outcome of sabbath living, is shalom 'the harmony of a caring community informed at every point by its awareness of God.'[777] He goes on to say 'Economically and socially this dream of shalom found expression in what I call the theology of enough.'[778]

Limits extend a courtesy of respect and wisdom in the myriad of interdependent relationships that make up human existence. As humanity accepts the limits implicit in transition to a community which lives with the future in mind there are significant challenges that go beyond curbing the obvious excessiveness of individual and national greed. Exercising its prophetic voice the Church must follow the moral principle argued in Chapter 2 that the common good must prevail, and prevail not simply in the here and now, but inter-generationally. If 'common good' is to prevail and to prevail into the future, the following must be challenged:

1. **The assumption that exponential growth is always and everywhere necessary.**

   It is beyond my capacity to argue what a global economy might look like that is not predicated on exponential growth. However I have argued as strongly as I am able that a global economy that accepts no limits, that is based upon levels of ever increasing consumption, is inconsistent with a sabbath world. 'Sabbath must be kept because sabbath is the key mark of existence outside imperial productivity.'[779] While my argument is theological, Jeffrey Sachs and Tim Jackson represent a growing body of economic opinion that argues the same case.

> The world's ability to combine long-term economic growth with environmental health is heavily debated. Yet one thing is certain: *the current trajectory of human activity is not sustainable.* ... The limits of the environment itself will defeat our global aspirations for prosperity.[780]
>
> The idea of a non-growing economy may be an anathema to an economist. But the idea of a continually growing economy is anathema to an ecologist ... we have no alternative but to question growth.[781]

2. **The assumption that production at the lowest cost is always in the best interest of human society.**

Capitalism relies on the assumption that profits that accrue from distribution will be greater than the cost of production. Pressure is therefore ubiquitous to achieve the lowest possible cost of production. However, low cost production achieved at environmental cost, or that is achieved through sweatshops, or that is achieved through mineral exploitation which disrupts cultures and rural livelihoods, is not in the best interests of human society. In contemporary times, and with notable exceptions, the Church does not have a good record in exercising its voice for the (human or non-human) oppressed in the face of (corporate) profit seeking. In *Rich Land, Wasteland*[782] Sharon Munro paints a picture of devastating consequences for both humanity and ecology as a result of the coal and coal gas excavation enterprise in Australia. Cavalier disregard for both human society and ecological health by the mining industry in underdeveloped countries in the cause of profit is notoriously even more damaging.[783]

3. **An advertising narrative that associates acquisition with meaning or value.**

The consumption industry relies upon the power of advertising to convince the public that their products enhance our lives. Social research indicates that this is not true and that happiness or fulfilment associated with acquisition is illusionary. There is no evidence that, apart from those who are very poor, additional wealth adds to an overall sense of well-being.[784]

> Addressing the social logic of consumerism is vital. This task is far from simple—mainly because of the way in which material goods are so deeply implicated in the fabric of our lives. Prosperity is not synonymous with material wealth.[785]

4. **A mindset that personal self-sufficiency is more desirable than cooperative sharing.**

In the 'west' we are inheritors of a culture which assumes that personal ownership is always desirable. This is not the biblical mindset, nor is it the mindset of ancient indigenous cultures worldwide. Chapter 5 noted that the religion of Yahweh, predicated on a collaborative, interdependent community, was constantly contrasted with the religion of Baal (owner). Chapter 1 drew attention to a significant feature of the new Christian community that 'all who believed were together and had all things in common; they would sell their possessions and goods and distribute the proceeds to all, as any had need' (Acts 2:44).

The enlightenment creed taught that every individual was free to pursue her own happiness, irrespective of what others thought. This approach had disastrous consequences. ... The individual is not a monad, but part of an organism. We live in one world. ... The 'me generation' has to give way to the 'us generation'. ... Here lies the pertinence of the rediscovery of the Church, the body of Christ, and of the Christian mission as building a community of those who share a common destiny.[786]

Critics of the 'principle of enough' have argued, and will argue, that its application implies the (intended or unintended) death of a 'free, aspirational, civil society' such as we have come to enjoy in the developed world. In other words that it implies a backward rather than a forward movement for humanity, perhaps even a return to the dark days of Marxist socialism.[787] I am arguing that embracing a principle of enough contributes to a rediscovery of human fulfilment in which relationship is more important than acquisition and the flourishing of community a prerequisite to the flourishing of an individual.

What was a 'stumbling block to the Jews and foolishness to Greeks' (1 Cor. 1:23) remains true in the 21st century environmentally challenged world. Truth lies with the counter-intuitive, at least with what is counter-intuitive to a consumerist society. Kenosis, is life giving. Emptying links humanity to the ongoing activity of creation, the enabling of space in which abundance flourishes. Taylor concludes his *Enough is Enough* with 'Behold I am making all things new' (Rev. 21:5). The truth is that within interdependence there is life, independence is death. Jesus warned against hoarding in barns (Lk. 12:18), such investment is easily lost. Investment in community (human and ecological) delivers compounding interest. Less is more. A life embraced by the sabbath ethic invested in common good, is investment in the fulfilment that is human destiny under God.[788]

Conclusions

Kenosis is a useful descriptor of the 'way things are'; that enabling space for that which is other than self is a necessity of life shared in the common space of the created order. Kenosis describes the nature of God in both creation and redemption and describes an essential characteristic of the 'human vocation'. Kenosis should be embraced as enhancement not diminishment.

The human vocation requires space to be enabled for generations that follow. Living with the future in mind has now also become a scientific imperative: accumulating data points to a crisis of the planet's ecological health. The threats to this future place moral obligations upon all humanity, but especially upon the Christian community, to live within limits.

The size of the human population is one of these threats. Christianity has traditionally been slow to consider limits to human expansion because of an intuitive or perceived trust in a biblical mandate to multiply. Scripture on the other hand carries a consistent mandate for each generation to steward freedoms and opportunities on behalf of the next generation. Given that the size of the population is now an existential threat to the well-being of future generations rather than a guarantor of its security, the Christian community has an obligation to revisit scripture in light of a changed context and to address circumstances which militate against a stabilised global population.

Sabbath commitment focusses upon healthy relationships at the heart of the human condition. We now live in a culture which appears to have replaced this priority with the priority of acquisition. A consumerist society is bombarded with encouragement to believe that acquisition not only enhances, but is essential to human identity. Given that excessive acquisition is a significant cause of the environmental crisis, encouraging limits can and should be promoted not simply as a means of dealing with the environmental crisis but as an essential element in the recovery of fulfilled humanity, a celebration of common good. Limits should therefore be embraced not reluctantly as diminishment, but gladly as contributing to the health and well-being of a fully functional, relational world in which individuals flourish. Limits contribute to common good.

CHAPTER 8

CONCLUSIONS

I have examined twenty-first century Christian existence and mission in light of the environmental crisis. Background to this examination has been ethical and theological research for a foundation upon which a Christian response to this crisis can confidently be made. While the parameters of this research have been focussed upon the Anglican Church, the conclusions are not specifically Anglican, but belong to the Church universal.

Christianity and christian mission are at one level changeless. Christianity is a proclamation, in word and action, of the redemptive love of God in light of the enduring human condition. At another level it is changing, shaped within specific historical contexts. To proclaim the gospel without proper reference to prevailing context is to sanction detachment, with the unintended consequence that faith can then be understood as other worldly, 'corralling souls to heaven', without commitment to the redemption and transformation of the world. It is to risk abandoning life's public and political struggles for equity and justice for withdrawal into personal piety and morality, a situation inconsistent with the biblical narrative.

The twenty-first century context is marked by the aspirational reach of the human footprint exceeding the earth's capacity for sustainability. For this to be sanctioned is to ignore the insight of the second creation narrative that unredeemed humanity has an insatiable appetite to consume and control, and that such consumption and control is ultimately destructive of self and human relationship with creation. (Gen. 3:1-24). This narrative makes clear that the human appetite has consequences in the loss of harmony and the rise of hostility and that it ultimately denies humanity its birthright and destiny, peaceful co-existence within creation's abundance.

This is a global context which presents Christianity with a contemporary challenge it is yet to fully grasp. It is however a challenge that can be met by arguing that creation, the dwelling place of God, is a single house within which blessing resides for life in all its diversity; and ethically by an imperative that good must prevail equitably and inter-generationally for creation in its entirety.

The environmental crisis and the necessary human response cannot be fully explained and responded to through ecological insights alone. Factors such as loss of diversity, desertification, sea level rise, temperature rise, are well documented. What must also be understood, and responded to, are human behaviours that arise from political and economic norms. These behaviours are embedded in an increasingly independent and unregulated market that demands increasing per capita consumption, without factoring its cost to the natural environment. These norms, articulated in Chapter 1, are what led Rowan Williams to say we do not have an environmental crisis, but a crisis of the human vocation.

Couched in the language of a crisis to the human vocation, a response to the environmental crisis must be far more than a simple adjustment of light globes and sources of energy. It must be founded in a well articulated ethical framework, and for the Christian community, a theological framework.

I have researched an ethical and theological framework that may be embraced by the Christian community generally, as well as the Anglican

community specifically. To do this, theological and ethical principles have
been sought from successive Lambeth Conferences over the last 140 years,
that have underpinned responses to various social challenges with the
intention that they might, with confidence, be applied in response to the
environmental crisis.

Four principles were identified that in turn have provided the
framework for this work:

1. A response to a social issue, deserving the widest possible
    support, cannot emerge at the whim of a sectional interest
    but should be an expression of the Church's catholicity.
    That is to say a response should be grounded in the essential
    and universal truths of the Christian faith. This principle
    undergirds my whole argument and in particular the choice of
    sabbath as the window through which ethical and theological
    principles are examined.

2. A response must be rooted in scripture. Scripture, especially
    as it is fulfilled in the revelation of God in Jesus, unfolds the
    character of God which, in turn, is to be imaged by humanity.
    Scripture is the vehicle through which the 'modern world
    can come to understand itself'.[789] This principle has been
    explored in Part 2.

3. A response must prioritise common good over self interest.
    This principle is considered to be inherent in belief that
    the creation is a single house; that in Jesus a boundary-less
    new community is established, that all life is to be drawn
    into a New Creation. Political implications of this principle
    have immediate application to the environmental crisis:
    environmental common good must prevail over national as
    well as individual self interest. In Part 2 sabbath is examined
    in light of this principle, as is the human vocation in Part 3.

4.   A response must enhance and fulfil the human vocation. That is to say, notwithstanding the plurality of post modern society, the biblical narrative presupposes a character of living for humanity as a whole that issues in blessedness, contentment, human fulfilment, and respect for God's creation. Understanding what this character is and applying it to the changing context of the twenty-first century is a search for wisdom that the Church can contribute to the whole of humanity. This is the subject of Part 3.

In my research, all four principles and their application to the environmental crisis have been explored through the concept of sabbath. Sabbath was chosen as a key concept for the following reasons:

1.   Sabbath in the two decalogues is rooted respectively in creation and human history (redemption). Recent theological emphasis has prioritised redemption theology over creation theology, leaving creation theology in a Cinderella position. An unintended consequence has been that redemption theology with its interpreted emphasis upon the individual has undergirded a trend towards individualism, one of the underlying issues that must be addressed in response to the environmental crisis. Sabbath brings creation and redemption theologies into conversation with one another, with the result that redemption theology is then called to reflect the relationality that lies at the heart of creation. An adequate response to the environmental crisis has to be couched theologically in language that connects God's intention in creating with God's intention in creation's destiny.

2.   Sabbath is not a celebration of rest in the sense of cessation from work, but rest in the sense of contentment that arises from presence. God is present to creation in sabbath and

the source of its blessing. Shekinah, God's presence, first understood and localised in cloud, fire and temple, becomes universal to the whole creation in sabbath and finally incarnate in the person of Jesus. Sabbath, shekinah and Jesus are one. Understanding sabbath as presence, engagement, challenges assumptions of modern commercial life, implicit or explicit, that the material world can be treated as a commodity that exists apart from humanity. Humanity is itself part of creation not apart from it and humanity must respond with empathy to creation's groaning.

3. The ethical requirements of sabbath cannot be plumbed through personal piety alone, however deep or sincere, for sabbath is not primarily about the individual it is about the community. The ethical requirements of sabbath are foundational to a community, local or global, that seeks in its flourishing to enjoying harmony and intergenerational longevity. The ethical requirements of sabbath serve justice, equity and mercy. The import of the biblical narrative is that the ethical principles inherent in sabbath are immutable, that is to say they might be ignored by humanity but they cannot be abrogated. The biblical narrative makes clear that ultimately the created order will 'call in' the sabbaths that have been denied to it. This is the message now disturbingly confirmed by scientific data.

4. 'Sabbath fulfilled' is both Jesus' self understanding and the understanding of the early Church about him, as expressed through New Testament writers. In Luke's Gospel Jesus commences his ministry by choosing to read the sabbath jubilee passage from Isaiah 61; and Mark and Matthew draw on the same imagery in answer to questions from John the Baptist

as to who he is and what he considers his mission to be. Sabbath jubilee imagery underlies key passages such as the Beatitudes and the Lord's Prayer. Jesus declares himself to be Lord of the Sabbath. The writer to the Hebrews claims Jesus fulfils the long awaited 'rest'. The Kingdom Jesus inaugurates is inclusive of all that emanates from God; however, it is popularly understood more narrowly because it has been anthropomorphised in biblical interpretation. The Kingdom in fact enfolds the whole created order—it is no less than a new creation. If sabbath is so central to the biblical narrative and as a consequence so central to Christian self understanding, it must shape the existential and missional objectives of the Church in every age.

5.   In 1998 and 2008 the Lambeth Conferences called for a recovery of the 'sabbath principle', and the development of a sabbath theology in order that the Church may more adequately respond to the environmental crisis. This book has become, in part, a response to this request, a request that intuitively infers an adequate response from the Church to the environmental crisis must be immersed in actions that identify 'true humanity' and are drawn from a theological and ethical rediscovery of sabbath.

The results of the above inquiry into Sabbath lead to three general conclusions about the human vocation, the subject of part three, dealt with respectively in Chapters, 5, 6 and 7.

First, in light of the environmental crisis humanity in the twenty-first century must balance, even move away from, its twentieth century propensity for competitive independence to a much more conscious collaborative interdependence. This interdependence may include the necessity of national goals and aspirations being tempered by the greater needs of global justice and equity. The sabbath principle as demonstrated in the Old Testament shows that which belongs to all, under God, has a higher priority for protection than that which is privately owned. Such a move will be strongly resisted, for the capitalist spirit that ubiquitously pervades contemporary global commerce aggressively guards individual rights against community responsibilities. If this move is not made it is clear that inequity both between humans and between humanity and the natural order will continue to escalate alarmingly. Capitalism has a proven track record to increase wealth, indeed large numbers in Asia in particular have been pulled out of a cycle of poverty, but it is far less certain that unregulated capitalism can undergird a just equitable and harmonious world for humanity and the non-human creation in the twenty-first century. Since the Enlightenment the Western world, for a long time the home of Christianity, has come to believe that true humanity, or the human vocation, is best expressed through independence. The insight of sabbath is that collaboration is a more accurate descriptor of that vocation.

Second, the goodness of each generation is to be judged by the manner in which it protects the well-being of the next generation. Each generation must live with the future in mind. Again, this is a great challenge to a culture in which the volume and growth of commercial exchange is paramount, indeed such is the perceived need for growth that factoring in the cost to future generations is discounted. Unregulated commercial enterprise seeks to maximise profit which means maximising value to the present, no matter the source from which that value is drawn. The conclusion that sabbath demands that each live with the future in mind is drawn both from specific and immediate sabbath requirements and also from an eschatological imperative. The immediate requirement is that generational poverty must not become entrenched, that poverty not be passed from one generation to another. In cycles that are annual, seven-yearly and each fifty years, debt and inequity are to be released. In our present context this does not simply mean human poverty, but it includes the poverty being imposed upon the natural environment. Both poverties are intertwined. Environmental poverty increases human poverty and human poverty can make environmental responsibility beyond reach. Environmental debt has the potential to become the greatest existential threat to long term sustainability and in this context has been called the 'greatest moral challenge of our time'.

But the requirement is also eschatological. Sabbath is both a present reality and a yet to be fulfilled future expectation. We do not yet live, but yearn for, the total harmony and well-being inherent in sabbath. Christian hope is premised in that what is hoped for is to be lived as if it were a present reality. That is to say, that which is intended in sabbath is to be lived now as a sign of hope by the Christian community. We, the Christian community, are to live as beacons of hope in a world that is yet to believe that environmental responsibility is not only possible but desirable, that quality of life will be enhanced and not diminished. This is a challenge to individual Christians and to the Church as an institution. Living these choices as a sign of hope is equally as important as advocating for change.

Third, individual human beings, and humanity as a whole, are vocationally fulfilled when appropriateness is understood and limits accepted. The current era has been called the age of the anthropocene because of the all pervading presence and intrusion of humanity into and over every aspect of life on the planet. Human beings are called not only to live spiritually without limit in ambition for a life of value and service, but also to live materially with limits in terms of acquisition and desired personal wealth.

Sabbath's contribution to this understanding is located in the revelation that God's presence imbues creation with its essential character. In creating God makes space for that which is not God. In redemption God 'empties himself' in order to embrace and lift fallen humanity.

This character, the character of *kenosis*, reveals not simply the incarnate nature of God, but the eternal nature of God. God is the 'self-emptying God'. Creation bares the same character; each part of creation empties itself into the well-being of the rest of creation. Using different language, this is the science of ecological systems.

Of all created species, humanity alone has the capacity to resist and insist that the rest of creation serve its purposes in isolation from the rest of creation. This truth lies at the heart of our present dilemma. The rate of consumption together with the size of the population and the technological capacity to exploit is placing a burden upon the natural order that it cannot sustain. My unfolding argument leads to the conclusion that humanity must accept limits in two respects.

Humanity must accept limits to consumption and in the process be freed from advertising's demeaning claim that identity is aligned to acquisition. Two sabbath based theological propositions have been presented to undergird the proposition that limits to consumption enhance rather than diminish a more noble humanity; the principle of 'today' and of 'enough'.

'Today' is a celebration of life, without diminishment of the past or loss for the future. 'Enough' is a life lived in the knowledge of abundance, in contrast to acquisition which is life lived out of the fear of scarcity. 'Enough' both acknowledges abundance and safeguards it. Exploitation corrals possession into private barns, diminishing the abundance that all have the right to enjoy.

Humanity must also accept limits to the size of the global population. What has been commonly assumed as a biblical injunction to multiply has been necessary for most of human history, where disease, natural disaster, and other calamities have kept the human population low. However, the primary biblical injunction to each generation has been the health and well-being of the next. In an entirely new situation where the size of the population is a threat, rather a guarantee of continuity, tackling this situation has become an imperative. The Christian community can do so in confidence that this is not only necessary, but an appropriate way of living the biblical narrative in the twenty-first century.

Sabbath is both a celebration of common good and a framework for each generation to live its human vocation. I conclude that sabbath, initially set in the primordial creation narrative, has significant implications for humanity in every generation. Focussing those implications in the twenty-first century warrants further research shaped around certain questions:

1. Sabbath principles critique economic systems. What does Christianity bring to dialogue about a twenty-first century economic system that might focus equity and justice and consequently minimise hostility and conflict?

2. Sabbath principles are global in their application. Does Christianity have a view about a form of governance that might more effectively tackle issues that are not confined to the boundaries of sovereign states? How does the concept of the catholicity of the church relate to the defence of the nation state?

3. Sabbath principles imply an intergenerational ethic. What does Christianity bring to a debate about global human population? What wisdom can Christianity bring to a conversation about global population?

Just as there are immutable laws of science that govern the predictability with which the physical world can be understood, so there are also relational principles that might be ignored but cannot be abrogated by humanity. Sabbath, a biblical insight into these principles, is a celebration of the world's relationality in the presence of God; a celebration of the priority of common good; a celebration of the human vocation, a celebration of the present, endowed by the past and shaped by its future destiny.

APPENDIX 1

SCRIPTURAL REFERENCES

Old Testament

Reference	Page	Reference	Page
Genesis		3:1-24	253
1	108	3:8	177
1-11	178	4:3	66
1:1-2:4	186	9	83
1:2	105, 166	9:8-17	100
1:3-5	109	29:15-35	102
1:22	111	41:1ff	110
1:25	138	Exodus	
1:26	83	13:21	96
1:27	187, 206, 215	16:1-35	114
1:28	10, 13, 111, 235	16:17-18	114
1:31	185	16:18	240
2:1	108, 120, 158, 211	16:20	114
2:1-2	141	19:5-6	190
2:1-4	19, 91, 98, 104, 120, 176, 229	20:1-17	92, 96
		20:8-10	106
2:2	121	23:10-12	99
2:15	83, 189	31:1ff	105
2:18-20	101	40:33	108
3	160		

New Testament

Appendix 2

Resolutions of the Lambeth Conferences that have a Bearing Upon a Theological and Ethical Response to the Environmental Crisis

1867 (Archbishop Charles Longley)

There were no resolutions on social policy.

1878 (Archbishop Archibald Tait)

There were no resolutions on social policy.

1888 (Archbishop Edward Benson)

Resolution 7[790]

That this conference receives the Report drawn up by the committee on the subject of socialism, and submits it to the consideration of the Churches of the Anglican Communion.

1897 (Archbishop Frederick Temple)

Resolution 13[791]

That this conference receives the report of the committee upon the critical study of Holy Scripture, and commends it to the consideration of all Christian people.

Resolution 44[792]

That this Conference receives the report of the committee on the duty of the Church in regard to industrial problems, and commends the suggestions embodied in it to the earnest and sympathetic consideration of all Christian people.

1908 (Archbishop Randall Davidson)

Resolution 1[793]

The conference commends to Christian people and all who seek after truth the Report of the Committee on the Faith and Modern Thought, as a faithful attempt to show how that claim of our Lord Jesus Christ, which the Church is set to present to each generation, may, under the characteristic conditions of our time, best command allegiance.

Resolution 45[794]

The social mission and social principles of Christianity should be given a more prominent place in the study and teaching of the Church, both for the clergy and the laity.

Resolution 48[795]

The Church should teach that the Christian who is the owner of a property should recognise the governing principle that, like all our gifts, our powers, and our time, property is a trust held for the benefit of the community, and its right use should be insisted upon as a religious duty.

Resolution 49[796]

The Conference urges upon the Church practical recognition of the moral responsibility involved in their investments. This moral responsibility extends to:

a.   the character and general social effect of any business or enterprise in which their money is invested;

b.   the treatment of the persons employed in that business or enterprise;

c.   the due observance of the requirement of the law relating thereto;

d.   the payment of a just wage to those who are employed therein.

Resolution 50[797]

The conference holds that it is the duty of the Church to press upon governments the wrong of sanctioning for the sake of revenue any forms of trade which involve the degradation or hinder the moral and physical progress of the races and peoples under their rule or influence.

1920 (Archbishop Randall Davidson)

Resolution 9[798]

[This is an unusually long resolution in the form of a manifesto calling for the visible unity of the Church. This appears to have been the main focus of the conference following the enormous divisions of war].

Resolution 73[799]

We desire to emphasise our conviction that the pursuit of mere self-interest, whether individual or corporate, will never bring healing to the wounds of society. ... Nor is this less true when this self-interest is equipped with every advantage of science and education ....

Resolution 74[800]

An outstanding and pressing duty of the Church is to convince its members of the necessity of nothing less than a fundamental change in the spirit and working of our economic life. This change can only be effected by accepting as the basis of industrial relations the principle of co-operation in service of the common good in place of unrestricted competition for private or sectional advantage.

Resolution 76[801]

In obedience to Christ's teaching as to covetousness and self-seeking, the conference calls upon members of his Church to be foremost both by personal action and sacrifice in maintaining the superiority of the claims of human life to those of property. ... In a word, they must set an example in subordinating the claim for rights to the call of duty.

1930 (Archbishop Cosmo Gordon Lang)

[Very surprisingly there were no motions similar to 1920 addressing the severe economic difficulties of the time]

1948 (Archbishop Geoffrey Fisher)

Resolution 4[802]

We fully share man's aspiration for fellowship in an ordered society and for freedom of individual achievement, but we assert that no view of man can be satisfactory which confines his interests and hopes to this world and his life alone; such views belittle man and blind him to the greatness of his destiny.

Resolution 5[803]

The conference believes that both the recognition of the responsibility of the individual to God and the development of his personality are gravely imperilled by any claim made either by the state or by any group within the state to control the whole of human life. Personality is developed in community, but the community must be one of free persons. The Christian must therefore judge every social system by its effect upon human personality.

Resolution 40[804]

The conference values the witness given by those who, in response to a special vocation, keep themselves apart from the life of the world. But we believe that Christians generally are called by God to take their part in the life of the world, and through the power of God's grace to transform it.

1958 (Archbishop Geoffrey Fisher)

Resolution 8[805]

The conference acknowledges gratefully the work of scientists in increasing man's knowledge of the universe, wherein is seen the majesty of God in his creative activity. It therefore calls upon Christian people both to learn reverently from every new disclosure of truth, and at the same time to bear witness to the biblical message of a God and Saviour apart from whom no gift can be rightfully used.

1968 (Archbishop Michael Ramsey)

Resolution 2[806]

The conference having considered and welcomed

    a.   the increasing extent of human knowledge,

    b.   the prospect of human control of the natural environment,

    c.   the searching enquiries of the theologians,

calls the Church to a faith in the living God which is adventurous, expectant, calm, and confident, and to faith in the standards of Christ, who was, and is, and is to come, as the criterion of what is to be welcomed and what is to be resisted in contemporary society.

Resolution 6[807]

The conference urges all Christians, in obedience to the doctrine of creation, to take all possible action to ensure man's responsible stewardship over nature; in particular in his relationship with animals, and with regard to the conservation of the soil, and the prevention of pollution of air, soil, and ocean.

Resolution 7[808]

The conference endorses the initiative of Dr Pardo, leader of the Maltese delegation at the United Nations, urging that steps be taken to draft a treaty embodying the following principles. That the seabed beyond the present limits of national jurisdiction:

    a.   be conserved against appropriation by nations or their nationals, so that the deep ocean floor should be allowed to become a stage for competing claims of national sovereignty;

    b.   be explored in a manner consistent with the principles and purposes of the charter of the United Nations;

    c.   be exploited economically or made use of with the aim of safeguarding the interests of mankind;

    d.   be conserved exclusively for peaceful purposes in perpetuity.

Resolution 69[809]

Established the Anglican Consultative Council.

1978 (Archbishop Donald Coggan)

Resolution 1 Today's world[810]

The conference approves the following statement as expressing some of the concerns of the bishops about today's world in which today's Church must proclaim a total Gospel. It is printed here for study, and action wherever possible, by the member Churches.

We, the bishops of the Anglican Communion gathered from many parts of the world, having experienced a deep unity in the conviction of our faith and in our calling as bishops, wish to share with all people some matters of universal concern.

On earlier occasions we have appealed not only to Anglicans but to all Christian people. Today because we have discovered a new dimension of unity in our intense concern for the future wellbeing for all mankind in the new era of history which we are now entering we dare to appeal also to governments, world leaders, and people, without distinction, because all countries, however nationalistic in sentiment, are now interdependent. No nation is an island unto itself.

The choices before us are real, and so are the consequences of them. On the one hand there are great potentialities for advance in human wellbeing but there are also real possibilities of catastrophic disaster if present attitudes and the expectations of individuals do not swiftly change and if vital problems of society are not confronted and resolved by governments and through international co-operation. We draw attention to the following areas where there is a need for change in attitude and practice:

1. We need to see the necessary exchange of commodities in the market place as an area where human values can be affirmed and not ignored; to seek to ensure that those involved are not treated merely as functional units but as being worthy of and able to enter into relationships of friendship.

2. We need to challenge the assumption that 'more is better' and 'having is being' which add fuel to the fire of human greed.

3. We need to stress that the wellbeing of the whole human family is more important than egoistic self-interest.

4. We need to change the focus on technology and see it not as the master with an insidious fascination of its own but as the servant of the world and its people, beginning with those in need. We must face the threat of science and technology as well as their promise.

5. We need to be diverting our planning and action to the development of a new kind of society. Much time is still spent in overtaking problems. We must direct our efforts to the achievement of a kind of society where the economy is not based on waste, but on stewardship, not on consumerism but conservation, one not only concerned with work but with the right use of leisure. We may need to contemplate a paradox: an increasing use of appropriate technology, while returning, where possible, to many of the values of pre-industrial society. In some places this can include home industries, the local market, the fishing village, and the small farm.

6. We need to recognise that at present all over the world there tends to be a growing urbanisation. Many cities are in crisis due to the growing number of people with little hope of freedom of choice. The gap between the rich and the poor, between the powerful and the powerless, continues to grow.

7. We need to recognise that some earlier evaluations of the place of work in human life are becoming dangerously obsolete. In many societies more goods are produced, but there is less employment. We need to orientate education so as to help people develop new attitudes both to work and leisure.

8. We need to help people in the parts of the world classed as economically underdeveloped not to mirror industrialised societies, but to retain or shape a style of life which affirms both the dignity of the person and the value of close human community.

9. We need to help the developed industrial nations and the people who live in them to face the necessity of a redistribution of wealth and trading opportunities. Such a redistribution could place the major burden on those groups within such societies which are already most vulnerable. We need, therefore, to urge such nations to face the challenge to work for much greater internal justice.

10. We need to recognise that expenditure on armaments is disproportionate to sums spent on such essentials as health and education and constitutes a vast misdirection of limited resources that are badly needed for human welfare, especially for the eradication of poverty. The escalation of weapons systems with their ever-increasing technological complexity diverts attention from the real needs of mankind. We call all people to protest, in whatever ways possible, at the escalation of the commerce in armaments of war and to support with every effort all international proposals and conferences designed to achieve progressive world disarmament in a way that recognises the need for power balances. New initiatives are urgently required for mutual co-existence and toleration which are essential if real justice and peace are to be established.

11. The resources of our planet are limited; delicate ecological balances can be disturbed by modern technology, or threatened by the toxic effects of human ingenuity. Ways must be found to stop waste, to recycle resources and to monitor

and control the manufacture of substances dangerous to life and health. The use of nuclear fuel must be subject to the safe and permanent disposal of its toxic by-products. Alternative sources of energy must be harnessed for use.

Such changes will not be easy to make and will require wise leadership from both secular and religious sources. Creative solutions will require both technical knowledge and moral insights. Decisions will be not only difficult but unpopular. ...

We believe that time is running out. Beneath all the choices lies the ultimate choice of life or death. We join with all men of goodwill in appealing that we shall choose life. We know that the tasks and situations which to human view seem hopeless can, with the boundless resources of God's grace, be transformed.

Resolution 2 was a response in the form of an appeal first to government, secondly to the Churches, and their decision making bodies and thirdly to members.[811]

1988 (Archbishop Robert Runcie)

Resolution 36: Poverty and debt[812]

This Conference:

1. Calls attention to the life-and-death urgency of the problem of world poverty.

2. Salutes the courage and solidarity of poor people who, at great personal cost, are struggling to achieve their own liberation from poverty and oppression.

3. Calls for an international, co-operating settlement, negotiated by both industrial and developing countries that will establish policies to reduce interest charges and the level of indebtedness, based on shared responsibility for the world debt and in accordance with Christian and humanitarian principles of economic justice and social and ecological interdependence.

4. Calls on national governments, transnational corporations, the International Monetary Fund and the World Bank together to re-examine all principles governing trade relationships, the transfer of technology and resources and all loan and aid policies in order to improve the economic viability and local autonomy of developing countries.

5. Requests these bodies to consider these and other creative ways of involving the global economy over time by:

    a. correcting demand imbalances;
        -   reducing protectionism;
        -   stabilising exchange rates;
        -   increasing resource transfers;

    b. offering relief from debt incurred with commercial banks in ways that will not leave debtor economies vulnerable to foreign manipulation, by
        -   lending directly to developing countries at reduced and subsidised interest rates;
        -   improved rescheduling of existing debt payments;
        -   establishing a multilateral body to co-ordinate debt relief;

    c. offering relief from official debts incurred with the World Bank and the International Monetary Fund through
        -   improved rescheduling of existing debt repayments;
        -   lending on conditions orientated to development objectives;
        -   refraining from making demands on debtor countries which would endanger the fabric of their national life or cause further dislocation to their essential human services.

Resolution 40: Environment, militarism justice and peace[813]

This conference:

1. Identifies four interrelated areas in which the misuse of people or resources poses a threat to the life system of the planet, namely (a) unjust distribution of the world's wealth, (b) social injustice within nations, (c) the rise of militarism, (d) irreversible damage to the environment; and therefore

2. Calls upon each province and diocese to devise a programme of study, reflection and action in which the following elements should play a part:

    a. as a matter of urgency, the giving of information to our people of what is happening to our environment, and to encourage them to see stewardship of God's earth for the care of our neighbours as a necessary part of Christian discipleship and a Christian contribution to citizenship;

    b. actively to support by public statement and in private dialogue, the engagement of governments, transnational corporations, management and labour in an examination of what their decisions are doing to our people, and our land, air and water;

    c. opposition to the increase in the arms trade, questioning both excessive expenditure of scarce resources on weapons and trade policies which look upon arms sales as a legitimate source of increased export revenue;

    d. the encouragement of Christians to re-examine the currently accepted economic policies which operate to the disadvantage of those with less bargaining power at every level from international to personal, and to use God's gifts of technology for the benefit of all;

e. the critical examination of the exercise of power, first within congregations and all other Church bodies, and then in secular institutions which affect the lives of all. Insofar as the aim is to achieve a just and sustainable society world-wide, priority must be given to those modes which nurture people's gifts and evoke responsible participation rather than those which dominate and exclude.

3. (a) Commends, in general, the participation by every province in the WCC's programme for 'Justice, Peace and Integrity of Creation'; (b) Urges Churches, congregations and individual Christians to actively support all other agencies which share this urgent concern. In particular we commend a widespread study of the United Nations report Our Common Future and participation by Church bodies in the local responses it requires; (c) Recommends that, in view of the resolutions passed by ACC-7, information concerning local needs and initiatives be shared throughout the provinces, possibly by extending the terms of reference for the existing Peace and Justice Network; (d) Encourages people everywhere to make changes ...

1998 (Archbishop George Carey)

Resolution 1.8. Creation[814]

This conference:

a. Reaffirms the Biblical vision of Creation according to which: creation is a web of interdependent relationships bound together in the covenant which God the Holy Trinity has established with the whole of the earth and every living being.

    i. The divine spirit is sacramentally present in creation,

which is therefore to be treated with reverence, respect and gratitude;

ii. Human beings are both co-partners with the rest of creation and living bridges between heaven and earth, with responsibilities to make personal and corporate sacrifices for the common good of all Creation;

iii. The redemptive purpose of God in Jesus extends to the whole creation.

b. Recognises

i. That unless human beings take responsibility for caring for the earth, the consequences will be catastrophic because of:

- overpopulation
- unsustainable levels of consumption by the rich
- poor quality and shortage of water
- air pollution
- eroded and impoverished soil
- forest destruction
- plant and animal extinction;

ii. that the loss of natural habitats is a direct cause of genocide amongst millions of indigenous peoples and is causing the extinction of thousands of plant and animal species. Unbridled capitalism, selfishness and greed cannot continue to be allowed to pollute, exploit and destroy what remains of the earth's indigenous habitats;

iii. that the future of human beings and life on the earth hangs in balance as a consequence of the present unjust economic structures, the injustice existing between the rich and the poor; the continuing exploitation of the natural environment and the threat of nuclear self-destruction;

iv.   that the servant-hood to God's creation is becoming the most important responsibility facing humankind and that we should work together with people of all faiths in the implementation of our responsibilities;

v.   that we as Christians have a God given mandate to care for look after and protect God's creation.

c.   Prays in the Spirit of Jesus Christ:

i.   For widespread conversion and spiritual renewal in order that human beings will be restored to a relationship of harmony with the rest of Creation and that this relationship might be informed by the principles of justice and the integrity of every living being, so that self centred greed is overcome; and

ii.   For the recovery of the sabbath principle, as part of the redemption of time and the restoration of the divinely intended rhythms of life.

Resolution I.9[815]

Ecology

a.   This conference:

i.   Calls upon all ecumenical partners and other faith communities, governments and transnational companies:

ii.   To work for a sustainable society in a sustainable world;

iii.   To recognise the dignity and rights of all people and the sanctity of life, especially the rights of future generations;

iv.   To ensure the responsible use and recycling of natural resources;

v.   To bring about economic reforms which will establish a just and fair trading system both for people and the environment.

b.   Calls upon the United Nations to incorporate the right of future generations to a sustainable future in the Universal Declaration of Human Rights

c. Asks the Joint Standing Committee of the ACC and the Primates to consider the appointment of a coordinator of an inter-national ecological network within the Anglican Communion who would:

    i. Work in cooperation with other ecumenical and interfaith agencies;

    ii. Be funded through and responsible to the Anglican Consultative Council;

    iii. Support those involved in grassroots environmental initiatives;

    iv. Gather and disseminate data and information on environmental issues so that the Church can play an informed role in lobbying for ecological justice in both the public and private sectors; and

    v. Contribute to the development of environmental educational programmes for use in the training of Christian leaders.

Resolution I.15 A substantial resolution on international debt.

Resolution V.2 A resolution on the cancellation of international debt and the alleviation of poverty.

Appendix 3

Declaration Accompanying the Commencement of the First Lambeth Conference 1867

We, Bishops of Christ's Holy Catholic Church, professing the faith of the primitive and undivided Church, as based on Scripture, defined by the first four General Councils and reaffirmed by the Fathers of the English Reformation, now assembled by the good providence of God at the Archiepiscopal Palace of Lambeth under the primacy of the Primate of All England, desire first to give hearty thanks to Almighty God for having thus brought us together for common counsels and united worship; Secondly we desire to express the deep sorrow with which we view the divided condition of the flock of Christ throughout the world: and, Lastly we do here solemnly declare our belief that the best hope of future reunion will be found in drawing each of us for ourselves closer to our common Lord, in giving ourselves to much prayer and intercession, in the cultivation of a spirit of charity, and in seeking to diffuse through every part of the Christian Community that desire and resolution to return to the Faith and Discipline of the undivided Church which was the principle of the English Reformation.

Appendix 4

Lambeth Origins

The nineteenth century witnessed a rapid expansion of British colonial interest on all continents. The colonial interest was not restricted to matters of trade but included the 'civilising' of colonised peoples. Christianity was considered a corner stone of this 'civilising' and being the state religion, the 'Church of England' a necessary conduit. Evangelising the new worlds under British colonial rule therefore was a matter of Gospel proclamation, but not simply so; it involved the ordering of Christian life according to the customs that pertained to the prevailing relationship of Church and State in Britain. New Dioceses were rapidly created and new bishops appointed. These Dioceses and Bishops came under the authority of the Bishop of London.[816]

Since the Reformation, the Church of England enjoyed the protection of the state through the sovereign; but the 'price' paid for this protection was being subject to state legislation.[817] The Church was not free to govern itself. This protection, together with its restriction, was understood to be imparted to newly established colonial Dioceses and their Bishops through Letters Patent from the sovereign. (The exceptions were the Episcopal Church of Scotland and the Episcopal Church of the Unites States of

America. The Episcopal Church of Scotland was not the established Church in Scotland and the United States was already a republic). The legal validity of powers inherent in 'Letters Patent' in countries which had established their own legislature was soon to be challenged.

In South Africa a dispute arose between the Bishops of Cape Town (Gray) and Natal (Colenso) over Colenso's widely published critique of the Mosaic authorship of the Pentateuch. Colenso's biblical criticism, while explosive to many in authority in his time, could be likened to the early stages of the biblical literary source criticism which became popularly accepted in the mid-20th century, argued by scholars such as Gerard Von Rad.[818] The vehemence with which Colenso felt the condemnation of some of his peers can be attributed not simply to what he had to say, but the manner in which he said it.

> He [Colenso] was more of a mathematician than a theologian. While he stumbled across some now widely accepted views, his manner of arguing them was neither subtle nor winning.[819]

Colenso claimed to have been strongly influenced by the writings of F.D. Maurice[820] and the publication of *Essays and Reviews*.[821] The primary criticism directed at the latter was that the essays inferred the Bible could not be considered 'The Word of God' but 'contained the Word of God'.[822] Also that teaching on 'eternal damnation' should not be supported. Archbishops Longley (Canterbury) and Thomson (York), supporting the conservative theological position, could not so persuade the judicial committee of the Privy Council that subsequently ruled the essays contained 'nothing contrary to the formularies of the Church of England'.[823] The more liberally minded Dean Stanley of Westminster wrote:

> That the Church of England does not hold—1) Verbal Inspiration, 2) Imputed Righteousness, 3) Eternity of Torment, is now, I trust, fixed forever. I hope that all will now go on smoothly, and that the Bible may be really read without those terrible nightmares. Thank God![824]

The theological dispute was not itself the reason why Archbishop Longley agreed to call the first conference. The issue became one of order. Bishop Gray, with the authority he believed he inherited through 'Letters Patent' had attempted to discipline an Evangelical priest, Walter Long, for refusing to attend the Cape Town synod.[825] The South African Supreme Court supported Gray, but Long took his case to the sovereign. On 24 June 1864 the Privy Council ruled that Letters Patent, issued after properly constituted Government had been established in the new territories, were invalid. This in effect declared that where legitimate government had been established and where no legislation had been enacted to establish the Church of England, it [the Church of England] was in 'no better, but no worse position'[826] than any other religious body. The authority Gray assumed in dealing with Long had evaporated. When the Colenso matter arose Gray was left with uncertain authority as to how to deal with the crisis and sought an ascending hierarchy of synods, crowned by an international synod. The Privy Council decision sent shock waves around the colonial Church, and the Canadian Church in particular became anxious that the Anglican Communion, now apparently lacking internal authority, would disintegrate. They wanted an international Anglican synod to overrule, where necessary, any decisions made at a national or diocesan level.

Longley agreed to call a worldwide conference of bishops in 1867, Sixty-two[827] accepted the invitation out of approximately one hundred and forty[828] who were invited. Those who declined to come were either opposed to the formation of synodical government on the grounds that it was a rebuttal of the Church's proper relationship with the state, or were opposed to a censure of Colenso. In reality Colenso's theological position and his biblical critique were not directly debated, nor was he directly censured by the conference. The consensus of the conference was not to establish any form of international governance. Encouragement given to autonomous national churches to establish their own forms of synodical government has prevailed to this day.

NOTES

1   Douglas John Hall, *Imaging God: Dominion as Stewardship* (Grand Rapids: Eerdmans, 1986), 22.

2   John F. Kennedy, *Address Before the Irish Parliament in Dublin, June 28 1963*, http://www.jfklibrary.org/Asset-Viewer/lPAi7jx2s0i7kePPdJnUXA.aspx (accessed 30 April 2014).

3   I have chosen to use the term 'environmental crisis' rather than an 'ecological crisis' although both are used in the literature and some of the quotations in the text speak of an 'ecological crisis'. Richard Bauckham prefers 'ecology' 'in the general sense of interconnectedness of all things, living and inanimate, on the planet'. Richard Bauckham, *Bible and Ecology: Rediscovering the Community of Creation*. (London: Darton, Longman & Todd, 2010), ix. I am using the term 'environment' to refer to the whole biosphere inclusive of human activity. The biosphere is generally understood to mean all that is associated with earth that enables the possibility of life, or that supports living organisms. 'Ecology' was introduced into biology as a term in 1866 by the German biologist, naturalist, philosopher, Ernst Haeckel. His definition of the term was 'The study of the relationship of organisms with their environment'. Cary Institute of Ecosystem Studies. *Definition of Ecology*, http://www.caryinstitute.org/discover-ecology/definition-ecology (accessed 10 November 2013).

4   Comprehensive yet written with a scientific layman in mind is John Houghton, *Global Warming*, 4th edition (Cambridge: Cambridge University Press, 2009).

5   Naomi Oreskes and Erik Conway, *Merchants of Doubt: How a Handful of Scientists Obscured the Truth on Issues from Tobacco Smoke to Global Warming* (New York: Bloomsbury Press, 2010) relates the history of special interest groups and their use of 'science' and the media to influence government and the wider population for their own commercial protection.

6   As the US Senator Daniel Patrick Moynihan is reputed to have said 'everyone is entitled to their own opinions, but they are not entitled to their own facts'.

7   Reference to the 'earth' in this book is generally used to refer to the whole created order. This is consistent with the creation narrative in which reference to 'heaven and earth' is to be understood as a reference to everything that comes under the sovereign interest of God.

8   Church and Christianity are not equated, however because Christianity is understood through the Church: its creedal formulations, its canonical scripture and its witness through the centuries, it assumes that truth implicit in Christianity must find expression through the life and witness of the Church. Therefore reference to Christianity and the Church is made with the understanding that Christianity's witness cannot be distinguished from the witness of the Church.

9   'Stewardship' is examined in Chapters 5 and 7.

10   The claim of the 2013 IPCC report. http://www.ipcc.ch/ (accessed 30 September 2013).

11   Intergovernmental Panel on Climate Change. *Climate Change 2013: The Physical Science Basis: Summary for Policymakers. 2013,* https://www.ipcc.ch/report/ar5/wg1/docs/review/WG1AR5-SPM_FOD_Final.pdf (accessed 30 April 2014).

12   Ibid., 3.

13   Ibid., 3.

14   Ibid., 7.

15   Ibid., 7.

16   Ibid., 7.

17   Ibid., 17.

18   Brad Gregory, *The Unintended Reformation: How a Religious Revolution Secularized Society* (Cambridge Massachusetts: Harvard University Press, 2012), 242.

19   'Client State is one of the several terms used to describe the subordination of one state to a more powerful state in international affairs'. http://www.princeton.edu/~achaney/tmve/wiki100k/docs/Client_state.html (accessed 7 March 2014).

20   'Every westerner lives in a society pervaded by consumerism ... in which the vast majority of manufactured goods for sale are made by poor labourers working for low wages in far away countries.' Gregory, *The Unintended Reformation*, 235.

21   Jeffrey Sachs, *The Price of Civilization: Economics and Ethics after the Fall* (London: Random House, 2011), xv.

22   Hinson-Hasty, Elizabeth. *As Any Might Have Need: Envisioning Communities of Shared Partnership*. 2011. http://www.kairoscanada.org/wp-content/uploads/2011/11/SUS-CJ-11-10-Hinson-Hasty.pdf (accessed 17 November 2011).

23   Ibid.

24   Sachs, *The Price of Civilisation,* 175.

25   'The conventional formula for achieving prosperity relies upon the pursuit of exponential growth'. Tim Jackson, *Prosperity without Growth: Economics for a Finite Planet* (London: Earthscan, 2009), 17.

26   See Jackson, *Prosperity without Growth*. Sachs, *The Price of Civilisation*.

27   Lesslie Newbigin, *Foolishness to the Greeks: the Gospel and Western Culture* (London: SPCK, 1986), *27*.

28   In the United States of America 10% of the population own almost three quarters of the wealth, while 1% owns 40% of the wealth.

29   Williams, *Faith in the Public Square*, 227, 228.

30   Professor Crutzen proposed the name Anthropocene, a change from the Holocene period which should be dated from the 18th Century when human changes to the biosphere as a result of the industrial revolution were first detected by scientists. Paul J. Crutzen and Eugene F. Stoermer. 'The 'Anthropocene', *Global Change Newsletter* no.41 (May 2000): 17-18, http://www.igbp.net/download/18.316f18321323470177580001401/NL41.pdf (accessed 16 November 2011).

31   The fifth mass extinction occurred approximately 65 million years ago and resulted in the loss of an estimated 76 percent of species including the

dinosaurs. All previous mass extinctions have resulted from natural causes; this is the first extinction to result from the activity of one species—humans.

32   From the fifth mark of Mission of the International Anglican Communion. Anglican Communion. *Mission—the Five Marks of Mission* http://www.anglicancommunion.org/ministry/mission/fivemarks.cfm (accessed 12 February 2014).

33   The connection of Australia's first citizens to land, their sense of responsibility for it, has never been fully understood or appreciated by European settlers.

34   Jürgen Moltmann, 'Creation and Redemption,' in *Creation, Christ and Culture*, ed. Richard W.A.McKinney (Edinburgh: T&T Clark, 1976), 119.

35   For example: 'Increasingly, it seems, the institutions of consumer society are designed to favour a particularly materialistic individualism and to encourage the relentless pursuit of consumer novelty because this is exactly what's needed to keep the economy going.' Jackson, *Prosperity Without Growth*, 163. Tim Jackson is Economics Commissioner on the Sustainable Development Commission, the UK Governments' independent adviser on sustainable development.

36   Jackson, *Prosperity Without Growth*, 77-82.

37   A theme promoted by the eminent American economist, Jeffrey Sachs, in his *Common Wealth: Economics for a Crowded Planet* (London: Penguin, 2008).

38   *World POP Clock Projection*, http://www.census.gov/population/popclockworld.html (accessed 4 November 2011).

39   Paul Ricoeur, *The Conflict of Interpretations: Essays in Hermeneutics* (Evanston, Ill: Northwestern University Press, 1974), 300.

40   Ibid., 302.

41   This statement was developed by the Anglican Consultative Council between 1984 and 1990 and has subsequently become the recognised mission statement of the member Churches of the Anglican Communion:

> To proclaim the good news of the kingdom
> To teach baptise and nurture new believers
> To respond to human need by loving service
> To seek to transform unjust structures of society
>
> To strive to safeguard the integrity of creation and sustain and renew the life of the earth.

42   Richard Heinberg, *The End of Growth: Adapting to Our New Economic Reality* (Gabriola Island: New Society Publishers, 2011), 171- 172. Here Heinberg argues that while changing to LED light globes should be encouraged, such efficiencies on their own will simply not be enough.

43   'Planting trees' or 'Direct Action' is the environmental policy of the current (2014) Australian Government. It is considered an insufficient instrument to achieve a scientifically prescribed carbon emissions reduction target, a target that requires a more generic solution, such as a price on carbon.

44   Michael J. Sandel, *What Money Can't Buy: the Moral Limits of Markets* (London: Allen Lane, 2012), 49-51. Sandel, drawing on the work of the Chicago economist Gary Becker, argues that human acquisitiveness is not simply about satisfying material need, it is about contributing to perceived well-being, status or identity.

45   Lynn White, 'The historical roots of our ecological crisis,' *Science* 155 (10 March 1967): 1203-1207, http://www.uvm.edu/~gflomenh/ENV-NGO-PA395/articles/Lynn-White.pdf (accessed 13 November 2011).

46   Max Weber, *The Protestant Ethic and the Spirit of Capitalism,* (London: Allen & Unwin, 1930).

47   Ibid.

48   On 21 July 2013 the ABC Compass programme was entitled 'What happened to the Charismatics?' It featured the development of the first major charismatic (Pentecostal Church) in Canberra under the leadership of Pastor Harry Westcott. Pastor Westcott told the programme that his charismatic conversion was demonstrably sealed through the purchase of a Mercedes car. 'The Prosperity gospel sure beats the poverty Gospel,' he said. *Whatever Happened to ... the Charismatics?',* http://www.abc.net.au/compass/s3795778.htm (accessed 25 September 2013).

49   Gregory, *The Unintended Reformation*, 262.

50   Ibid., 258.

51   Ibid., 251.

52   Ibid., 252.

53   Ibid., 266.

54   Ibid., 277ff.

55   Ibid., 272.

56   Ibid., 284.

57   John Ruddick, a long time member of the NSW Liberal Party was threatened with a five year suspension by the party for suggesting that 'in-house lobbyists' should not hold positions within the party. It was further suggested that political parties now exist primarily to provide a safe working place for lobbyists. Matt Peacock, *Liberal Party Member John Ruddick Threatened With Suspension After Reform Push,* http://abc.net.au/news/2013-10-03-liberal-john-ruddick-threatened-with-suspension/4997440 (accessed 5 October 2013).

58   Gregory, *The Unintended Reformation*, 285.

59   In my experience of over 40 years in Anglican leadership, this position has been expressed in response to synod resolutions, letters to the editor, and in Church teaching that focusses upon personal salvation at the expense of a theology of creation.

60   An analysis of the media statements and lobbying of the 'Australian Christian Lobby' amplifies this statement. Australian Christian Lobby [website], http://www.acl.org.au/ (accessed 3 December 2013).

61   'Sex matters enormously, but global justice matters far, far more' N.T. Wright, *Surprised by Hope* (London: SPCK, 2007), 228.

62   'It is God's *shekinah* that will make the heavens and the earth new.' Jürgen Moltmann, *Ethics of Hope* (Minneapolis: Fortress Press, 2012), 121.

63   Ibid., 54.

64   Daniel W. Hardy, 'Created and Redeemed Sociality,' in *On Being the Church: Essays on the Christian Community,* ed. Colin E. Gunston and Daniel W. Hardy (Edinburgh: T&T Clark, 1989), 42.

65   Kevin Treston, *A Modern Credo: Telling the Christ Story within the Context of Creation* (Mulgrave, Victoria: John Garrett Publishing, 2010), 113.

66   Williams, *Faith in the Public Square*, 199.

67   Arthur Campbell Ainger, 'Hymn 548,' in *The English Hymnal* (London: Oxford University Press, 1960), 710.

68   Newbigin, *Foolishness to the Greeks*, 19.

69   Jürgen Moltmann's commentary on the 'two worlds' is taken up in Chapter 6.

70   Newbigin, *Foolishness to the Greeks*, 19.

71   Williams, *Faith in the Public Square*, 181.

72   Ibid., 229.

73   Ibid., 200.

74   Andrew Carnegie, *The Gospel of Wealth and Other Timely Essays* (New York: The Century Co.,1900) https://archive.org/stream/ cu31924001214539 (accessed 23 November 2013).

75   Williams, *Faith in the Public Square*, 194.

76   Moltmann, *Ethics of Hope*, 135.

77   Ibid .,135, 136.

78   White, 'The historical roots of our ecological crisis,' 1203-1207.

79   Alister McGrath is Professor in Science and Religion in the faculty of Theology and Religion at the University of Oxford. His many books include: *Surprised by meaning: Science, Faith and How We Make Sense of Things* (Louisville, Kentucky: Westminster John Knox Press, 2011) and *Science and Religion, a New Introduction* (Oxford: Wiley-Blackwell, 2009)

80   John Polkinghorne held the chair of mathematical physics at Cambridge University. He is an Anglican priest and author of five books on physics and many publications on the relationship between science and religion. He has been knighted for his contribution to science and religion.

81   John Polkinghorne, 'Bridging the Divide,' *Encounter (radio program)*, 18 September 2011. http://www.abc.net.au/rn/encounter/ stories/2011/3316531.htm (accessed 13 November 2011).

82   Pierre Teilhard De Chardin was a Jesuit, scientist, anthropologist and theologian. He is best known for his publication *The Phenomenon of Man* (London: Fontana, 1965).

83   For example: Thomas Berry, *The Dream of the Earth* (San Francisco: Sierra Club Books, 1988);

      Jürgen Moltmann, *God in Creation* (London: SCM, 1985); John Haught, *Making Sense of Evolution: God Darwin and the Dream of Life* (Westminster:

John Knox Press 2010); Sallie McFague, *A New Climate for Theology: God the World and Global Warming* (Minneapolis: Augsburg Fortress, 2008).

84   In the text I follow the habit of the Revised Standard Version of the Bible in referring to sabbath in the lower case unless a quotation or other circumstance dictate otherwise.

85   'A number [of theologians] have built upon rich scriptural resources to [develop] a responsible ecological attitude. Walter Brueggemann on the land, Jürgen Moltmann on the Sabbath, Elizabeth Johnson on the indwelling spirit of wisdom, Denis Edwards on the Wisdom of God and Douglas Hall on Stewardship', Gregory Brett, 'Humanity and Ecology in the Light of Christian Hope', in *Earth Revealing—Earth Healing; Ecology and Christian Theology,* ed. Denis Edwards (Minnesota: Liturgical Press, 2001), 160.

86   Charles Raven, *Looking Forward (Towards 1940)* (London: James Nisbet, 1931), 25.

87   J.W.C. Wand, *Anglicanism in History and Today* (London: Weidenfeld and Nicholson, 1961), 74.

88   It is the view of John Hart that Barth and Brunner differed not so much in theological fundamentals but in the manner of doing theology. Barth remained essentially a Dogmatic Theologian while Brunner, wishing to engage with emerging philosophies, turned towards philosophical theology. John Hart, *Karl Barth vs Emil Brunner: The Formation and Dissolution of a Theological Alliance, 1916—1936* (New York: Peter Lang, 2001), 218, 219.

89   'The Holy Spirit which proceeds from the Father and the Son, and is thus revealed and believed in as God, needs no other point of contact than that which he himself establishes'. Correspondence from Barth to Brunner quoted in: Eberhard Busch, *Karl Barth: His Life from Letters and Autobiographical Texts* (London: SCM Press, 1976), 248.

90   Moltmann, *Ethics of Hope,* 137.

91   Colin Gunton, 'Salvation,' in *The Cambridge Companion to Karl Barth,* ed. John Webster (Cambridge: Cambridge University Press, 2000), 143.

92   Ibid., 156.

93   Karl Barth, *Church Dogmatics, vol.3: The Doctrine of Creation* (London: T&T Clark, 2009), 175.

94   Ibid., 226.

95   'Remember the Sabbath Day and keep it holy' (Ex. 20:8). 'Observe the sabbath day and keep it holy' (Deut. 5:12).

96   Kathryn Tanner, 'Creation and Providence,' in *The Cambridge Companion to Karl Barth,* ed. John Webster (Cambridge: Cambridge University Press, 2000), 112.

97   Gunton, 'Salvation,' 143.

98   Tanner, 'Creation and Providence,' 116.

99   Ibid., 111.

100   Abraham Joshua Heschel, *The Sabbath, its Meaning for Modern Man.* (New York: Farrar Strauss and Giroux, 2005), 17.

101   Ibid., 73.

102   The theme of God's indwelling is explored in Chapter 6. Moltmann consistently links *shekinah* and sabbath, particularly in his latest book the *Ethics of Hope*. In *God in Creation* he poses the question: 'What does sabbath add to creation.' His answer: 'Sabbath is God's present existence.' Jürgen Moltmann, *God in Creation: An Ecological Doctrine of Creation: the Gifford Lectures 1984-1985.* (London: SCM Press, 1985), 280.

103   'The Common Good,' http://www.scu.edu/ethics/practicing/decision/commongood.html (accessed 6 September 2013).

104   Literal meaning: *eu* good, *daimon* spirit.

105   Miriam Bruning, 'A Theology of the Common Good: What has Endured?' (B.A. Hons Thesis, Charles Sturt University, 2012).

106   William French, 'Grace is Everywhere: Thomas Aquinas on Creation and Salvation,' in *Creation and Salvation,* ed. Ernst Conradie (Zurich: Lit Verlag, 2012), 165.

107   'Without the virtues there could be no sustained community, which meant no common good, thus no individual good and no salvation.' Gregory, *The Unintended Reformation*, 192.

108   Ibid., 231.

109   French, 'Grace is everywhere,' 165.

110   Gregory, *The Unintended Reformation*, 225.

111 Aquinas' application of 'common good' within Church and politics differentiated him from Augustine for whom the purpose of good was directed specifically towards the 'heavenly city' or human destiny beyond earthly life.

112 Luther ridiculed Aristotle.

113 'Whatever divided Christians from one another doctrinally was of cardinal moral significance because of its social implications'. Gregory, *The Unintended Reformation*, 205.

114 'From the outset of the reformation until the present day the insistence on sola scriptura has produced and continues to yield an open-ended range of incompatible interpretations of the bible with centrifugal social and wide-ranging substantive implications for morality'. Gregory, *The Unintended Reformation*, 205.

115 Gregory, *The Unintended Reformation*, 184.

116 The Declaration of Independence http://www.ushistory.org/declaration/document (accessed 10 February 2014); quoted in Pauline Maier, *American Scripture: Making the Declaration of Independence* (New York: Vintage, 1998), 135, 144.

117 See Alisdair MacIntyre, *After Virtue: A Study of Moral Theory,* 2nd ed. (Indiana: University of Notre Dame Press, 1984).

118 Ibid., 256-264.

119 'The Common Good', http://www.scu.edu/ethics/practicing/decision/commongood.html (accessed 6 September 2013).

120 Brueggemann, *Journey to the Common Good,* 1.

121 Ibid., 46.

122 Dr. Mary M. Keys' research is in the interrelatedness of human rights, mental health and law at the University of Galway. Mary M. Keys *Aquinas, Aristotle and the Promise of the Common Good* (Cambridge: Cambridge University Press, 2006).

123 Glenn W. Olsen, *The Turn to Transcendence: The Role of Religion in the Twenty-First Century* (Washington D.C.: Catholic University of America Press, 2010), 62.

124 Gregory, *The Unintended Reformation,* 211.

125   It is a salutary aspect of contemporary public discourse that not only is a
      religiously drawn meta narrative increasingly rejected within a pluralistic
      society, so also a narrative drawn from science appears to be in danger of
      experiencing the same fate.

126   Roger Scruton, *Green Philosophy: How to Think Seriously about the Planet*
      (London: Atlantic Books, 2012) writes an apologia from the point of
      view of conservative, or right wing, politics for what he calls 'oikophilia'.
      By this he means love of home understood as the nation state as being the
      basis of an environmental ethic. In the process he writes a polemic against
      what he calls 'oikophobia', meaning attempts (by the left of politics)
      for regulation beyond the nation state. To use Scruton's terminology, I
      argue (Chapter 7) that 'oikophilia' must refer to the planet as our home.
      However in doing so, citizens must express that care in tending their own
      'back-yard'.

127   E.M. Conradie, *An Ecological Christian Anthropology: At Home on Earth?*
      (Aldershot: Ashgate, 2005), 28.

128   Moltmann, *Ethics of Hope,* 121.

129   'Goodness in existence is only experienced through relational sharing—a
      common good'. Bruning, 'A Theology of the Common Good', v.

130   Houghton, *Global warming,* 254-255.

131   Moltmann, 'Creation and Redemption', 134.

132   'The Common Good', http://www.scu.edu/ethics/practicing/decision/
      commongood.html (accessed 6 September 2013).

133   'The Nicene Creed', in *A Prayer Book for Australia* (Sydney: Broughton
      Books), 123.

134   Christopher D. Ringwald, *A Day Apart: How Jews, Christians, and Muslims
      Find Faith, Freedom, and Joy on the Sabbath* (New York: Oxford University
      Press, 2007). The contribution of Ringwald lies in his capacity to show
      that each of the three faiths have in some way or another continued to
      keep the Sabbath tradition alive. Where he fails is that he restricts his
      findings to the historical and contemporary ways in which each faith has
      kept one day in seven sacred.

135   Daisuke Kitagawa, 'Faith and Society', in *Lambeth Essays on Faith,* ed.
      Michael Ramsey (London: SPCK, 1969), 76, 78.

136   Through Act 25 Henry VIII gave the crown control over all ecclesiastical assemblies. Diocesan synods became a thing of the past and the provincial synods of Canterbury and York met only at the pleasure of the Crown. Alan M. G. Stephenson, *The First Lambeth Conference, 1867*. (London: SPCK, 1967), 27.

137   Letters Patent (from the Latin *pateo*—lie open) were legal instruments, in this case from the crown, granting an office, title or entitlement. They were deemed void in a country which had achieved its own legitimate government.

138   Apart from the period of tension that led to the Second World War.

139   The Lambeth Quadrilateral—Resolution 11 of 1888:

'The Holy Scriptures as containing all things necessary for salvation and as being the rule and ultimate standard of faith.

The Apostles' Creed as the baptismal symbol and the Nicene Creed as the sufficient statement of the Christian Faith.

The two sacraments ordained by Christ himself—Baptism and the Supper of the Lord, ministered with unfailing use of Christ's words of institution and of the elements ordained by him.

The historic Episcopate, locally adapted in the methods of its administration to varying needs of the nations and peoples called by God into the unity of the Church'.

Lambeth Conference. *The Lambeth Conferences (1867–1948)*, 296-297.

140   Anglican Church of Australia, *The Constitution Canons and Rules of the Anglican Church of Australia 2010* (Mulgrave, Victoria: Broughton Publishing, 2011), 3.

141   Inter-Anglican Theological and Doctrinal Commission. *Report*. London: Anglican Consultative Council, 1997. http://www.lambethconference. org/1998/documents/report-1.pdf (accessed 10 February 2014).

142   *The Windsor Report 2004: The Instruments of Unity*, http://www. anglicancommunion.org/windsor2004/section_c/p1.cfm (accessed 25 May 2014).

143   Anglican Consultative Council meetings are listed at: http://www. anglicancommunion.org/communion/acc/meetings/index.cfm, (accessed 4 February 2014).

144 *The Windsor Report 2004: The Instruments of Unity,* http://www. anglicancommunion.org/windsor2004/section_c/p1.cfm (accessed 25 May 2014).

145 *Primates' Meetings,* http://www.anglicancommunion.org/communion/ primates/index.cfm (accessed 4 February 2014).

146 Lambeth Conference, *The Lambeth Conferences (1867–1948),* 23.

147 The Virginia conference advised against trying to be inclusive of all facets of the Church for fear that the Conference might then be confused with decision-making synods at a Diocesan and national level.

148 The 1958 Conference was the most resolution heavy with 131 resolutions and 1878 the lightest with 12. The 2008 Lambeth Conference did not express its findings through formal resolutions. The style of the conference was *indaba* or conversation. Consensus from these conversations is recorded in *Lambeth Indaba: Capturing Conversations and Reflections from the Lambeth Conference 2008,* http:// www.lambethconference.org/vault/Reflections_Document_(final).pdf (accessed 25 May 2014).

149 From the outset the Lambeth Conferences have been concerned with the order of the Church as an expression of the Church's catholicity. The encyclical letters that followed the Lambeth Conferences up until 1948 invariably commenced 'We Bishops and Archbishops of the Holy Catholic Church'. 1958 began with 'We, Archbishops and Bishops of the Holy Catholic and Apostolic Church'.

150 The Colenso affair is detailed in appendix 3.

151 Relationship with other Churches was seen to be derivative of the claim for catholicity. Relationships which have received considerable focus have included the Scandinavian churches, the Latin Church and the Church(es) of India.

152 See: Lambeth Conference, *The Lambeth Conferences (1867–1948),* 63.

153 Ibid., 72.

154 Ibid., 72.

155 Ibid., 66.

156 Ibid., 1948, 6.

157   Resolution 1.8c *The Official Report of the Lambeth Conference 1998: Transformation and Renewal* (Harrisburg, Pa: Moorehouse Publishing, 1998), 380.

158   *Lambeth Indaba: Capturing Conversations and Reflections from the Lambeth Conference 2008,* 19. http://www.lambethconference.org/vault/Reflections_Document_(final).pdf (accessed 25 May 2014).

159   Graham James, 'Resolving to Confer and Conferring to Resolve: the Anglican Way,' in *A Fallible Church: Lambeth Essays,* ed. Kenneth Stevenson (London: Darton, Longman and Todd, 2008), 80.

160   Ibid., 81,82.

161   The Articles of Religion agreed by the Archbishops, Bishops and Clergy of the Provinces of Canterbury and York in London 1562.

162   Introduction to: *Deep Engagement, Fresh Discovery: Report of the Anglican Communion 'Bible in the Life of the Church' Project. 2012,* http://www.anglicancommunion.org/communion/acc/meetings/acc15/downloads/bible_in_the_life_of_the_church.pdf (accessed 23 November 2013).

163   *Essays and Reviews* (London: John W. Parker and Son, 1860) was published a year after Darwin's *Origin of Species.* Much of the material would now be deemed innocuous but then the publication created a storm necessitating 10 rapid reprints. Frederick Temple, by the end of the century Archbishop of Canterbury, wrote the first of the seven essays, another was written by Baden Powell, the father of the founder of the scouting movement.

164   Mark D. Chapman, *Anglican Theology* (London: T&T Clark, 2012), 182.

165   The fourteenth meeting of the Anglican Consultative Council.

166   The study was *Deep Engagement, Fresh Discovery* http://www.anglicancommunion.org/communion/acc/meetings/acc15/downloads/bible_in_the_life_of_the_church.pdf (accessed 23 November 2013).

167   *Conference of Bishops of the Anglican Communion 1897, Holden at Lambeth Palace, in July, 1897: Encyclical Letter from the Bishops, with the Resolutions and Reports.* (London: SPCK, 1897), 63-67.

168   Ibid., 65.

169   Ibid., 63, 64.

170   *Deep Engagement, Fresh Discovery,* 42.

171   He was later to become Rector of St Bride's Fleet Street, 1962–1984.

172   Dewi Morgan, *Lambeth Speaks* (London: Mowbray, 1958), 102.

173   *The Lambeth Conference 1958: The Encyclical Letter from the Bishops together with the Resolutions and Reports* (London: SPCK, 1958).

174   Ibid., page 1 of the report

175   *The Lambeth Conference 1958*, part 2, 5.

176   Ibid., part 2, 6.

177   Williams, *Faith in the Public Square*, 175.

178   Ibid., 179.

179   Frederick Denison Maurice, *Theological Essays* (1853) (London: James Clarke, 1957), 403.

180   James Carpenter, *Gore: A Study in Liberal Catholic Thought* (London: Faith Press, 1960), 45.

181   The 30 page report of the committee appointed by the Conference is entitled *The Holy Bible: its Authority and Message.*

182   Lambeth Conference, *Resolutions of the Twelve Lambeth Conferences, 1867–1988* (Toronto: Anglican Book Centre, 1992), 121, 122.

183   Stephen Pickard, *Seeking the Church: An Introduction to Ecclesiology* (London: SCM, 2012), 139.

184   Ibid., 140.

185   Lambeth Conference. *The Lambeth Conferences (1867–1948)*, 23.

186   Ibid., 1948, 21.

187   The First Vatican Council was held from 1869-70 and included the promulgation and definition of Papal Infallibility.

188   Chapman, *Anglican Theology*, 187.

189   Ibid., 188.

190   Ibid., 191.

191   Ibid., 193.

192   Accepting the authority of The '39 Articles of Faith', first established by a convocation of the Church in 1563 under the leadership of the then Archbishop of Canterbury Matthew Parker, has been legally required of licensed clergy and lay people in the Church of England and the wider Anglican Communion.

193   E.J. Bicknell, *A Theological Introduction to the Thirty-Nine Articles of the Church of England* (London: Longmans, 1961), 125.

194   Lambeth Conference. *The Lambeth Conferences (1867–1948)*, 296-297.

195   The second statement of the Lambeth Quadrilateral.

196   P.H.E. Thomas, 'The Lambeth Conferences and the Development of Anglican Ecclesiology 1867-1978' (PhD Thesis, Department of Theology, University of Durham, 1982), 82.

197   Paul Avis, 'What is Anglicanism,' in *The Study of Anglicanism,* ed. Stephen Sykes and John Booty (London: SPCK, 1988), 411, 412.

198   Charles Gore, *St. Paul's Epistle to the Ephesians: A Practical Exposition* (London: Murray, 1898), 14.

199   F.D. Maurice, Charles Gore, William Temple and Michael Ramsey all embraced the Liberal Catholic tradition of Anglicanism. All have been described as 'incarnational', all seeking to embed Christianity as a transforming force within society.

200   Charles Gore, *Christian Moral Principles: Seven Sermons Preached in Grosvenor Chapel as a Lenten Course in 1921* (London: Mowbray, 1921), 47.

201   Carpenter, *Gore,* 249.

202   Charles Gore, *Christ and Society.* (London: Allen & Unwin, c.1928.), 93ff.

203   Walter Brueggemann, *Journey to the Common Good* (Louisville, Ky: Westminster John Knox Press, 2010), 111.

204   Alan M.G. Stephenson, *Anglicanism and the Lambeth Conferences* (London: SPCK, 1978), 240. Stephenson was quoting from James B. Simpson and Edward M. Story, *The Long Shadows of Lambeth* X (New York, McGraw-Hill, 1969), 285.

205   Michael Ramsey, *The Gospel and the Catholic Church,* 2nd ed. (London: Longmans, 1956), 180.

206   Benjamin Myers, *Christ the Stranger: The Theology of Rowan Williams* (London: T&T Clark, 2012), 59.

207   Rowan Williams, *On Christian Theology* (Oxford: Blackwell, 2000), 226.

208   Rowan Williams, *A Margin of Silence: The Holy Spirit in Russian Orthodox Theology* (Québec: Éditions du Lys Vert, 2008), 43.

209   Timothy Gorringe, 'Keeping the Commandments: The Meaning of
Sustainable Countryside,' in *Ecological Hermeneutics: Biblical, Historical,
and Theological Perspectives,* edited by David Horrell, Cherryl Hunt,
Christopher Southgate, and Francesca Stavrakopoulou (London: T & T
Clark, 2010), 284.

210   James B. Simpson and Edward M. Story, *Discerning God's Will: The
Complete Eyewitness Report of the Eleventh Lambeth Conference* (New York:
Thomas Nelson, 1979), 130.

211   Daisuke Kitagawa (1910–1970), a Japanese born Anglican priest,
exercised his ministry in the USA. He developed a reputation for
outspokenness on matters of Christian social justice
and ecumenism.

212   Kitagawa, 'Faith and Society,' 92.

213   Lambeth Conference. *Resolutions of the Twelve Lambeth Conferences,
1867–1988,* 13. 'That this conference receives the report drawn up
by the Committee on the subject of Socialism, and submits it to the
consideration of the Churches of the Anglican Communion.'

214   William Sachs, *The Transformation of Anglicanism: From State Church to
Global Communion* (Cambridge: Cambridge University Press, 1993),
221.

215   Randall T. Davidson, ed., *The Lambeth Conferences of 1867, 1878 and 1888:
With the Official Reports and Resolutions together with the Sermons Preached
at the Conferences* (London: SPCK, 1889), 267.

216   Ibid., 304.

217   Ibid., 304.

218   Ibid., 309.

219   Ibid., 373/374. Archbishop Thomson was speaking on Saturday July 28
1888 in St Paul's London.

220   Lambeth Conference. *The Lambeth Conferences (1867–1948),* 62-78.

221   Ibid., 71.

222   Ibid., 72.

223   Ibid., 62.

224   Ibid., 63.

225   *Conference of the Bishops of the Anglican Communion 1920: Encyclical Letter from the Bishops with the Resolutions and Reports.* (New York: SPCK, 1920), 18.

226   *Lambeth Conference 1948: The Encyclical Letter from the Bishops together with Resolutions and Reports* (London: SPCK 1948), 20.

227   Vinay Samuel and Christopher Sugden, *Lambeth: A View from the Two-Thirds World* (London: SPCK, 1989), 74.

228   *Conference of the Bishops of the Anglican Communion 1920*, 22.

229   Ibid., 22.

230   Morgan, *Lambeth Speaks*, 7.

231   Ibid., 23.

232   *The Lambeth Conference 1958*, 125.

233   *Resolutions and Reports [of the] The Lambeth Conference 1968* (London: SPCK, 1968), 79.

234   Ibid., 75.

235   *Today's Church and Today's World: The Lambeth Conference 1978 Preparatory Articles* (London: CIO Publishing, 1977).

236   Hugh Montefiore, 'Nationalism and Internationalism,' in *Today's Church and Today's World*, 88. Montefiore is quoting C.M. Woodhouse from *The New Concert of Nations* (London: Bodley Head, 1964), 20.

237   Ibid.

238   Ibid., 90.

239   Ibid., 91.

240   James Simpson and Edward Story, *Discerning God's Will*, 131.

241   *The Report of the Lambeth Conference 1978* (London: CIO Publishing, 1978), 33.

242   *The Truth Shall Make You Free: The Lambeth Conference of 1988* (London: Church House Publishing, 1988), 23.

243   Ibid., 157.

244   *The Official Report of the Lambeth Conference 1998*, 87.

245   Ibid., 87.

246   Ibid. 87.

247   Rowan Williams, 'Renewing the Face of the Earth: Human Responsibility
       and the Environment' (Ebor Lecture, 25 March 2009) http://
       rowanwilliams.archbishopofcanterbury.org/articles.php/816/renewing-
       the-face-of-the-earth-human-responsibility-and-the-environment
       (accessed 13 May 2014).

248   Ibid.

249   Ibid.

250   Stephenson, *Anglicanism and the Lambeth Conferences*, 35.

251   James Moorehouse was Melbourne's second bishop (1877 -1866). His
       remarkable legacy has endured to the present.

252   C.H. Simpkinson, *The Life and Work of Bishop Thorold* (London: Isbister,
       1896), 290.

253   Stephenson, *Anglicanism and the Lambeth Conferences*, 106.

254   *Conference of Bishops of the Anglican Communion 1897*, 139.

255   Ibid., 139.

256   Stephenson, *Anglicanism and the Lambeth Conferences,* 128.

257   Lambeth Conference. *The Lambeth Conferences (1867–1948)*, 62-78.

258   Ibid., 68.

259   Ibid., 68.

260   Ibid., 70.

261   Ibid., 68.

262   Ibid., 73.

263   John V Taylor, *Enough is Enough* (London: SCM Press, 1975).

264   Lewis Carroll, *Alice's Adventures in Wonderland* (London: Macmillan,
       1872).

265   *The Report of the Lambeth Conference 1978,* 33-35.

266   Taylor, *Enough is Enough,* 63-84.

267   Ibid., 71.

268   Brueggemann, *Journey to the Common Good.*

269   *The Official Report of the Lambeth Conference 1998*, 107-118.

270   Ibid., 108.

271   In 2012 'Earth overshoot day' the approximate date our resource consumption for a given year exceeds the planet's ability to replenish fell on August 22. 'Earth Overshoot Day was August 22, and Yes, We're Still in Overshoot', Footprint Network News, issue 30, 3 October, 2012. http://www.footprintnetwork.org/en/index.php/newsletter/det/earth_overshoot_day_was_august_22_and_yes_were_still_in_overshoot (accessed 15 October 2012).

272   'The term 'environmental debt' is defined as polluting and or damaging actions that will cost other parties (people, businesses or governments) real money in the future. And just like any other debt, at some point the bill will come due'. Amy Larkin, *Environmental Debt: The Hidden Costs of the Changing Global Economy* (New York: Palgrave Macmillan, 2013), 5.

273   Williams, Rowan, 'Time for us to challenge the idols of high finance', Financial Times 1 November 2011. http://rowanwilliams. archbishopofcanterbury.org/articles.php/2236/time-for-us-to-challenge-the-idols-of-high-finance (accessed 6 June 2013).

274   Williams, *Faith in the Public Square*, 215.

275   David Jenkins, *The Humanum Studies 1969–1975* (Geneva: World Council of Churches, 1975), 17.

276   Richard Bauckham, *Ecological Hope in Crisis?* http://www.jri.org.uk/wp-content/uploads/JRI_23_Hope_Bauckham.pdf (accessed 19 March 2013).

277   Williams, *Faith in the Public Square*, 176.

278   Moltmann, *Ethics of Hope*, 160.

279   *Lambeth Conference 1948*, 6.

280   *The Lambeth Conference 1958*, 136.

281   *Resolutions and Reports [of the] The Lambeth Conference 1968*, 71.

282   Kosoke Koyama, 'Traditional Cultures and Technology', in *Today's Church and Today's World*, 69.

283   Ibid., 70.

284   *The Report of the Lambeth Conference 1978*, 34.

285   Michael Marshall, *Church at the Cross Roads: Lambeth 1988* (London: Collins, 1988), 73. Marshall is quoting Robert Runcie from lecture 2: 'The Anglican Response' in Robert A.K. Runcie, *Authority in Crisis: An Anglican Response* (London: SCM, 1988).

286   Moltmann, *Ethics of Hope*, 67.

287   Lambeth Conference. *The Lambeth Conferences 1867–1930: The Reports of the 1920 and 1930 Conferences, with Selected Resolutions from the Conferences of 1867, 1878, 1888, 1897, and 1908.* (London: SPCK, 1948), 64.

288   Ibid., 70.

289   *The Lambeth Conference 1958*, 163.

290   *Today's Church and Today's World*, 70.

291   Margaret Dewey, 'Dominant Influences in the Current World', in *Today's Church and Today's World: The Lambeth Conference 1978 Preparatory Articles* (London: CIO Publishing, 1977), 46.

292   Moltmann, *Ethics of Hope*, 134.

293   Kitagawa, 'Faith and Society,' 75.

294   *The Report of the Lambeth Conference 1978*, 35.

295   *Lambeth Conference 1948*, 6.

296   *Resolutions and Reports [of the] The Lambeth Conference 1968*, 72.

297   *The Lambeth Conference 1958*, 161, 162.

298   *Conference of the Bishops of the Anglican Communion 1920*, 64.

299   Archbishop William Thomson speaking at St Paul's Cathedral London on Saturday 28 July 1888.

300   Randall Davidson, *The Lambeth Conferences of 1867, 1878 and 1888*, 366ff.

301   Ibid., 364.

302   David Jenkins was Director of Humanum Studies for the World Council of Churches 1969-1975 and later Bishop of Durham 1984–1994.

303   Jenkins, *The Humanum Studies 1969–1975*, 43.

304   Lambeth Conference. *The Lambeth Conferences 1867–1930*, 63.

305   Lambeth Conference. *The Lambeth Conferences (1867–1948)*, 5,6.

306   *Lambeth Conference 1968: Preparatory Information* (London: SPCK, 1968).

307   *Resolutions and Reports [of the] The Lambeth Conference 1968*, 77.

308   Ibid., 30.

309   *The Report of the Lambeth Conference 1978*, 35.

310   *Today's Church and Today's World*, 71.

311   Anglican Communion. *Mission—the Five Marks of Mission* http://www.
       anglicancommunion.org/ministry/mission/fivemarks.cfm (accessed 12
       February 2014).

312   *The Truth Shall Make You Free*, 174.

313   Lambeth Conference. *Lambeth Conferences 1867–1988*, 219.

314   *The Official Report of the Lambeth Conference 1998*, 89.

315   Ibid., 73ff.

316   Williams, *Faith in the Public Square*, 199.

317   This position is challenged by Normal Habel. He argues that in the first
       place we should treat this text with 'suspicion', recognising that it needs to
       be freed from an anthropocentric focus, allowing the 'voice of the earth'
       to be retrieved. Norman Habel 'Introducing Ecolgical Hermeneutics',
       Exploring Ecological Hermeneutics ED. Norman Habel and Peter Trudinger
       (Atlanta: Society of Biblical Literature, 2008), 1-8.

318   *The Official Report of the Lambeth Conference 1998*, 90.

319   Ibid.

320   Ibid.

321   Ibid., 87.

322   Ibid., 89.

323   Ibid., 92.

324   *Lambeth Indaba: Capturing Conversations and Reflections from the Lambeth
       Conference 2008,* 19. http://www.lambethconference.org/vault/
       Reflections_Document_(final).pdf (accessed 25 May 2014)..

325   Ibid.

326   Conradie, *An Ecological Christian Anthropology,* 240.

327   Norman Wirzba, *Living the Sabbath: Discovering the Rhythms of Rest and
       Delight* (Grand Rapids, Mich.: Brazos Press, 2006), 31.

328   Brian Brock, *Christian Ethics in a Technological Age* (Grand Rapids, Mich.:
       William B. Eerdmans, 2010), 291.

329   Barth, *Church Dogmatics, vol.3: The Doctrine of Creation,* 226.

330   Wirzba, *Living the Sabbath*, 30.

331   The work of God outside of God.

332 Gnana Robinson, *The Origin and Development of the Old Testament Sabbath: A Comprehensive Exegetical Approach* (Frankfurt am Main: Peter Lang, 1988).

333 Numbers requires the sacrifice of four lambs on the sabbath day and two bulls, one ram, seven lambs and one goat on the new moon festival; while Ezekiel requires six lambs and a ram on the sabbath day, and on the new moon one bull, six lambs and a ram.

334 Victor Hamilton, *The Book of Genesis, Chapters 1-17* (Grand Rapids: William B. Eerdmans, 1990), 142.

335 'The origin and history of the Sabbath has still not been fully explained. However there is much to suggest that in the pre-exilic period the Sabbath was the Israelite New Moon festival (11 Kings 4:23; Isa. 1:13; Hos. 2:13 Amos 8:5). As such it was celebrated regularly in the cult by the priests in the temple (Isa. 1:13; Hos. 2:13) in a way—comparable to the tamid sacrifice—which probably excluded the public. The Sabbath was significant for the public only to the degree that it was a good time for the getting of omens. Thus in pre-exilic times the Sabbath was largely part of the official cult and came to an end with the destruction of the Jerusalem temple. ... Alongside this in the pre-exilic period there had been a family custom of interrupting agricultural work every seven days for a day of rest. It probably had something to do with an old taboo about not exploiting animals until their last breath. There is something to be said for the thesis that the two institutions became combined in the exile. The festival which was once limited to the official temple cult was opened up so that families everywhere could participate in it, the rest from work therefore took on cultic and religious dignity.' Rainer Albertz, *A History of Israelite Religion in the Old Testament Period, vol 2: From the Exile to the Maccabees* (Louisville: Westminster/John Knox Press, 1994), 408ff.

336 Andreas Schuele, 'Sabbath,' in *The New Interpreter's Dictionary of the Bible*, vol. 5 (Nashville, Ten.: Abingdon Press, 2009), 1-13.

337 Ibid., 7.

338 *Theological Dictionary of the Old Testament, vol. xiv* (Grand Rapids: William B. Eerdmans, 2004), 389.

339 'There is no evidence that connects these moon festivals with Sabbath origins in the text.' Paul A Barker 'Sabbath, sabbatical year, jubilee,' in *Dictionary of the Old Testament: Pentateuch,* ed. David Baker and T. Desmond Alexander (Illinois: InterVarsity Press, 2003), 699.

340   Heather McKay, *Sabbath and Synagogue: The Question of Sabbath Worship in Ancient Judaism* (Leiden: Brill, 1994).

341   Margaret Barker, *Creation: A Biblical Vision for the Environment* (London: T&T Clark International, 2010).

342   Richard H. Lowery, *Sabbath and Jubilee* (St. Louis: Chalice Press, 2000), 4.

343   Barker, *Creation,* 51.

344   'P'—priestly the designation given to the editor of the Pentateuch post the exile.

345   Frank Crüsemann, *The Torah: Theology and Social History of Old Testament Law* (Edinburgh: T&T Clark, 1996), 366.

346   Detailed legal interpretation of Talmudic literature.

347   Joel Shuman, *The Body of Compassion: Ethics, Medicine and the Church* (Boulder, Co.: Westview, 1999), Chapter 3.

348   Atkinson, *Renewing the Face of the Earth*, 36.

349   Patrick Logan, *Biblical Reflections on the Political Economy of Jubilee* (London: Diocese of Southwark, 1997), 11.

350   An example of this benevolence can be demonstrated in the English village system where benevolent landholders have provided for their labourers regardless of their usefulness (post sickness or old age) to the landowner.

351   John Howard Yoder, *The Politics of Jesus*, 2nd ed. (Grand Rapids: Eerdmans, 1994), 41.

352   Brueggemann, *The Word that Redescribes the World,* 161, quoting Crüsemann, *The Torah*, 224.

353   *Theological Dictionary of the Old Testament, vol. xiv*, 385.

354   Barth, *Church Dogmatics, vol.3: The Doctrine of Creation,* 180.

355   *Theological Dictionary of the Old Testament, vol. xiv*, 385.

356   Claus Westermann, *Genesis 1-11: A Commentary*, (London: SPCK, 1984), 169.

357   Jürgen Moltmann, *Creating a Just Future: The Politics of Peace and the Ethics of Creation in a Threatened World* (London: SCM Press, 1989), 61.

358   'The Sabbath as a cultic institution is quite outside the purview' [of Genesis 2.1-4a]. Gerhard von Rad, *Genesis: A Commentary* (London: SCM Press, 1972), 62.

359   Michael Fishbane, *Biblical Text and Texture: A Literary Reading of Selected Texts* (Oxford: Oneworld 1998), 11.

360   Ibid., 12.

361   Bauckham, *Bible and Ecology*, 83.

362   'The creation is described as a building in the Old Testament, presumably because the temple 'was' the creation...in the time of Jesus the Jews were still thinking of the creation in terms of the temple'. Margaret Barker, *Creation*, 42-43.

363   Brueggemann, *Journey to the Common Good*, 49.

364   Genesis 9:8ff; Exodus 23:10-12; Exodus 31:12-17; Leviticus 25; Deuteronomy 5:12-15.

365   John Polkinghorne, ed., *The Work of Love: Creation as Kenosis* (Grand Rapids: William B. Eerdmans, 2001).

366   'God never appears mightier than in the act of his self-limitation, and never greater than in the act of self-humiliation' Moltmann, *God in Creation*, 148.

367   Malcom Jeeves, 'The Nature of Persons and the Emergence of Kenotic Behaviour,' in *The Work of Love: Creation as Kenosis*, ed. John Polkinghorne, (London: SPCK, 2001), 66-89.

368   Westermann, *Genesis 1-11*, 174.

369   'Sabbath rest is at the centre of YHWH's alternative intention for creation, the defining mark of creation in Gen 2.1-4a': Walter Brueggemann, *The Word that Redescribes the World: The Bible and Discipleship.* (Minneapolis: Fortress Press, 2006), 128.

370   Heschel, *The Sabbath, its Meaning for Modern Man*, 74.

371   Willem A. VanGemeren, ed. *New International Dictionary of Old Testament Theology and Exegesis, vol 2*, (Grand Rapids: Zondervan Publishing House, 1997), 641.

372   Ibid., 641.

373   Rad, *Genesis,* 60.

374   'The seventh day has no morning or evening because just as creation began in the eternal rest of God, so it ends in the same repose'. Robert Farrar Capon, *Genesis the Movie* (Grand Rapids: William B. Eerdmans, 2003), 161.

375   Alexander Heidel, *The Babylonian Genesis: The Story of the Creation* (Chicago: University of Chicago Press, 1951), 127.

376   Westermann, *Genesis 1-11*, 169.

377   Umberto Cassuto, *From Adam to Noah* (Jerusalem: Magnes Press The Hebrew University, 1961).

378   'In *De Genesi ad Litteram*, Augustine spends quite a bit of time insisting that God's *Requies* on the seventh day should not be taken as mere cessation from labour'. Capon, *Genesis the Movie*, 169.

379   VanGemeren, *New international Dictionary of Old Testament Theology and Exegesis, vol. 4*, 144.

380   Ibid., 495.

381   *Interpreters Dictionary of the Bible, vol.4*, (New York: Abingdon Press, 1962), 294.

382   Lunar months do not neatly divide into four seven day weeks.

383   *Interpreters Dictionary of the Bible, vol.4*, 294.

384   'Seven is a period of time so the seventh day completes the first period of time': Cassuto, *From Adam to Noah*, 64.

385   Crüsemann, *The Torah*, 299.

386   Terence E. Fretheim, 'Genesis,' in *New Interpreter's Bible* (New York: Abingdon Press, 1994), 346.

387   Ibid., 170.

388   *New International Dictionary of Old Testament Theology and Exegesis, vol. 1*, (Grand Rapids, Zondervan, 1997), 758.

389   Ibid.

390   Westermann, *Genesis 1-11*, 172.

391   'No organism has the power to consider self limitation on behalf of others as one of its options. That level of choice only appears with humans'. Holmes Rolston, 'Kenosis and Nature,' in *The Work of Love: Creation as Kenosis,* ed. John Polkinghorne (London: SPCK, 2001), 62.

392   This point is picked up and addressed in Chapter 6 where consideration of scripture and its apparent mandate for endless population expansion is discussed in the context of a prior responsibility for the well-being of the next generation.

393   Nahum N. Sarna, *Genesis* (Philadelphia: Jewish Publication Society, 1989), 15.

394   Donna Orsuto, *Holiness* (London: Continuum, 2006), 12.

395   Barth, *Church Dogmatics, vol.3: The Doctrine of Creation,* 215.

396   Ibid., 48.

397   Capon, *Genesis the Movie,* 166.

398   Jacob Milgrom, 'Holy, Holiness, NT.,' in *New Interpreter's Dictionary of the Bible, vol.2*, Nashville, Tenn.: Abingdon Press, 2007), 854.

399   Ibid.

400   The Israelites in transit claimed they would rather return to slavery in Egypt than suffer what they considered to be the privation of the wilderness. (Ex. 16: 1-4)

401   'The 'bread of heaven' was like nothing they knew, and so they said to one another, as they saw the gift of bread fall on them, what is it? The Hebrew for that question in *man hu*', and so the bread is called manna.' Brueggemann, *Journey to the Common Good*, 14.

402   The prophetic tradition considered the actualising of these events in the lives of successive generations to be the heart of the faith.

403   These words are mirrored in the words that open the Psalter (Psalm 1.3).

404   Moltmann, *Creating a Just Future*, 64.

405   Ecological debt is a term used to describe both the estimated dollar value of remedial work necessary to put right environmental damage and degradation, but more particularly it is a term used to describe the level of human activity which exceeds the earth's annual capacity for renewal. Humanity's footprint first exceeded global bio-capacity in the mid-1980's and has done so every year since. By 2008 this annual overshoot had accrued into an ecological debt that exceeded 2.5 years of the Earth's total productivity. *World Footprint: Do We Fit on the Planet?* http://www.footprintnetwork.org/en/index.php/GFN/page/world_footprint (accessed 29 May 2014).

406   Timothy Gorringe of Exeter University argues for a different economic world view and uses the Ahab and Naboth narrative to argue his case. His argument is that an economic system should be devised to maximise quality of life and that quality life is accessed through harmonious

relationship not acquisition. 'A denial of the untamed commodity-money mechanisms of the world market is, therefore, the most important precondition for a change in direction towards a life sustaining economy'. Timothy Gorringe, *Idolatry and Redemption: Economics in Biblical Perspective*. 2013. Page 8.   http://www.operationnoah.org/sites/default/files/Idolatry & Redemption T.Gorringe Mar2013_0.pdf (accessed 23 November 2013).

407   Bauckham, *Bible and Ecology*, 26.

408   In his campaign to abolish slavery William Wilberforce was confronted by the captains of industry and commerce with the argument that freeing of slaves could not be afforded, that economic and social order which slavery protected, would collapse.

409   Brueggemann, *The Word that Redescribes the World*, 128.

410   Church of England Mission and Public Affairs Council, *Sharing God's Planet: A Christian Vision for a Sustainable Future* (London: Church House Publishing, 2005), 27.

411   He appears to have confused the rationale for the fourth commandment in Exodus which roots the commandment in creation, with the rationale in Deuteronomy which roots it in the Exodus.

412   St Augustine's wrestling with the relationship between '*finished*' in Genesis 2:2, Jesus' words from the cross '*it is finished*', and Jesus words '*My father is working up till now*' is dealt with by Robert Capon in *Genesis the Movie*, 170-172.

413   W. H. Vanstone, *The Stature of Waiting* (London: Darton, Longman & Todd, 1982).

414   The 'sabbath day miracles" are examined in some detail in Chapter 5.

415   Hugh Montefiore, *A Commentary on the Epistle to the Hebrews* (London: A&C Black, 1964), 86.

416   Brueggemann, *The Word that Redescribes the World*, 116.

417   T.S. Eliot, *Four Quartets: no2: East Coker,* (London: Faber & Faber, 1959), line 1.

418   Wirzba, *Living the Sabbath*, 23.

419   'We must take as our starting point that when P arranged the works of creation in a seven day pattern he was not concerned merely with a

succession of seven days, but with a whole, a unit of time, which becomes a whole in the climax of the seventh day': Westermann, *Genesis 1-11*, 171.

420   Elizabeth Barrett Browning, *Aurora Leigh*. 1864. http://digital.library. upenn.edu/women/barrett/aurora/aurora.html (accessed 23 November 2013).

421   David Jenkins, *The Glory of Man: Bampton Lectures for 1966* (Bristol: SCM, 1967), 85.

422   Bauckham, *Bible and Ecology*, 141.

423   Jewish Law. The path one walks.

424   Eduard Lohse, 'σάββατον,' in *Theological Dictionary of the New Testament, vol vii*, ed. Gerhard Friedrich (Grand Rapids: Eerdmans, 1971), 25.

425   John Meier, *A Marginal Jew: Rethinking the Historical Jesus, vol.4: Law and Love* (New Haven: Yale University Press 2009), 263.

426   'The early Christian movement was characterised by the bursting of boundaries.' Henry Sturcke, *Encountering the Rest of God: How Jesus Came to Personify the Sabbath* (Zurich: Theologischer Verlag Zurich, 2005), 346.

427   '*Cosmos*' occurs 78 times in John's Gospel alone'. Bauckham, *Bible and Ecology*, 163. In the creation narrative God's resting is set within the context of the 'heavens and the earth' (Gen. 2:1 and 2:4). Col: 1:16 claims that heavens and the earth come into being through Jesus.

428   Keith Weber, *The Lord of the Sabbath: The Riches of God's Rest* (Leominster: Day One Publications, 2007).

429   Sturcke, *Encountering the Rest of God*.

430   Ibid., 344.

431   Ibid., 346.

432   Meier, *A Marginal Jew*, 282.

433   Ibid., 246.

434   Richard John Neuhaus, *The Naked Public Square: Religion and Democracy in America* (Grand Rapids: Eerdmans, 1984) 269.

435   Bauckham, *Bible and Ecology*, 145.

436   Barth, *Church Dogmatics, vol.3: The Doctrine of Creation*, 93–227.

437   Bauckham, *Bible and Ecology*, 144.

438   Williams, *On Christian Theology*, 63.

439   Joseph Sittler, 'Called to Unity,' *The Ecumenical Review* 14 (January 1962), 178.

440   Brueggemann, *The Word that Redescribes the World*, 114.

441   See for example Psalms 8, 19 and 104.

442   Heschel, *The Sabbath, its Meaning for Modern Man*, 20.

443   Meier, *A Marginal Jew, vol. 4*, 269.

444   Lohse, 'σάββατον,' in *Theological Dictionary of the New Testament, vol. vii*, 23.

445   Meier, *A Marginal Jew*, 282-283.

446   Ibid., 125.

447   Heschel, *The Sabbath, its Meaning for Modern Man*, 53.

448   Meier, *A Marginal Jew*, 281.

449   Robert A. Guelich, *Mark 1:8-26* (Dallas: Word Books, 1989), 126.

450   Meier, *A Marginal Jew*, 286.

451   Schweizer, *The Good News According to Matthew*, 277.

452   Eduard Schweizer, *The Good News According to Mark* (London: SPCK, 1987), 73.

453   Meier, *A Marginal Jew*, 259.

454   Lohse, 'σάββατον,' in *Theological Dictionary of the New Testament, vol. vii*, 24.

455   Guelich, *Mark 1:8-26*, 139.

456   Lohse, 'σάββατον,' in *Theological Dictionary of the New Testament, vol. vii*, 27.

457   Brueggemann, *The Word that Redescribes the World*, 188.

458   Ibid., 194.

459   Guelich, *Mark 1:8-26*, 136.

460   Bonhoeffer, *Ethics*, 193.

461   Ibid., 188.

462   Ibid., 193.

463   'Sabbath and eternity are one ... the sabbath is an example of the world to come'. Heschel, *The Sabbath, its Meaning for Modern Man*, 73.

464   Eduard Schweizer, *The Good News According to Luke* (Atlanta: John Knox Press, 1973), 222.

465   Lohse, 'σάββατον,' in *Theological Dictionary of the New Testament, vol. vii*, 26.

466   Schweizer, *The Good News According to Luke*, 222.

467   Meier, *A Marginal Jew*, 296.

468   Ernst Haenchen, *John 1: A Commentary on the Gospel of John* (Philadelphia: Fortress Press, 1984), 248.

469   Lohse, 'σάββατον,' in *Theological Dictionary of the New Testament, vol. vii*, 27.

470   Ibid., 28.

471   Williams, *On Christian Theology*, 65.

472   Ernst Haenchen, *John 1: A Commentary on the Gospel of John*, 249.

473   Bauckham, *Bible and Ecology*, 113.

474   Walter Brueggemann, 'Editors Foreword,' in *Jesus, Liberation and the Biblical Jubilee: Images for Ethics and Christology*, by Sharon H. Ringe (Philadelphia: Fortress Press, 1985), x.

475   *We Can End Poverty: Millennium Development Goals and Beyond 2015.* http://www.un.org/millenniumgoals/ (accessed 3 December 2013).

476   Paul Ricoeur, *The Symbolism of Evil* (New York: Harper and Row, 1967), 10.

477   John Nolland, *Luke, vol. 1: Luke 1–9: 20* (Waco: Word Books, 1989), 193.

478   Ibid., 202.

479   Yoder, *The Politics of Jesus*, 60.

480   Sharon Ringe, *Jesus, Liberation and Biblical Jubilee: Images for Ethics and Christology* (Philadelphia: Fortress Press, 1985), 34.

481   Eduard Schweizer, *The Good News According to Matthew* (London: SPCK, 1976), 83.

482   Ringe, *Jesus, Liberation and Biblical Jubilee*, 51.

483   Schweizer, *The Good News According to Matthew*, 79-98.

484   Yoder, *The Politics of Jesus*, 60.

485   Ibid., 62.

486   Ibid., 65.

487   Ringe, *Jesus, Liberation and Biblical Jubilee*, 59.

488   The Global Footprint Network estimated that in 2012 the global community had exceeded its sustainably defensible draw down on annual

resources in that year by 22 August. The draw down after that date was equivalent to debt added to the accumulating burden. 'Earth Overshoot Day was August 22, and Yes, We're Still in Overshoot,' Footprint Network News, issue 30, 3 October, 2012. http://www.footprintnetwork.org/en/index.php/newsletter/det/earth_overshoot_day_was_august_22_and_yes_were_still_in_overshoot (accessed 15 October 2012).

489   Kevin Rudd, *Address to the 64th Session of the United Nations General Assembly 23 September 2009,* http://www.smh.com.au/opinion/politics/rudd-speech-to-the-united-nations-20090924-g3nn.html (accessed 15 October 2012).

490   Ringe, *Jesus, Liberation and Biblical Jubilee,* 36.

491   Yoder, *The Politics of Jesus,* 63.

492   Heschel, *The Sabbath, its Meaning for Modern Man,* 90.

493   Schweizer, *The Good News According to Matthew,* 389-390.

494   Yoder, *The Politics of Jesus,* 71.

495   Judith Hoch Wray, *Rest as a Theological Metaphor in the Epistle to the Hebrews and the Gospel of Truth: Early Christian Homiletics of Rest* (Atlanta: Scholars Press, 1998), 173.

496   Harold Attridge, *The Epistle to the Hebrews: A Critical Commentary on the Epistle to the Hebrews* (Philadelphia: Fortress Press, 1989), 123.

497   Sturcke, *Encountering the Rest of God,* 278.

498   William Taylor, 'Psalm 95,' in *The Interpreter's Bible, vol. 4* (Nashville: Abingdon Press, 1955), 516.

499   Ibid., 517.

500   Wray, *Rest as a Theological Metaphor in the Epistle to the Hebrews and the Gospel of Truth,* 91.

501   Attridge, *The Epistle to the Hebrews,* 131.

502   Bauckham, *Bible and Ecology,* 164.

503   Ibid., 166.

504   Wright, *Surprised by Hope,* 213-215.

505   Wright, *The Lord and His Prayer,* 31.

506   C.H. Dodd, *The Coming of Christ; Four Broadcast Addresses for the Season of Advent* (Cambridge: Cambridge University Press, 1951), 7.

507   Bauckham, *Bible and Ecology*, 165.

508   Ibid., 165

509   Jürgen Moltmann, 'God's Kenosis in the Creation and Consummation of the World,' in *The Work of Love: Creation as Kenosis,* ed. John Polkinghorne (London: SPCK, 2001), 151.

510   Heschel, *The Sabbath, its Meaning for Modern Man*, 83.

511   Thorwald Lorenzen, *Resurrection and Discipleship: Interpretive Models, Biblical Reflections, Theological Consequences* (Maryknoll, N. Y.: Orbis Books, 1995), 275.

512   Wilhelm Gesenius, *A Hebrew and English Lexicon of the Old Testament* (Oxford: Clarendon Press, 1959), 675.

513   Ringe, *Jesus, Liberation and Biblical Jubilee,* 32.

514   Denis Edwards, *Jesus the Wisdom of God: An Ecological Theology* (Sydney: St Pauls, 1995), 33.

515   Wendell Berry, *Two Economies.* 2005. http://www.worldwisdom.com/public/viewpdf/default.aspx?article-title=Two_Economies_by_Wendell_Berry.pdf (accessed 4 October 2012).

516   Raymond Brown, *The Gospel According to John* (Garden City, New York: Doubleday, 1996), 523.

517   Moltmann, 'God's Kenosis in the Creation and Consumption of the World,' in *The Work of Love: Creation as Kenosis,* ed. John Polkinghorne (London: SPCK, 2001), 142.

518   'These observations lead to the conclusion that the history of religious background of the conceptions in this hymn is to be sought in Hellenistic Judaism'. Eduard Lohse, *Colossians and Philemon: A Commentary on the Epistles to the Colossians and to Philemon* (Philadelphia: Fortress Press, 1982), 42.

519   Vicki Balabanski, 'Hellenistic Cosmology and the Letter to the Colossians,' in *Ecological Hermeneutics : Biblical, Historical, and Theological Perspectives,* ed. David Horrell, Cherryl Hunt, Christopher Southgate, and Francesca Stavrakopoulou (London: T&T Clark, 2010), 100.

520   Lohse, *Colossians and Philemon*, 42.

521   Bauckham, *Bible and Ecology*, 153.

522   Joseph Sittler, *Evocations of Grace: Writings on Ecology, Theology and Ethics* (Grand Rapids: Eerdmans, 2000), 39.

523   Kathleen O'Connor, *The Wisdom Literature* (Wilmington Delaware: Liturgical Press, 1993), 59.

524   Balabanski, 'Hellenistic Cosmology and the Letter to the Colossians,' 104.

525   Ibid., 103.

526   Lohse, *Colossians and Philemon*, 53, 54.

527   Ibid., 55.

528   Edwards, *Jesus the Wisdom of God*, 82.

529   Cf. J.B. Lightfoot, *St Paul's Epistles to the Colossians and Philemon* (New York: Macmillan 1879), 257-273.

530   Lohse, *Colossians and Philemon*, 57, quoting Hippolytus (ref. 6.34.2).

531   Balabanski, 'Hellenistic Cosmology and the Letter to the Colossians,' 100.

532   Edwards, *Jesus the Wisdom of God*, 34.

533   Thomas Berry, *The Dream of the Earth* (San Francisco: Sierra Club, 1998), 216-217.

534   Wright, *Surprised by Hope*, 215.

535   Conradie, *An Ecological Christian Anthropology*, 171.

536   Barth, *Church Dogmatics, vol.3: The Doctrine of Creation* 47.

537   Moltmann, *Creating a Just Future*, 62.

538   Steven Bouma-Prediger, *For the Beauty of the Earth: A Christian Vision for Creation Care* (Grand Rapids: Baker Academic, 2010), 111.

539   Northcott, *A Moral Climate*, 11.

540   Rudolf Otto, *The Idea of the Holy: An Inquiry into the Non-rational Factor in the Idea of the Divine*, 2nd ed. (New York: Oxford University Press, 1950).

541   Otto understood religion as an experience of the numinous which he described as wholly other (mysterium), provoking terror or fear (tremendum) and yet merciful and gracious (fascinans).

542   Barth, *Church Dogmatics, vol.3: The Doctrine of Creation*, 53.

543   Ibid., 114.

544   Ibid., 212.

545   Not a single, first man, but humanity, all humanity.

546   Barth, *Church Dogmatics, vol.3: The Doctrine of Creation*, 182.

547   Ibid., 198.

548   Westermann, *Genesis 1-11,* 276, 277.

549   Barth, *Church Dogmatics, vol.3: The Doctrine of Creation,* 214.

550   Moltmann, *God in Creation,* 285.

551   The controversial Australian Senator with a strongly espoused Christian faith, Cory Bernardi, states that environmentalism is one of the greatest threats to Christianity because it places plants and animals above humanity. Cori Bernardi, *The Conservative Revolution* (Ballarat: Connor Court Publishing, 2013).

552   Brueggemann, *Journey to the Common Good,* 28.

553   David Atkinson, *Renewing the Face of the Earth: A Theological and Pastoral Response to Climate Change* (Norwich: Canterbury Press, 2008), 35.

554   Wirzba, *Living the Sabbath,* 24.

555   Brueggemann, *The Word that Redescribes the World,* 187.

556   Moltmann, *God in Creation,* 187-189.

557   'The Greek is tricky, but Matthew's version [of the Lord's Prayer] seems to mean give us today our bread for tomorrow'. Tom Wright, *The Lord and His Prayer* (London: SPCK, 1996), 40.

558   *A Prayer Book for Australia* (Netley, South Australia: Broughton Books, 1995), 144.

559   Wendell Berry, *Sex, Economy, Freedom and Community* (New York: Pantheon, 1992), 115.

560   J. Morgenstern, 'Sabbath,' in *The Interpreters Dictionary of the Bible, vol. 4.* (New York: Abingdon Press 1962), 135-137.

561   At the 2008 Lambeth Conference of Anglican Bishops, Sir Jonathan Sacks (Lord Sacks), Britain's chief rabbi, spoke to the dilemma imposed on Judaism by its culture of separation, when he expressed gratitude to Christianity for taking to the world a message of universal love and reconciliation which Judaism has not.

562   James Alison, *Knowing Jesus* (London: SPCK, 1993), 61-87.

563   Michael Stafford, 'The Heresy of Religious Opposition to Global Warming' http://www.abc.net.au/religion/articles/2012/03/19/3456911.htm (accessed 14 October 2012).

564   Brueggemann, *The Word that Redescribes the World,* 187.

565 Michael Northcott addresses the manner in which opposition to the science of climate change has become a political rallying point in *A Moral Climate: The Ethics of Global Warming* (London: Darton Longman and Todd, 2007); see especially pages 269ff.

566 James Hansen deals extensively with this political dilemma in *Storms of My Grandchildren: The Truth about the Coming Climate Catastrophe and Our Last Chance to Save the Planet* (London: Bloomsbury, 2009); see for example page 241. From 2011–2013 the conservative Australian Federal Opposition has consistently opposed the Government policy for a market based price on carbon, preferring to put its own policy of Government intervention, a position to which it would normally be ideologically opposed.

567 W.J. Harrelson, 'Blessings and Cursings,' in *The Interpreters Dictionary of the Bible, vol 1* (New York: Abingdon Press, 1962), 446.

568 Ibid.

569 Bauckham, *Bible and Ecology*, 32.

570 Walter Brueggemann, 'The Liturgy of Abundance, the Myth of Scarcity,' *Christian Century*, 24-31 March 1999, http://www.religion-online.org/showarticle.asp?title=533 (accessed 3 September 2010).

571 Walter Brueggemann, *Theology of the Old Testament: Testimony, Dispute, Advocacy* (Minneapolis: Fortress, 1997), 156.

572 Taylor, *Enough is Enough*.

573 Carroll, *Alice's Adventures in Wonderland*, 1872.

574 Taylor, *Enough is Enough*, 1.

575 Jackson, *Prosperity Without Growth*, 121.

576 Heinberg, *The End of Growth*.

577 Brueggemann, *The Word that Redescribes the World*, 162.

578 James Lovelock, *The Vanishing Face of Gaia: A Final Warning* (London: Allan Lane, 2009), 21.

579 Bauckham, *Bible and Ecology*, 90.

580 Atkinson, *Renewing the Face of the Earth*, 35.

581 Fishbane, *Biblical Text and Texture*.

582 *Theological Dictionary of the Old Testament, vol. xiii*, 335.

583   Teilhard De Chardin, *The Phenomenon of Man*.

584   'Thus when the creator ceases work on the seventh day, it is not the abdication of a petty deity from a burdensome task, as in some Mesopotamian creation accounts. Rather God's rest in Genesis 2 represents the delegation to humanity of the royal task of administering the world on his behalf. Humans are delegated with nothing less than God's own proper work, as the creator's authorised representatives on earth. Whatever other meanings God's rest has elsewhere in the Old testament (for example justification for the Sabbath as in Exodus 20:11), in the context of Genesis 1 creation story it appropriately symbolises the beginning of the rule of the human race, their coming into their true power as makers of history, as representatives and emissaries of God, called to shape the world in imitation of the creator's own primordial activity in the first six days of creation': J. Richard Middleton, *The Liberating Image: The Imago Dei in Genesis 1* (Grand Rapids: Brazos Press, 2005), 294.

585   Dietrich Bonhoeffer, *Ethics* (London: Collins Fontana, 1964), 224.

586   Desmond Tutu, *No Future Without Forgiveness* (London: Random House, 1999), 34-35.

587   Bonhoeffer, *Ethics*, 225.

588   Kristin M. Swenson, 'Earth Tells the Lessons of Cain,' in *Exploring Ecological Hermeneutics*, ed. Norman C. Habel and Peter Trudinger (Atlanta, Ga: Society of Biblical Literature, 2008), 34.

589   Bauckham, *Bible and Ecology*, 24.

590   Philip Sherrard, *The Rape of Man and Nature: An Enquiry into the Origins and Consequences of Modern Science* (Ipswich: Golgonooza Press, 1991), 40.

591   William G Witt, *George Herbert's Approach to God: The Faith and Spirituality of a Country Priest* http://willgwitt.org/george-herberts-approach-to-god/ (accessed 27 August 2012).

592   John Zizioulas, 'Priest of Creation,' in *Environmental Stewardship: Critical Perspectives, Past and Present.* ed. R. J. Berry (New York: Continuum International, 2006), 290.

593   Moltmann, *God in Creation*, 71.

594   David Atkinson, quoting Arnold Toynbee in 1974, Atkinson, *Renewing the Face of the Earth*, 44.

595   John Haught, *The Promise of Nature: Ecology and Cosmic Purpose* (New York: Paulist Press, 1993), 101.

596   Bauckham, *Bible and Ecology*, 89.

597   Wirzba, *Living the Sabbath*, 30.

598   John Marks Templeton, *Riches for the Mind and Spirit* (San Francisco: Harper Collins, 1990), 209.

599   Tim Flannery, *We are the Weather Makers: the Story of Global Warming* (Melbourne: Text Publishing, 2006), 70.

600   Sachs, *The Price of Civilization*, 176.

601   '[Modern conservationism] stems from seventeenth century humanism with its Pelagian emphasis on what can be accomplished by the human will and its playing down of original sin, rather than from the standard Augustinian tradition'. John Passmore, *Man's Responsibility for Nature: Ecological Problems and Western Traditions* (London: Duckworth, 1974), 30-31.

602   C.H. Dodd, *The Parables of the Kingdom* (Glasgow: Fount, 1978), 151.

603   Dodd's Realised Eschatology has been critiqued as a diminishment of future hope. As will be argued later in the chapter, hope is enhanced by living the present in light of future destiny.

604   Williams, *On Christian Theology*, 65.

605   Brueggemann, *Journey to the Common Good*, 28-35.

606   Gustavo Gutiérrez, *A Theology of Liberation: History Politics and Salvation*, rev. ed. (Maryknoll, N.Y: Orbis, 1988), 92.

607   Ibid., 81.

608   'While Tutu does not extend the family model to Earth community the extension is natural'. Kapya Kaoma, *God's Family, God's Earth: Christian Ecological Ethics of Ubuntu* (Zomba, Malawi: Kachere, 2013), 106.

609   'Ubuntu emphasises right relationships in the universe; it recognises that we are all inextricably bound up in each other's being, and we are one family in creation'. Kaoma, *God's Family, God's Earth*, 103.

610   Tutu, *No Future Without Forgiveness*, 34.

611   Ibid., 34.

612   Ibid., 35.

613   Ibid., 226.

614   'Trade was nothing new to Africans, but the Enlightenment theory that
       viewed trade as individual and competitive, rather than a community
       enterprise, was alien'. Kaoma, *God's Family, God's Earth*, 95.

615   Hans Schwarz, *Theology in a Global Context: The Last Two Hundred Years*
       (Grand Rapids: Eerdmans, 2005), 543.

616   Barth, *Church Dogmatics, vol.3: The Doctrine of Creation,* 514.

617   Bonhoeffer, *Ethics*, 220.

618   Scott A. Dunham, 'Creaturely Salvation in Augustine,' in *Creation and
       Salvation* ed. Ernst Conradie (Zurich: Lit Verlag, 2012), 86.

619   Julian of Norwich (1342- ca.1416) in her *Showings* https://www.
       christianhistoryinstitute.org/incontext/article/julian (accessed 29
       January 2014).

620   Brett, 'A Timely Reminder,' 159.

621   While support for climate change action appears to have waned in the
       last three years a 2012 report 'Climate change in the American mind'
       conducted by Yale University found that the majority of Americans
       believe more decisive action should be taken to reduce carbon emissions
       and reduce global warming. *Extreme Weather and Climate Change in
       the American Mind*, September 2012 http://environment.yale.edu/
       climate-communication/files/Extreme-Weather-Public-Opinion-
       September-2012.pdf (accessed 23 May 2014). The same analysis appears
       to be true in Australia, even within the business community, see *Open for
       Business*, Q&A, 11 November 2013 http://www.abc.net.au/tv/qanda/
       txt/s3873461.htm (accessed 23 May 2014).

622   As a result of his *Theology of Hope* Moltmann has been accused of
       panentheism. (Jürgen Moltmann, *Theology of Hope: On the Ground and the
       Implications of a Christian Eschatology*. (London: SCM Press, 1967)). I find the
       accusation ill-founded as a way of critiquing his essential Christian orthodoxy.
       Panentheism is a midpoint between pantheism and theism: theism being
       belief in God who is separate from creation, and pantheism belief that 'all is
       God'. Panentheism is a teaching that all things dwell in God and God dwells
       in all things. It is considered by its accusers to be a belief in universalism, or, at
       its worst, a belief in 'new age religion'. I find it an ill-founded accusation against
       Moltmann by those who continue to insist that Christianity is exclusively

about the salvation of the individual out of this world, a form of Christianity which is primarily about 'heaven' out of this world rather than a commitment to the transformation of this world in Christ's name. As an example of this criticism see Ken Silva, 'Brian McLaren and evangelical panentheism (part 2)' http://apprising.org/2009/08/23/brian-mclaren-and-evangelical-panentheism-part-2/ (accessed 22 August 2013).

623   Alasdair I.C. Heron, *A Century of Protestant Theology* (Guildford: Lutterworth Press, 1980), 162.

624   Ibid., 162-163.

625   Schwarz, *Theology in a Global Context*, 546.

626   Ernst Bloch, *The Principle of Hope* (Cambridge: MIT Press, 1986), 3:1375.

627   In the lead up to the 2013 Australian Federal Election the Public Affairs Commission of the Anglican Church in Australia issued a paper which commenced 'We need a government who will determine the truly critical issues that should be addressed for the national and global good and then go about achieving progress collaboratively.' Anglican Church of Australia Public Affairs Commission. *Issues and Questions for the 2013 Federal Election Process.* 2013. http://www.anglican.org.au/docs/commissions/public_affairs/Issues and Questions for the 2013 Federal Election Process.pdf (accessed 21 November 2013).

628   'If love is the ultimate source of goodness in our lives, it follows that the good life is primarily about others. What else could it be about?' Hugh Mackay, *The Good Life* (Sydney: Macmillan, 2013), 128.

629   At the 2013 Australian Federal Election both political leaders espoused strong Christian faith but rather than finding this an advantage, both sought to minimise the influence this conviction has on their public life.

630   The religion of society, or the protector of sacredness at the heart of public life.

631   Moltmann, *Theology of Hope,* 310.

632   'The eschatology of the period we know of as Christendom was so concerned with going to heaven that this earth was neglected'. *The Triune Creator* (Grand Rapids: Eerdmans, 1998), 226.

633   Lesslie Newbigin, *The Open Secret: An Introduction to the Theology of Mission* rev. ed. (Grand Rapids: Eerdmanns, 1995), 16-17.

634   John Dominic Crossan, 'Jesus and the Challenge of Collaborative Eschatology,' in *The Historical Jesus: Five Views* ed. James K. Beilby and Paul Rhodes Eddy (Downers Grove, Ill.: IVP Academic, 2009), 125.

635   Crossan is appropriately (although with some exaggeration) criticised by his respondents in *The Historical Jesus: Five Views* for almost totally ignoring any future aspect of the eschaton.

636   Crossan, 'Jesus and the Challenge of Collaborative Eschatology,' 125.

637   Wright, *Surprised by Hope*, 57.

638   Moltmann, *Theology of Hope*, 325.

639   John, Metropolitan of Pergamon, 'Preserving God's Creation,' in *Christianity and Ecology* ed. Elizabeth Breuilly and Martin Palmer (London: Cassell, 1992), 62.

640   Moltmann, *Ethics of Hope,* 117-118, 121, 129, 150.

641   'The indwelling of the spirit is evident in the sabbath presence of God, in the Salvation History of Israel, in Jesus Christ, in the Church, and ultimately in the earth where righteousness dwells.' Conradie, *An Ecological Christian Anthropology,* 71.

642   Bauckham, *Bible and Ecology*, 151-157.

643   Conradie, *An Ecological Christian Anthropology*, 13.

644   Moltmann, *God in Creation*, 5.

645   Sigurd Bergmann, 'Now the Spirit Dwells amongst us ...: The Spirit as Liberator of Nature in the Trinitarian Cosmology of Gregory of Nazianz,' in *Creation and Salvation* ed. Ernst Conradie (Zurich: Lit Verlag, 2012), 68.

646   Moltmann, *Ethics of Hope*, 150.

647   Literally 'in God'.

648   http://plato.stanford.edu/entries/panentheism (accessed 18 November 2013).

649   Several websites provide a critique of panentheism. That provided by Intervarsity Press is helpful. http://www.ivpbooks.com/9781844741748 (accessed 18 November 2013).

650   For a full articulation of a theology of 'embrace' see Miroslav Volf *Exclusion and Embrace: A Theological Exploration of Identity, Otherness, and Reconciliation* (Nashville: Abingdon Press, 1996).

651   Leonardo Boff and Virgil Elizondo, *Ecology and Poverty: Cry of the Earth, Cry of the Poor* (Maryknoll, NY: Orbis Books, 1997), 81.

652   Moltmann, 'Creation and Redemption,' 126, 127.

653   'The earth, our planet is indeed a single *oikos.*' Conradie, *An Ecological Christian Anthropology*, 7.

654   Ibid., 70.

655   Ibid., 39.

656   Sallie McFague, *The Body of God: An Ecological Theology* (London: SCM Press, 1993), 112.

657   Larry Rasmussen, 'Theology of Life and Ecumenical Ethics,' in *Ecotheology: Voices from South and North,* ed. David G. Hallman. (Geneva: WCC Publications, 1994), 118.

658   The G20 conferences such as the one concluded in September 2013 have lacked the capacity to do more than encourage cooperation for common good, without real effect.

659   David Hollenbach, *The Common Good and Christian Ethics* (Cambridge: Cambridge University Press, 2002), 244.

660   Berry, 'Two Economies', 219-235.

661   In 2009 the astronaut Sandra Magnus reflected: 'We are all there together as human beings and other organisms and we have to take care of each other'. Tariq Malik, *Planet Earth a Fragile Oasis, Astronauts Say*. 2009. http://www.space.com/6603-planet-earth-fragile-oasis-astronauts.html (accessed 23 November 2013).

662   McFague, *The Body of God*, 105.

663   Conradie, *An Ecological Christian Anthropology,* 138.

664   Charles Murphy, *At Home on Earth: Foundations for a Catholic Ethic of the Environment* (New York: Crossroads, 1989), 117.

665   Conradie, *An Ecological Christian Anthropology*, 51.

666   Elizabeth Theokritoff, 'The High Word's Mystery Play: Creation and Salvation in St Maximus the Confessor,' in *Creation and Salvation*, ed. Ernst Conradie (Zurich: Lit Verlag, 2012), 93-107.

667   House size impacts the human footprint, both in construction, maintenance, and running costs. In square metres comparative house

sizes per nation are: UK 76, Sweden 83, US 201, Australia 214. *How Big is a House? Average House Size by Country* http://shrinkthatfootprint.com/how-big-is-a-house (accessed 23 May 2014).

668   Conradie, *An Ecological Christian Anthropology,* 171.

669   'Environmental problems must be addressed by all of us in our everyday circumstances and should not be confiscated by the state. Their solution is only possible if people are motivated to confront them and the task of government is to create the conditions in which the right kind can emerge and solidify. I describe this motive as oikophilia, the love and feeling for home, and I set out the conditions in which oikophilia arises and the task of the state in making room for it'. Scruton, *Green Philosophy,* 3.

670   'Nationality ... is the only form of membership that has shown itself able to sustain a democratic process and a liberal rule of law'. Scruton, *Green Philosophy,* 240.

671   Edmund Burke, *Reflections on the French Revolution* (London: JM Dent, 1935).

672   Scruton, *Green Philosophy,* 218.

673   Ibid., 387-391.

674   Jonathan Sacks, *The Home We Build Together: Recreating Society* (London: Continuum, 2007), 240.

675   He refers to Col. 3:12-17 Hall, *Imaging God,* 84.

676   Ibid., 26.

677   Bauckham, *Bible and Ecology,* 11.

678   'The fundamental problem with the metaphor [of stewardship] is the implication that humans are effectively in control of nature'. Northcott, *The Environment and Christian Ethics,* 129.

679   .'Modern humanity does not experience itself as part of nature, but as an outside force destined to dominate and conquer it. Humans even talk of a battle with nature, forgetting that, if they won the battle, they would find themselves on the losing side'. Ernst Schumacher, *Small is beautiful: A study in Economics as if people mattered* (London: Blond and Biggs, 1973), 11.

680   Ibid., 218.

681   'The task of humans is that of serving or cultivating the soil. The place of the human species within the earth community may therefore be understood in terms of the metaphor of *humus*. Ibid., 42.

682   'Orthodox Perspectives on Creation: Report of the WCC Inter-Orthodox Consultation, Sofia, Bulgaria October 1987' (extracts). http://www.goarch.org/ourfaith/ourfaith8050 (accessed 19 November 2013).

683   Pickard, *Seeking the Church*, 118.

684   John, Metropolitan of Pergamon, 'Preserving God's Creation', 47.

685   Hall, *Imaging God*, 42.

686   Volf, *A Public Faith*, 97.

687   The fifth 'mark of mission' for the international Anglican Communion as defined by the Consultative Council of the Anglican Church in Australia in 1984.

688   'When I hope, I expect something from the future' Volf, *A Public Faith*, 55.

689   Charles Gutenson, *Christians and the Common Good: How Faith Intersects with the Public Life* (Grand Rapids: Brazos Press, 2011), 72.

690   'The Common Good', http://www.scu.edu/ethics/practicing/decision/commongood.html (accessed 6 September 2013).

691   Karl Rahner, *Foundations of Christian Faith: An Introduction to the Idea of Christianity* (New York: Seabury Press, 1978), 197.

692   Marianne Meye Thompson, *A Commentary on Colossians and Philemon* (Grand Rapids: Eerdmans, 2005), 113.

693   John V. Taylor, *The Christlike God* (London: SCM Press, 1992), 191.

694   Ibid., 192. Here Taylor is quoting the Jewish mystic, Isaac Luria

695   Ibid., 192-193.

696   C.K. Barrett, *A Commentary on the First Epistle to the Corinthians* (London: Adam and Charles Black, 1968), 54.

697   Simone Weil, *First and Last Note Books* (London: OUP, 1970), 120.

698   Emil Brunner, *The Christian Doctrine of Creation and Redemption* (London: Lutterworth Press, 1952), 20.

699   Sixteenth Century Kabbalist Rabbi (1534—1572).

700   Paul Badde, *The Face of God: The Rediscovery of the true face of Jesus* (San

Francisco: Ignatius Press, 2010), 222.

701 Jürgen Moltmann *God in Creation* 87.

702 Jürgen Moltmann 'God's Kenosis in the Creation and Consummation of the World' in The Work of Love: Creation as Kenosis Ed John Polkinghorne (London: SPCK, 2001), 142

703 Ibid., 143.

704 Matthew Anstey, *Four sermons on Genesis 1* (unpublished manuscript, 2006), 3.

705 Ernst Käsemann, *Exegetische Verusche und Besinnungen: Erste Band* (Göttingen, Vandenhoeck und Ruprecht, 1960), 70. (cited in Sarah Coakley, *Powers and Submissions: Spirituality, Philosophy and Gender.* (Oxford: Blackwell Publishers, 2002), 7).

706 Hans Urs von Balthasar, *Mysterium Paschale* (Edinburgh: T&T Clark, 1990), 23–36.

707 Balthasar, *Mysterium Paschale*, 11.

708 C.F.D. Moule, 'Further Reflections on Philippians 2: 5-11,' in *Apostolic History and the Gospel* ed. W.W. Gasque and R.A. Martin (Grand Rapids: Eerdmans, 1970), 265. (Cited in Coakley, *Powers and Submissions*, 10.).

709 Sarah Coakley, 'Kenosis: Theological Meanings and Gender Connotations,' in *The Work of Love: Creation as Kenosis,* ed. John Polkinghorne (London, SPCK, 2001), 203.

710 Coakley, *Powers and Submissions*, 3–39.

711 John Macquarrie, 'Kenoticism Reconsidered,' *Theology* 77 (1974), 24, cited in Coakley, *Powers and Submissions*, 23.

712 George F.R. Ellis, 'Kenosis as a Unifying Theme for Life and Cosmology,' in *The Work of Love: Creation as Kenosis,* ed. John Polkinghorne (London: SPCK, 2001), 107-126.

713 Ibid., 115.

714 Ibid., 110.

715 Charles Gore, *The Incarnation of the Son of God: Being the Bampton Lectures for the year 1891.* 2nd ed. (London: John Murray, 1892).

716 Charles Gore, *The Sermon on the Mount: A Practical Exposition* 2nd ed. (London: John Murray, 1910).

717   Charles Gore, *The Social Doctrine of the Sermon on the Mount* (London: Percival, 1892), 5.

718   Gore, *The Incarnation of the Son of God*, 89.

719   Mark D. Chapman, 'Charles Gore, Kenosis and the Crisis of Power', *Journal of Anglican Studies* 3 (November 2005): 204.

720   George Newlands, *Generosity and the Christian Future* (London: SPCK, 1997), 266.

721   The very Sabbath that is good news for ex-slaves is a worrying disruption for quintessential consumers as Amos understood so well (Amos 8: 4-5), Brueggemann, *The Word that Redescribes the World*, 129.

722   Taylor, *The Christlike God*, 203. Quoting Andrew Elphinstone, *Freedom, Suffering and Love* (London: SCM, 1976), 106.

723   Ricoeur, *The Conflict of Interpretations*, 301.

724   Brueggemann, *The Word that Redescribes the World*, 122.

725   Jackson, *Prosperity Without Growth*, 44.

726   Conradie, *An Ecological Christian Anthropology*, 233.

727   The Micah Challenge is an ecumenical alliance devoted to the alleviation of poverty.

728   *Chambers Dictionary of Etymology* (New York: Chambers Harrap Publishers, 1988), 653

729   Hollenbach, *The Common Good and Christian Ethics*, 216.

730   Ibid., 217.

731   Kaoma, *God's Family, God's Earth*, 133.

732   Ibid., 142.

733   Heinberg, *The End of Growth*, 15.

734   Mark O'Connor and William J. Lines *Overloading Australia: How Governments and Media Dither and Deny on Population* (Canterbury, NSW: Envirobook, 2008), 25.

735   The Haber Bosh process, said to be the greatest invention of the 20th century, produces 500 million tons of fertiliser per year and supports 40% of the world's population. Using 1% of the world's energy it extracts hydrogen and nitrogen out of the air to make ammonia.

736   Thomas Malthus published 'An Essay on the Principle of Population' in 1798 in response to William Godwin's assertions that the rational capacity of humanity for perfection was unlimited and that the stumbling blocks were not in the nature of humanity per se, but in the evils of human institutions. Thomas Malthus, *An Essay on the Principle of Population as it Affects the Future Improvement of Society*. (London: Printed for J. Johnson, 1798).

737   The Club of Rome was founded as an independent think tank in 1968. Its initial work on 'limits to growth' has been ridiculed in light of enormous human expansion in recent decades. Its current work is focussed on an analysis of a new economy which delivers stability and real prosperity without causing environmental degradation.

738   Malthus, *An Essay on the Principle of Population*, 9.

739   Ibid., 49.

740   James Hansen, *Storms of My Grandchildren*, 221.

741   Tim Flannery, *Beautiful Lies: Population and Environment in Australia*. (Melbourne: Schwartz Publishing, 2003), 58.

742   Executive Director of the Climate Change Institute at the Australian National University.

743   Will Steffen has used a statement like this in many of his addresses. These words are taken from correspondence between Professor Steffen and the author 25 November 2013.

744   Andrew J.B. Cameron, 'Is Growth Good? Toward a Christian Ethical Interrogation of a Dominant Paradigm,' *St Mark's Review* 214 (November 2010), 15-32.

745   Hall, *Imaging God*, 26.

746   Christopher Flavin, 'The Legacy of Rio,' in *the State of the World 1997* ed. Linda Starke (New York: Norton, 1997), 18.

747   Flannery, *Beautiful Lies*, 56.

748   Bouma-Prediger, *For the Beauty of the Earth*, 27.

749   Beth Heyde, 'Care for Creation: Population and Environment,' *St Mark's Review*, 214 (November 2010), 44.

750   All of the eight millennium development goals directly or indirectly

impact this challenge. *We Can End Poverty: Millennium Development Goals and Beyond 2015,* http://www.un.org/millenniumgoals/ (accessed 3 December 2013).

751   United Nations. Department of Economic and Social Affairs. Population Division. *World Population to 2300.* 2004. http://www.un.org/esa/population/publications/longrange2/WorldPop2300final.pdf (accessed 21 November 2013).

752   Heyde, 'Care for Creation,' 48.

753   Newbigin, *The Open Secret,* 94-95.

754   Heyde, 'Care for Creation,' 46.

755   This is the argument of Margaret Heffernan in her *A bigger Prize.* 'Collaboration is a habit of mind, solidified by routine and predicated on openness, generosity, rigour and patience. It requires precise and fearless communication without status, awe or intimidation. It's hard because it allows no passengers: everyone must bring their best'. Margaret Heffernan, *A Bigger Prize* (London: Simon and Schuster, 2014), 373.

756   Michael Sandel, *What Money Can't Buy:The Moral Limits of Markets (London: Allen and Lane, 2012).*

757   Ibid., 51.

758   Gregory Brett, 'A Timely Reminder: Humanity and Ecology in the Light of Christian Hope,' in *Earth Revealing—Earth Healing: Ecology and Christian Theology* Ed Denis Edwards (Collegeville, Minn.: Liturgical Press, 2001), 172.

759   Heyde, 'Care for Creation,' 43.

760   Tutu, *No Future Without Forgiveness.*

761   'Our ecological debts are as unstable as our financial debts. Neither is properly accounted for in the relentless pursuit of consumption growth'. Jackson, *Prosperity Without Growth,* 33.

762   One of the shortcomings of GDP as a measurement of wealth is that it does not factor in the loss implied in depletion of finite resources.

763   'About 50% of an increase in atmospheric carbon dioxide will be removed within 30 Years, a further 30% within a few centuries and the remaining 20% may remain for thousands of years' Houghton, *Global Warming,* 37.

764   'Increase in greenhouse gases is by far the largest of the factors that

can lead to climate change in the 21st century' John Houghton, *Global Warming* (Cambridge: Cambridge University Press, 2009), 167.

765   Hansen, *Storms of My Grandchildren*, 101.

766   Sweden already produces 50% of it energy from renewable sources. Most European countries are on track to meet their 2020 targets. Some had done so by 2012. The US and China are committing to new targets.

767   Oxfam has reported that the combined riches of the world's 85 most wealthy individuals is equal to the combined wealth of the poorest half of the world's population. Graeme Wearden, 'Oxfam: 85 Richest People as Wealthy as Poorest Half of the World.' *The Guardian* 20 January 2014. http://www.theguardian.com/business/2014/jan/20/oxfam-85-richest-people-half-of-the-world (accessed 30 January 2014).

768   Paul Gilding, *The Great Disruption: How the Climate Crisis will Transform the Global Economy (for the Better)* (London Bloomsbury, 2011), 225-227.

769   David Suzuki, 'Tony Abbott will Doom Future Generations if he Ditches Carbon Tax', Sydney Morning Herald 18 September 2013. http://www.smh.com.au/comment/tony-abbott-will-doom-future-generations-if-he-ditches-carbon-tax-20130917-2tx0j.html (accessed 24 September 2013).

770   Bonhoeffer, *Ethics*, 267.

771   Rise Svein, 'Irenaeus on Creation and Salvation,' in *Creation and Salvation*, ed. Ernst Conradie (Zurich: Lit Verlag, 2012), 34.

772   Hall, *Imaging God,* 200.

773   Conradie, *An Ecological Christian Anthropology,* 135.

774   Walter Brueggemann, 'The Creatures Know,' in *The Wisdom of Creation* ed. Edward Foley and Robert Schreiter (Collegeville, Minn.: Liturgical Press, 2004), 1-12.

775   Bauckham, *Bible and Ecology,* 89.

776   Taylor, *Enough is Enough.*

777   Ibid., 41.

778   Ibid., 42.

779   Brueggemann, *Journey to the Common Good*, 108.

780   Sachs, *Common Wealth*, 57.

781   Jackson, *Prosperity Without Growth*, 14-15.

782 Sharyn Munro, *Rich Land, Wasteland: How Coal is Killing Australia* (Sydney: Pan Macmillan, 2012).

783 Anglican Communion Environment Network. *Crisis and Commitment: Final Report, Lima Statement and Action Plan, The Anglican Communion Environment Network Meeting, Lima, Peru, 4 to 10 August 2011.* 2012. http://acen.anglicancommunion.org/resources/docs/peru/ACEN%20Peru%20report%20final%20rev.pdf (accessed 17 August 2013).

784 Mackay, *The Good Life.*

785 Jackson, *Prosperity Without Growth*, 143.

786 David Bosch, *Transforming Mission: Paradigm Shifts in Theology of Mission* (New York: Orbis Books, 1991), 362.

787 Bernardi, *The Conservative Revolution*, 60.

788 'With its rest and rhythm of time, the sabbath is also the strategy which will take us out of ecological crisis and after one sided progress at the expense of others show us the value of abiding equilibrium and accord with nature'. Moltmann, *Creating a Just Future*, 66.

789 *The Lambeth Conference 1958* Page 1 of the Report The Holy Bible, its Authority and Message.

790 Lambeth Conference. *Resolutions of the Twelve Lambeth Conferences, 1867–1988*, 13.

791 Ibid., 18.

792 Ibid., 24.

793 Ibid., 27.

794 Ibid., 36.

795 Ibid., 36.

796 Ibid., 36.

797 Ibid., 37.

798 Ibid., 45-48.

799 Ibid., 66.

800 Ibid., 66.

801 Ibid., 67.

802 Ibid., 91.

803 Ibid., 92.

804   Ibid., 99.

805   Ibid., 122.

806   Ibid., 152.

807   Ibid., 153.

808   Ibid., 153.

809   Ibid., 171.

810   Ibid., 174.

811   Ibid., 176-178.

812   Ibid., 216.

813   Ibid., 219.

814   *The Official Report of the Lambeth Conference 1998*, 378-380.

815   Ibid., 380-381.

816   Stephenson, *The First Lambeth Conference, 1867*, 36.

817   Act 25 Henry VIII gave the crown control over all ecclesiastical assemblies, so that diocesan synods became a thing of the past and the provincial synods of Canterbury and York met only at the pleasure of the Crown. Stephenson, *The First Lambeth Conference, 1867*, 27.

818   Von Rad became a well known proponent of source criticism which proposed four major literary sources to the Pentateuch, J.E.P and D.

819   James, 'Resolving to confer and conferring to resolve,' 69.

820   English Theologian and Christian Socialist 1805 -1872.

821   *Essays and Reviews* (London: John W. Parker and Son, 1860).

822   Stephenson, *The First Lambeth Conference, 1867*, 115-118.

823   Stephenson, *The First Lambeth Conference, 1867*, 116.

824   Dean Arthur Stanley was Dean of Westminster. Rowland E. Prothero, *The Life and Correspondence of Arthur Penrhyn Stanley, D.D., Late Dean of Westminster, vol.11.* 3rd ed. (London: John Murray, 1894), 44.

825   The Colenso dispute and its impact upon the developing Anglican Communion is well told by Stephenson, *The First Lambeth Conference 1867*.

826   Charles Gray, *Life of Robert Gray, Bishop of Cape Town and Metropolitan of Africa, vol II* (London: Rivingtons, 1876), 586.

827   Stephenson, *The First Lambeth Conference, 1867*, 209.

828   Ibid., 191.

REFERENCES

Ainger, Arthur Campbell. 'Hymn 548.' In *The English Hymnal*, 710. London: Oxford University Press, 1960.

Albertz, Rainer. *A History of Israelite Religion in the Old Testament Period*. Louisville: Westminster/John Knox Press, 1994.

Alison, James. *Knowing Jesus*. London: SPCK, 1993.

Anglican Church of Australia. *The Constitution Canons and Rules of Anglican Church of Australia 2010*. Mulgrave, Victoria: Broughton Publishing, 2011.

Anglican Church of Australia Public Affairs Commission. *Issues and Questions for the 2013 Federal Election Process*. 2013. http://www.anglican. org.au/docs/commissions/public_affairs/Issues and Questions for the 2013 Federal Election Process.pdf (accessed 21 November 2013).

Anglican Communion. *Mission—the Five Marks of Mission* http://www. anglicancommunion.org/ministry/mission/fivemarks.cfm (accessed 12 February 2014)

Anglican Communion Environment Network. *Crisis and Commitment: Final Report, Lima Statement and Action Plan, The Anglican Communion*

Environment Network Meeting, Lima, Peru, 4 to 10 August 2011. 2012. http://acen.anglicancommunion.org/resources/docs/peru/ACEN%20 Peru%20report%20final%20rev.pdf (accessed 17 August 2013).

Anstey, Matthew. *Four Sermons on Genesis 1.* (unpublished manuscript, 2006).

Atkinson, David. *Renewing the Face of the Earth: A Theological and Pastoral Response to Climate Change.* Norwich: Canterbury Press, 2008.

Attridge, Harold. *The Epistle to the Hebrews: A Critical Commentary on the Epistle to the Hebrews.* Philadelphia: Fortress Press, 1989.

Australian Christian Lobby [website], http://www.acl.org.au/ (accessed 3 December 2013).

Avis, Paul. 'What is Anglicanism.' In *The Study of Anglicanism,* edited by Stephen Sykes and John Booty, 405-423. London: SPCK, 1988.

Balabanski, Vicki. 'Hellenistic Cosmology and the Letter to the Colossians: Towards an Ecological Hermeneutic.' In *Ecological Hermeneutics: Biblical, Historical, and Theological Perspectives,* edited by David Horrell, Cherryl Hunt, Christopher Southgate, and Francesca Stavrakopoulou, 94-107. London: T & T Clark, 2010.

Balthasar, Hans Urs von. *Mysterium Paschale.* Edinburgh: T&T Clark, 1990.

Barker, Margaret. *Creation: A Biblical Vision for the Environment.* London: T&T Clark International, 2010.

Barker, Paul A. 'Sabbath, sabbatical year, jubilee.' In *Dictionary of the Old Testament: Pentateuch,* edited by David Baker and T. Desmond Alexander, 695-706. Downers Grove, Ill.: InterVarsity Press, 2003.

Barrett, C.K. *A Commentary on the First Epistle to the Corinthians.* London: Adam and Charles Black, 1968.

Barth, Karl. *Church Dogmatics, vol.3: The Doctrine of Creation.* London: T & T Clark, 2009.

Bauckham, Richard. *Bible and Ecology: Rediscovering the Community of Creation.* London: Darton, Longman & Todd, 2010.

Bauckham, Richard. *Ecological Hope in Crisis?* http://www.jri.org.uk/wp/wp-content/uploads/JRI_23_Hope_Bauckham.pdf (accessed 19 March 2013).

Bergmann, Sigurd. 'Now the Spirit Dwells Amongst us ...: The Spirit as Liberator of Nature in the Trinitarian Cosmology of Gregory of Nazianz.' In *Creation and Salvation,* edited by Ernst Conradie, 53-73. Zurich: Lit Verlag, 2012.

Bernardi, Cori. *The Conservative Revolution.* Ballarat: Connor Court Publishing, 2013.

Berry, Thomas. *The Dream of the Earth.* San Francisco: Sierra Club, 1998.

Berry, Wendell. *The Art of the Commonplace: The Agrarian Essays of Wendell Berry.* Berkeley, Ca: Counterpoint, 2002.

Berry, Wendell. *Home Economics.* San Francisco: North Point Press, 1987.

Berry, Wendell. *Sex, Economy, Freedom and Community.* New York: Pantheon, 1992.

Berry, Wendell. *Two Economies. 2005.* http://www.worldwisdom.com/public/viewpdf/default.aspx?article-title=Two_Economies_by_Wendell_Berry.pdf (accessed 4 October 2012).

Bicknell, E.J. *A Theological Introduction to the Thirty-Nine Articles of the Church of England.* London: Longmans, 1961.

Bloch, Ernst. *The Principle of Hope.* Cambridge: MIT Press, 1986.

Boff, Leonardo and Virgil Elizondo. *Ecology and Poverty: Cry of the Earth, Cry of the Poor.* Maryknoll, NY: Orbis Books, 1997.

Bonds of Affection: proceedings of ACC-6, Badagry, Nigeria, 1984. London: Anglican Consultative Council, 1985.

Bonhoeffer, Dietrich. *Ethics.* London: Collins Fontana, 1964.

Bosch, David J. *Transforming Mission: Paradigm Shifts in Theology of Mission.* New York: Orbis Books, 1991.

Bouma-Prediger, Steven. *For the Beauty of the Earth: A Christian Vision for Creation Care.* Grand Rapids: Baker Academic, 2010.

Brett, Gregory. 'A Timely Reminder: Humanity and Ecology in the Light of Christian Hope.' In *Earth Revealing—Earth Healing: Ecology and Christian Theology,* edited by Denis Edwards, 159-176. Collegeville, Minn.: Liturgical Press, 2001.

Brock, Brian. *Christian Ethics in a Technological Age.* Grand Rapids, Mich.: William B. Eerdmans, 2010.

Brown, Raymond. *The Gospel According to John.* Garden City, New York: Doubleday, 1996.

Browning, Elizabeth Barrett. *Aurora Leigh.* 1864. http://digital.library.upenn.edu/women/barrett/aurora/aurora.html (accessed 23 November 2013).

Brueggemann, Walter. 'The Creatures Know.' In *The Wisdom of Creation,* edited by Edward Foley and Robert Schreiter, 1-12. Collegeville, Minn.: Liturgical Press, 2004.

Brueggemann, Walter. 'Editors Foreword.' In *Jesus, Liberation and the Biblical Jubilee: Images for Ethics and Christology,* by Sharon H. Ringe, ix-xi. Philadelphia: Fortress Press, 1985.

Brueggemann, Walter. *Journey to the Common Good.* (Louisville, Ky: Westminster John Knox Press, 2010.

Brueggemann, Walter. 'The Liturgy of Abundance, the Myth of Scarcity.' *Christian Century* 24-31 March 1999. http://www.religion-online.org/showarticle.asp?title=533 (accessed 3 September 2010).

Brueggemann, Walter. *Theology of the Old Testament: Testimony, Dispute, Advocacy.* Minneapolis: Fortress Press, 1997.

Brueggemann, Walter. *The Word that Redescribes the World: The Bible and Discipleship.* Minneapolis: Fortress Press, 2006.

Bruning, Miriam. 'A Theology of the Common Good: What has Endured?' B.A. Hons. Thesis, Charles Sturt University, 2012.

Brunner, Emil. *The Christian Doctrine of Creation and Redemption.* London: Lutterworth Press, 1952.

Burke, Edmund. *Reflections on the French Revolution.* London: JM Dent, 1935.

Busch, Eberhard. *Karl Barth: His Life from Letters and Autobiographical Texts.* London: SCM Press, 1976.

Cameron, Andrew J.B. 'Is Growth Good? Toward a Christian Ethical Interrogation of a Dominant Paradigm,' *St Mark's Review* 214 (November 2010), 15-32.

Capon, Robert Farrar. *Genesis the Movie.* Grand Rapids: William B. Eerdmans, 2003.

Carnegie, Andrew. *The Gospel of Wealth and Other Timely Essays.* New York: The Century Co., 1900. https://archive.org/stream/cu31924001214539 (accessed 23 November 2013).

Carpenter, James. *Gore: A Study in Liberal Catholic Thought.* London: Faith Press, 1960.

Carroll, Lewis. *Alice's Adventures in Wonderland.* London: Macmillan, 1872.

Cary Institute of Ecosystem Studies. *Definition of Ecology*, http://www. caryinstitute.org/discover-ecology/definition-ecology (accessed 10 November 2013).

Cassuto, Umberto. *From Adam to Noah*. Jerusalem: Magnes Press The Hebrew University, 1961.

Chambers Dictionary of Etymology. New York: Chambers Harrap Publishers, 1988.

Chapman, Mark D. *Anglican Theology*. London: T&T Clark, 2012.

Chapman, Mark D. 'Charles Gore, Kenosis and the Crisis of Power.' *Journal of Anglican Studies* 3 (November 2005): 197-218.

Church of England Mission and Public Affairs Council. *Sharing God's Planet: A Christian Vision for a Sustainable Future*. London: Church House Publishing, 2005.

Coakley, Sarah. 'Kenosis: Theological Meanings and Gender Connotations.' In *The Work of Love: Creation as Kenosis*, edited by John Polkinghorne, 192 -210. London: SPCK, 2001.

Coakley, Sarah. *Powers and Submissions: Spirituality, Philosophy and Gender.* Oxford: Blackwell Publishers, 2002.

'The Common Good.' http://www.scu.edu/ethics/practicing/decision/ commongood.html (accessed 6 September 2013).

Conference of Bishops of the Anglican Communion 1897, Holden at Lambeth Palace, in July, 1897: Encyclical Letter from the Bishops, with the Resolutions and Reports. London: SPCK, 1897.

Conference of Bishops of the Anglican Communion: Encyclical Letter from the Bishops with the Resolutions and Reports 1908. Brighton: SPCK, 1908.

Conference of the Bishops of the Anglican Communion 1920: Encyclical Letter from the Bishops with the Resolutions and Reports. New York: SPCK, 1920.

Conradie, E.M. *An Ecological Christian Anthropology: At Home on Earth?* Aldershot: Ashgate, 2005.

Crossan, John Dominic. 'Jesus and the Challenge of Collaborative Eschatology.' In *The Historical Jesus: Five Views,* edited by James K. Beilby and Paul Rhodes Eddy, 105-132. Downers Grove, Ill.: IVP Academic, 2009.

Crüsemann, Frank. *The Torah: Theology and Social History of Old Testament Law.* Edinburgh: T & T Clark, 1996.

Crutzen, Paul J. and Eugene F. Stoermer. 'The 'Anthropocene'', *Global Change Newsletter,* no.41, May, 2000: 17-18, http://www.igbp.net/ download/18.316f18321323470177580001401/NL41.pdf (accessed 16 November 2011).

Davidson, Randall T, ed. *The Lambeth Conferences of 1867, 1878 and 1888: With the Official Reports and Resolutions together with the Sermons Preached at the Conferences.* London: SPCK, 1889.

Deep Engagement, Fresh Discovery: Report of the Anglican Communion 'Bible in the Life of the Church' Project. 2012, http://www.anglicancommunion. org/communion/acc/meetings/acc15/downloads/bible_in_the_life_ of_the_church.pdf (accessed 23 November 2013).

Dewey, Margaret. 'Dominant Influences in the Current World.' In *Today's Church and Today's World: The Lambeth Conference 1978 Preparatory Articles,* 46-55. London: CIO Publishing, 1977.

Dodd, C.H. *The Coming of Christ: Four Broadcast Addresses for the Season of Advent.* Cambridge: Cambridge University Press, 1951.

Dodd, C.H. *The Parables of the Kingdom.* Glasgow: Fount, 1978.

Dunham, Scott A. 'Creaturely Salvation in Augustine.' In *Creation and*

Salvation, edited by Ernst Conradie, 75-91. Zurich: Lit Verlag, 2012.

'Earth Overshoot Day was August 22, and Yes, We're Still in Overshoot', *Footprint Network News,* issue 30, 3 October, 2012. http://www. footprintnetwork.org/en/index.php/newsletter/det/earth_overshoot_ day_was_august_22_and_yes_were_still_in_overshoot (accessed 15 October 2012).

Edwards, Denis. *Jesus the Wisdom of God: An Ecological Theology.* Sydney: St Pauls, 1995.

Eliot, T.S. *Four Quartets.* London: Faber & Faber, 1959.

Ellis, George F.R. 'Kenosis as a Unifying Theme for Life and Cosmology.' In *The Work of Love: Creation as Kenosis,* edited by John Polkinghorne, 107-126. London: SPCK, 2001.

Elphinstone, Andrew. *Freedom, Suffering and Love.* London: SCM Press, 1976.

Essays and Reviews. London: John W. Parker and Son, 1860.

Extreme Weather and Climate Change in the American Mind, September 2012 http://environment.yale.edu/climate-communication/files/ Extreme-Weather-Public-Opinion-September-2012.pdf (accessed 23 May 2014).

Fishbane, Michael. *Biblical Text and Texture: A Literary Reading of Selected Texts.* Oxford: Oneworld, 1998.

Flannery, Tim. *Beautiful Lies: Population and Environment in Australia.* Melbourne: Schwartz Publishing, 2003.

Flannery, Tim. *We are the Weather Makers: the Story of Global Warming.* Melbourne: Text Publishing, 2006.

Flavin, Christopher. 'The Legacy of Rio.' In *State of the World 1997,* edited by Linda Starke, 3-22. New York: Norton, 1997.

French, William. 'Grace is Everywhere: Thomas Aquinas on Creation and Salvation.' In *Creation and Salvation,* edited by Ernst Conradie, 147-172. Zurich: Lit Verlag, 2012.

Fretheim, Terence E. *Genesis.* In *New interpreter's Bible.* New York: Abingdon Press, 1994.

Gesenius, Wilhelm. *A Hebrew and English Lexicon of the Old Testament.* Oxford: Clarendon Press, 1959.

Gilding, Paul. *The Great Disruption: How the Climate Crisis will Transform the Global Economy (for the Better).* London: Bloomsbury, 2011.

Gore, Charles. *Christ and Society.* London: Allen & Unwin, c.1928.

Gore, Charles. *Christian Moral Principles: Seven Sermons Preached in Grosvenor Chapel as a Lenten Course in 1921.* London: Mowbray, 1921.

Gore, Charles. *The Incarnation of the Son of God: Being the Bampton Lectures for the year 1891.* 2nd ed. London: John Murray, 1892.

Gore, Charles. *St. Paul's Epistle to the Ephesians: A Practical Exposition.* London: Murray, 1898.

Gore, Charles. *The Sermon on the Mount: A Practical Exposition.* 2nd ed. London: Murray, 1910.

Gore, Charles. *The Social Doctrine of the Sermon on the Mount.* London: Percival, 1892.

Gorringe, Timothy. *Idolatry and Redemption: Economics in Biblical Perspective.* 2013. http://www.operationnoah.org/sites/default/files/Idolatry%20&%20Redemption%20T.Gorringe%20Mar2013_0.pdf (accessed 23 November 2013).

Gorringe, Timothy. 'Keeping the Commandments: The Meaning of

Sustainable Countryside.' In *Ecological Hermeneutics: Biblical, Historical, and Theological Perspectives*, edited by David Horrell, Cherryl Hunt, Christopher Southgate, and Francesca Stavrakopoulou, 283-294. London: T & T Clark, 2010.

Gray, Charles. *Life of Robert Gray, Bishop of Cape Town and Metropolitan of Africa, vol.11*. London: Rivingtons, 1876.

Gregory, Brad. *The Unintended Reformation: How a Religious Revolution Secularized Society,* Cambridge, Massachusetts: Harvard University Press, 2012.

Guelich, Robert A. *Mark 1:8-26*. Dallas: Word Books, 1989.

Gunton, Colin. 'Salvation.' In *The Cambridge Companion to Karl Barth,* edited by John Webster, 143-158. Cambridge: Cambridge University Press, 2000.

Gunton, Colin E. *The Triune Creator.* Grand Rapids: Eerdmans, 1998.

Gutenson, Charles E. *Christians and the Common Good: How Faith Intersects with Public Life.* Grand Rapids: Brazos Press, 2011.

Gutiérrez, Gustavo. *A Theology of Liberation: History Politics and Salvation.* rev.ed. Maryknoll, N.Y: Orbis, 1988.

Habel, Norman and Trudinger, Peter. Eds 'Introducing Ecolgical Hermeneutics', *Exploring Ecological Hermeneutics.* Atlanta: Society of Biblical Literature, 2008.

Haenchen, Ernst. *John: A Commentary on the Gospel of John.* Philadelphia: Fortress Press, 1984.

Hall, Douglas John. *Imaging God: Dominion as Stewardship.* Grand Rapids: Eerdmans, 1986.

Hamilton, Victor P. *The Book of Genesis, Chapters 1-17.* Grand Rapids:

William B. Eerdmans, 1990.

Hansen, James. *Storms of My Grandchildren: The Truth about the Coming Climate Catastrophe and Our Last Chance to Save Humanity*. London: Bloomsbury, 2009.

Hardy, Daniel W. 'Created and Redeemed Sociality.' In *On being the Church: Essays on the Christian Community*, edited by Colin E. Gunston and Daniel W. Hardy, 21-47. Edinburgh: T&T Clark, 1989.

Harrelson, W.J. 'Blessings and Cursings.' In *The Interpreters Dictionary of the Bible, vol.1*, 446448. New York: Abingdon Press, 1962.

Hart, John W. *Karl Barth vs Emil Brunner: The Formation and Dissolution of a Theological Alliance, 1916–1936*. New York: Peter Lang, 2001.

Haught, John F. *The Promise of Nature: Ecology and Cosmic Purpose*. New York: Paulist Press, 1993.

Heffernan, Margaret. *A Bigger Prize*. London: Simon and Schuster, 2014.

Heidel, Alexander. *The Babylonian Genesis: The Story of the Creation*. Chicago: University of Chicago Press, 1951.

Heinberg, Richard. *The End of Growth: Adapting to Our New Economic Reality*. Gabriola Island: New Society Publishers, 2011.

Heron, Alasdair I.C. *A Century of Protestant Theology*. Guildford: Lutterworth Press, 1980.

Heschel, Abraham Joshua. *The Sabbath, its Meaning for Modern Man*. New York: Farrar Strauss and Giroux, 2005.

Heyde, Beth. 'Care for Creation: Population and Environment.' *St Mark's Review* 214 (November, 2010), 40-52.

Hinson-Hasty, Elizabeth. *As Any Might Have Need: Envisioning Communities of Shared Partnership*. 2011. http://www.kairoscanada.

org/wp-content/uploads/2011/11/SUS-CJ-11-10-Hinson-Hasty.pdf (accessed 17 November 2011).

Hollenbach, David. *The Common Good and Christian Ethics.* Cambridge: Cambridge University Press, 2002.

Houghton, John. *Global Warming.* 4th ed. Cambridge: Cambridge University Press, 2009.

How Big is a House? Average House Size by Country. http://shrinkthatfootprint.com/how-big-is-a-house (accessed 23 May 2014).

Inter-Anglican Theological and Doctrinal Commission. *Report.* London: Anglican Consultative Council, 1997.

Intergovernmental Panel on Climate Change. *Climate Change 2013: The Physical Science Basis: Summary for Policymakers.* 2013. https://www.ipcc.ch/report/ar5/wg1/docs/review/WG1AR5-SPM_FOD_Final.pdf (accessed 30 April 2014).

Interpreter's Dictionary of the Bible. New York: Abingdon Press, 1962-1976.

Jackson, Tim. *Prosperity Without Growth: Economics for a Finite Planet.* London: Earthscan, 2009.

James, Graham. 'Resolving to Confer and Conferring to Resolve: the Anglican Way.' In *A Fallible Church: Lambeth Essays,* edited by Kenneth Stevenson, 65-85. London: Darton, Longman and Todd, 2008.

Jeeves, Malcolm. 'The Nature of Persons and the Emergence of Kenotic Behaviour.' In *The Work of Love: Creation as Kenosis,* edited by John Polkinghorne, 66-89. London: SPCK, 2001.

Jenkins, David. *The Glory of Man: Bampton Lectures for 1966.* Bristol: SCM, 1967.

Jenkins, David. *The Humanum Studies 1969–1975.* Geneva: World Council of Churches, 1975.

Kaoma, Kapya J. *God's Family, God's Earth: Christian Ecological Ethics of Ubuntu.* Zomba, Malawi: Kachere, 2013.

Käsemann, Ernst. *Exegetische Versuche und Besinnungen: Erste Band.* Göttingen, Vandenhoeck und Ruprecht, 1960.

Kennedy, John F. *Address Before the Irish Parliament in Dublin, June 28 1963,* http://www.jfklibrary.org/Asset-Viewer/lPAi7jx2s0i7kePPdJnUXA.aspx (accessed 30 April 2014).

Keys, Mary M. *Aquinas, Aristotle and the Promise of the Common Good.* Cambridge: Cambridge University Press, 2006.

Kitagawa, Daisuke. 'Faith and Society.' In *Lambeth Essays on Faith*, edited by Michael Ramsey, 75-101. London: SPCK, 1969.

Koyama, Kosuke. 'Traditional Cultures and Technology.' In *Today's Church and Today's World: The Lambeth Conference 1978 Preparatory Articles*, 64-72. London: CIO Publishing, 1977.

Lambeth Conference 1948: The Encyclical Letter from the Bishops together with Resolutions and Reports. London: SPCK 1948.

The Lambeth Conference 1958: The Encyclical Letter from the Bishops together with the Resolutions and Reports. London: SPCK, 1958.

Lambeth Conference 1968: Preparatory Information. London: SPCK, 1968.

Lambeth Conference 1968: Resolutions and Reports. London: SPCK, 1968.

Lambeth Conference. *The Lambeth Conferences 1867–1930: The Reports of the 1920 and 1930 Conferences, with Selected Resolutions from the Conferences of 1867, 1878, 1888, 1897, and 1908.* London: SPCK, 1948..

Lambeth Conference. *The Lambeth Conferences (1867–1948): The Reports of the 1920, 1930 and 1948 Conferences, with Selected Resolutions from the Conferences of 1867, 1878, 1888, 1897 and 1908.* London: SPCK, 1948.

Lambeth Conference. *Resolutions of the Twelve Lambeth Conferences,*

1867–1988. Toronto: Anglican Book Centre, 1992.

Lambeth Indaba: Capturing Conversations and Reflections from the Lambeth Conference 2008, http://www.lambethconference.org/vault/Reflections_Document_(final).pdf (accessed 25 May 2014).

Larkin, Amy. *Environmental Debt: The Hidden Costs of the Changing Global Economy.* New York: Palgrave Macmillan, 2013.

Lawrence (Brother). *The Practice of the Presence of God.* Seaside, Oregon: Rough Draft Printing, 2009.

Lightfoot, J.B. *St Paul's Epistles to the Colossians and Philemon.* New York: Macmillan, 1879.

Logan, Patrick. *Biblical Reflections on the Political Economy of Jubilee.* London: Diocese of Southwark, 1997.

Lohse, Eduard. *Colossians and Philemon: A Commentary on the Epistles to the Colossians and to Philemon.* Philadelphia: Fortress Press, 1982.

Lohse, Eduard. 'σάββατον.' In *Theological Dictionary of the New Testament, vol.vii,* edited by Gerhard Friedrich, 1-35. Grand Rapids: Eerdmans, 1971.

Lorenzen, Thorwald. *Resurrection and Discipleship: Interpretive Models, Biblical Reflections, Theological Consequences.* Maryknoll, N. Y.: Orbis Books, 1995.

Lovelock, James. *The Revenge of Gaia: Why the Earth is Fighting Back—and How We Can Still Save Humanity.* London: Allen Lane, 2006.

Lovelock, James. *The Vanishing Face of Gaia; A Final Warning.* London: Allan Lane, 2009.

Lowery, Richard H. *Sabbath and Jubilee.* St Louis: Chalice Press, 2000.

McFague, Sallie. *The Body of God: An Ecological Theology.* London: SCM Press, 1993.

McGrath, Alister. *Science and Religion: A New Introduction.* London: Wiley

Blackwell, 2009.

McGrath, Alister. *Surprised by Meaning: Science, Faith and How We Make Sense of Things*. Louisville, Kentucky: Westminster, John Knox Press, 2011

MacIntyre, Alasdair. *After Virtue: A Study in Moral Theory*, 2nd ed. Indiana: University of Notre Dame Press, 1984.

McKay, Heather. *Sabbath and Synagogue: The Question of Sabbath Worship in Ancient Judaism*. Leiden: Brill, 1994.

Mackay, Hugh. *The Good Life*. Sydney: Macmillan, 2013.

Macquarrie, John. 'Kenoticism Reconsidered.' *Theology* 77 (March 1974), 115-124.

Maier, Pauline. *American Scripture: Making the Declaration of Independence*. New York: Vintage, 1998.

Malik, Tariq. *Planet Earth a Fragile Oasis, Astronauts Say*. 2009. http://www.space.com/6603-planet-earth-fragile-oasis-astronauts.html (accessed 23 November 2013).

Malthus, Thomas. *An Essay on the Principle of Population as it Affects the Future Improvement of Society*. London: Printed for J. Johnson, 1798.

Marshall, Michael. *Church at the Crossroads: Lambeth 1988*. London: Collins, 1988.

Martini, Bruno. *'Anthropocene' Period Would Recognize Humanity's Impact on Earth'* http://www.space.com/21916-anthropocene-period-humanity-effect-earth.html (accessed 17 September 2013).

Maurice, Frederick Denison. *Theological Essays*. London: James Clarke, 1957.

Meier, John P. *A Marginal Jew: Rethinking the Historical Jesus, vol.4: Law and Love*. New Haven: Yale University Press, 2009.

Middleton, J. Richard. *The Liberating Image: The Imago Dei in Genesis 1*.

Grand Rapids: Brazos Press, 2005.

Milgrom, Jacob. 'Holy, Holiness, NT.' In *New Interpreter's Dictionary of the Bible, vol.2,* 847-858. Nashville, Tenn.: Abingdon Press, 2007.

Miller, Patrick D. *Deuteronomy.* Louisville: J. Knox Press, 1990.

Moltmann, Jürgen. *Creating a Just Future: The Politics of Peace and the Ethics of Creation in a Threatened World.* London: SCM Press, 1989.

Moltmann, Jürgen. 'Creation and Redemption' In *Creation, Christ and Culture,* edited by Richard W.A. McKinney, 119-134. Edinburgh: T&T Clark, 1976.

Moltmann, Jürgen. *Ethics of Hope.* Minneapolis: Fortress Press, 2012.

Moltmann, Jürgen. *God in Creation: An Ecological Doctrine of Creation: the Gifford Lectures 1984-1985.* London: SCM Press, 1985.

Moltmann, Jürgen. 'God's Kenosis in the Creation and Consummation of the World.' In *The Work of Love: Creation as Kenosis,* edited by John Polkinghorne, 137-151. London: SPCK, 2001.

Moltmann, Jürgen. *Theology of Hope: On the Ground and the Implications of a Christian Eschatology.* London: SCM Press, 1967.

Montefiore, Hugh. *A Commentary on the Epistle to the Hebrews.* London: A & C Black, 1964.

Montefiore, Hugh. 'Nationalism and Internationalism.' In *Today's Church and Today's World: The Lambeth Conference 1978 Preparatory Articles,* 88-94. London: CIO Publishing, 1977.

Morgan, Dewi. *Lambeth Speaks.* London: Mowbray, 1958.

Morgenstern, J. 'Sabbath,' In *The Interpreters Dictionary of the Bible, vol.4,* 135-141. New York: Abingdon Press 1962.

Moule, C.F.D. 'Further Reflections on Philippians 2: 5-11.' In *Apostolic History and the Gospel,* edited by W. Ward Gasque and Ralph P. Martin,

264-276. Grand Rapids: Eerdmans, 1970.

Munro, Sharyn. *Rich Land, Wasteland: How Coal is Killing Australia.* Sydney: Pan Macmillan, 2012.

Murphy, Charles. *At Home on Earth: Foundations for a Catholic Ethic of the Environment.* New York: Crossroads, 1989.

Myers, Benjamin. *Christ the Stranger: The Theology of Rowan Williams.* London: T & T Clark, 2012.

Neuhaus, Richard John. *The Naked Public Square: Religion and Democracy in America.* Grand Rapids: Eerdmans, 1984.

New International Dictionary of Old Testament Theology and Exegesis. Grand Rapids, Zondervan, 1997.

Newbigin, Lesslie. *Foolishness to the Greeks: the Gospel and Western Culture.* London: SPCK, 1986.

Newbigin, Lesslie. *The Open Secret: An Introduction to the Theology of Mission.* Grand Rapids: Eerdmanns, 1995.

Newlands, George. *Generosity and the Christian Future.* London: SPCK Publishing, 1997.

'The Nicene Creed.' In *A Prayer Book for Australia,* 123. Sydney: Broughton Books, 1995.

Nolland, John. *Luke, vol.1: Luke 1–9:20.* Waco: Word Books, 1989.

Northcott, Michael S. *The Environment and Christian Ethics.* Cambridge: Cambridge University Press, 1996.

Northcott, Michael S. *A Moral Climate: The Ethics of Global Warming.* London: Darton, Longman and Todd, 2007.

O'Connor, Kathleen. *The Wisdom Literature.* Wilmington, Delaware: Liturgical Press, 1993.

O'Connor, Mark and William J. Lines. *Overloading Australia: How Governments and Media Dither and Deny on Population.* Canterbury, NSW: Envirobook, 2008.

The Official Report of the Lambeth Conference 1998: Transformation and Renewal. Harrisburg, Pa: Moorehouse Publishing, 1999.

Olsen, Glenn W. *The Turn to Transcendence: The Role of Religion in the Twenty-First Century.* Washington, D.C.: Catholic University of America Press, 2010.

Open for Business, Q&A, 11 November 2013 http://www.abc.net.au/tv/qanda/txt/s3873461.htm (accessed 23 May 2014).

Oreskes, Naomi and Erik M. Conway. *Merchants of Doubt: How a Handful of Scientists Obscured the Truth on Issues from Tobacco Smoke to Global Warming.* New York: Bloomsbury Press, 2010.

Orsuto, Donna. *Holiness.* London: Continuum, 2006.

'Orthodox Perspectives on Creation: Report of the WCC Inter-Orthodox Consultation, Sofia, Bulgaria October 1987 (extracts)'. http://www.goarch.org/ourfaith/ourfaith8050 (accessed 19 November 2013).

Otto, Rudolf. *The Idea of the Holy: An Inquiry into the Non-rational Factor in the Idea of the Divine and its Relation to the Rational.* 2nd ed. New York: Oxford University Press, 1950.

Pascal, Blaise. *Pascal's Pensées,* translated by W.F. Trotter. London: Dent, 1932.

Passmore, John. *Man's Responsibility for Nature: Ecological Problems and Western Traditions.* London: Duckworth, 1974.

Peacock, Matt. *Liberal Party Member John Ruddick Threatened With Suspension After Reform Push,* http://abc.net.au/news/2013-10-03-liberal-john-ruddick-threatened-with-suspension/4997440 (accessed 5 October 2013).

Peterson, Anna L. *Being Human: Ethics, Environment and Our Place in the World.* Berkeley: University of California Press, 2001.

Pickard, Stephen. *Seeking the Church: An Introduction to Ecclesiology.* London: SCM, 2012.

Polkinghorne, John. 'Bridging the Divide'. *Encounter (radio program)*, 18 September 2011, http://www.abc.net.au/rn/encounter/ stories/2011/3316531.htm (accessed 13 November 2011).

Polkinghorne, John, ed. *The Work of Love: Creation as Kenosis.* London: SPCK, 2001.

A Prayer Book for Australia. Netley, South Australia: Broughton Books, 1995.

Primates' Meetings, http://www.anglicancommunion.org/communion/ primates/index.cfm (accessed 4 February 2014).

Prothero, Rowland E. *The Life and Correspondence of Arthur Penrhyn Stanley, D.D., Late Dean of Westminster, vol.11.* 3rd ed. London: John Murray, 1894.

Rad, Gerhard von. *Genesis: A Commentary.* London: SCM Press, 1972.

Rahner, Karl. *Foundations of Christian Faith: An Introduction to the Idea of Christianity.* New York: Seabury Press, 1978.

Ramsey, Michael. *The Gospel and the Catholic Church,* 2nd ed. London: Longmans, 1956.

Rasmussen, Larry. 'Theology of Life and Ecumenical Ethics.' In *Ecotheology: Voices from South and North,* edited by David G. Hallman, 112-129. Geneva: WCC Publications, 1994.

Raven, Charles. *Looking Forward (Towards 1940).* London: James Nisbet, 1931.

The Report of the Lambeth Conference 1978. London: CIO Publishing, 1978.

Resolutions and Reports [of the] Lambeth Conference 1968. London: SPCK. 1968.

Ricoeur, Paul. *The Conflict of Interpretations: Essays in Hermeneutics.* Evanston, Ill.: Northwestern University Press, 1974.

Ricoeur, Paul. *The Symbolism of Evil.* New York: Harper and Row, 1967.

Ringe, Sharon H. *Jesus, Liberation and Biblical Jubilee: Images for Ethics and Christology.* Philadelphia: Fortress Press, 1985.

Ringwald, Christopher D. *A Day Apart: How Jews, Christians, and Muslims Find Faith, Freedom, and Joy on the Sabbath.* New York: Oxford University Press, 2007.

Rise, Svein. 'Irenaeus on Creation and Salvation.' In *Creation and Salvation,* edited by Ernst Conradie, 21-35. Zurich: Lit Verlag, 2012.

Robinson, Gnana. *The Origin and Development of the Old Testament Sabbath: A Comprehensive Exegetical Approach.* Frankfurt am Main: Peter Lang, 1988.

Rolston, Holmes. *Kenosis and Nature* In *The Work of Love: Creation as Kenosis,* edited by John Polkinghorne. London: SPCK, 2001.

Rudd, Kevin. *Address to the 64th Session of the United Nations General Assembly 23 September 2009,* http://www.smh.com.au/opinion/politics/rudd-speech-to-the-united-nations-20090924-g3nn.html (accessed 15 October 2012).

Runcie, Robert A.K. *Authority in Crisis: An Anglican Response.* London: SCM, 1988.

Sachs, Jeffrey. *Common Wealth: Economics for a Crowded Planet.* London: Penguin, 2008.

Sachs, Jeffrey. *The Price of Civilization: Economics and Ethics after the Fall.* London: Random House, 2011.

Sachs, William. *The Transformation of Anglicanism: From State Church to Global Communion.* Cambridge: Cambridge University Press, 1993.

Sacks, Jonathan. *The Home We Build Together: Recreating Society.* London: Continuum, 2007.

Samuel, Vinay and Christopher Sugden. *Lambeth: A View from the Two-Thirds World.* London: SPCK, 1989.

Sandel, Michael J. *What Money Can't Buy: the Moral Limits of Markets.* London: Allen Lane, 2012.

Sarna, Nahum N. *Genesis.* Philadelphia: Jewish Publication Society, 1989.

Schuele, Andreas. 'Sabbath.'. In *The New Interpreter's Dictionary of the Bible,* *vol.5,* 1-13. Nashville, Tenn.: Abingdon Press, 2009.

Schumacher, Ernst. *Small is Beautiful: Economics as if People Mattered.* London: Blond & Biggs, 1973.

Schwarz, Hans. *Theology in a Global Context: The Last Two Hundred Years.* Grand Rapids: Eerdmans, 2005.

Schweizer, Eduard. *The Good News According to Luke.* Atlanta: John Knox Press, 1973.

Schweizer, Eduard. *The Good News According to Mark.* London: SPCK, 1987.

Schweizer, Eduard. *The Good News According to Matthew.* London: SPCK, 1976.

Scruton, Roger. *Green Philosophy: How to Think Seriously about the Planet.* London: Atlantic Books, 2012.

Sherrard, Philip. *The Rape of Man and Nature: An Enquiry into the Origins and Consequences of Modern Science.* Ipswich: Golgonooza Press, 1991.

Shuman, Joel. *The Body of Compassion: Ethics, Medicine and the Church.* Boulder, Co: Westview, 1999.

Silva, Ken. 'Brian McLaren and evangelical panentheism (part 2).' http://apprising.org/2009/08/23/brian-mclaren-and-evangelical-panentheism-part-2/ (accessed 22 August 2013).

Simpkinson, C.H. *The Life and Work of Bishop Thorold.* London: Isbister, 1896.

Simpson, James B. and Edward M. Story. *Discerning God's Will: The Complete Eyewitness Report of the Eleventh Lambeth Conference.* New York: Thomas Nelson, 1979.

Simpson, James B. and Edward M. Story. *The Long Shadows of Lambeth* X. New York, McGraw-Hill, 1969.

Sittler, Joseph. 'Called to Unity.' *The Ecumenical Review* 14 (January 1962): 177-187.

Sittler, Joseph. *Evocations of Grace: Writings on Ecology, Theology and Ethics.* Grand Rapids: Eerdmans, 2000.

Stafford, Michael. *The Heresy of Religious Opposition to Global Warming.* 2012. http://www.abc.net.au/religion/articles/2012/03/19/3456911.htm (accessed 14 October 2012).

Stephenson Alan M.G. *Anglicanism and the Lambeth Conferences.* London: SPCK, 1978.

Stephenson Alan M.G. *The First Lambeth Conference, 1867.* London: SPCK, 1967.

Sturcke, Henry. *Encountering the Rest of God: How Jesus Came to Personify the Sabbath.* Zurich: Theologischer Verlag, 2005.

Suzuki, David, 'Tony Abbott will Doom Future Generations if he Ditches Carbon Tax', *Sydney Morning Herald* 18 September 2013. http://www.smh.com.au/comment/tony-abbott-will-doom-future-generations-if-he-ditches-carbon-tax-20130917-2tx0j.html (accessed 24 September 2013).

Swenson, Kristin M. 'Earth Tells the Lessons of Cain.' In *Exploring Ecological Hermeneutics*, edited by Norman C. Habel and Peter Trudinger, 31-39. Atlanta, GA: Society of Biblical Literature, 2008.

Tanner, Kathryn. 'Creation and Providence.' In *The Cambridge Companion to Karl Barth,* edited by John Webster, 111-126. Cambridge: Cambridge University Press, 2000.

Taylor, John V. *The Christlike God.* London: SCM Press, 1992.

Taylor, John V. *Enough is Enough.* London: SCM Press, 1975.

Taylor, William R. 'Psalm 95.' In *The Interpreter's Bible, vol.4,* 516. Nashville: Abingdon Press, 1955.

Teilhard De Chardin, Pierre. *The Phenomenon of Man.* London: Fontana, 1965.

Temple, Frederick, ed. *Essays and Reviews.* 5th ed. London: Longman, Green, Longman, and Roberts, 1861.

Templeton, John Marks. *Riches for the Mind and Spirit.* San Francisco: Harper Collins, 1990.

Theokritoff, Elizabeth. 'The High Word's Mystery Play: Creation and Salvation in St Maximus the Confessor.' In *Creation and Salvation,* edited by Ernst Conradie, 93-107. Zurich: Lit Verlag, 2012.

Theological Dictionary of the Old Testament. Grand Rapids: William B. Eerdmans, 1995.

Thomas, Philip H.E. 'The Lambeth Conferences and the Development of Anglican Ecclesiology 1867 -1978.' PhD Thesis, Department of Theology, University of Durham, 1982.

Thompson, Marianne Meye. *A Commentary on Colossians and Philemon.* Grand Rapids: Eerdmans, 2005.

Today's Church and Today's World: The Lambeth Conference 1978 Preparatory Articles. London: CIO Publishing, 1977.

Treston, Kevin. *A Modern Credo: Telling the Christ Story within the Context of Creation.* Mulgrave, Victoria: John Garrett Publishing, 2010.

The Truth Shall Make You Free: The Lambeth Conference of 1988. London: Church House Publishing, 1988.

Tutu, Desmond. *No Future Without Forgiveness.* London: Random House, 1999.

United Nations. Department of Economic and Social Affairs. Population Division. *World Population to 2300.* 2004. http://www.un.org/esa/population/publications/longrange2/WorldPop2300final.pdf (accessed 21 November 2013).

VanGemeren, Willem A, ed. *New International Dictionary of Old Testament Theology and Exegesis.* Grand Rapids: Zondervan Publishing House, 1997.

Vanstone, W.H. *The Stature of Waiting.* London: Darton, Longman & Todd, 1982.

Volf, Miroslav. *Exclusion and Embrace: A Theological Exploration of Identity, Otherness, and Reconciliation.* Nashville: Abingdon Press, 1996.

Volf, Miroslav. *A Public Faith: How the Followers of Christ Should Follow the Common Good.* Grand Rapids: Brazos Press, 2011.

Wand, J.W.C. *Anglicanism in History and Today.* London: Weidenfeld and Nicholson, 1961.

We Can End Poverty: Millennium Development Goals and Beyond 2015. http://www.un.org/millenniumgoals/ (accessed 3 December 2013).

Wearden, Graeme. 'Oxfam: 85 Richest People as Wealthy as Poorest Half of the World.' *The Guardian* 20 January 2014. http://www.theguardian.com/business/2014/jan/20/oxfam-85-richest-people-half-of-the-world (accessed 30 January 2014).

Weber, Keith. *The Lord of the Sabbath: The Riches of God's Rest.* Leominster: Day One Publications, 2007.

Weber, Max. *The Protestant Ethic and the Spirit of Capitalism.* London: Allen & Unwin, 1930.

Weil, Simone. *First and Last Notebooks.* London: OUP, 1970.

Westermann, Claus. *Genesis 1-11: A Commentary.* London: SPCK, 1984.

Whatever Happened to ... the Charismatics, http://www.abc.net.au/compass/s3795778.htm (accessed 25 September 2013).

White, Lynn. 1967. 'The historical roots of our ecological crisis,' *Science* 155 (10 March 1967): 1203-1207, http://www.uvm.edu/~gflomenh/ENV-NGO-PA395/articles/Lynn-White.pdf (accessed 13 November 2011).

Williams, Rowan. *Faith in the Public Square.* London: Bloomsbury Press, 2012.

Williams, Rowan. *A Margin of Silence: The Holy Spirit in Russian Orthodox Theology.* Québec: Éditions du Lys Vert, 2008.

Williams, Rowan. *On Christian Theology.* Oxford: Blackwell, 2000.

Williams, Rowan, 'Renewing the Face of the Earth: Human Responsibility and the Environment' (Ebor Lecture, 25 March 2009) http://rowanwilliams.archbishopofcanterbury.org/articles.php/816/renewing-the-face-of-the-earth-human-responsibility-and-the-environment (accessed 13 May 2014).

Williams, Rowan, 'Time for us to challenge the idols of high finance', *Financial Times* 1 November 2011. http://rowanwilliams.archbishopofcanterbury.org/articles.php/2236/time-for-us-to-challenge-the-idols-of-high-finance (accessed 6 June 2013).

The Windsor Report 2004: The Instruments of Unity. http://www.anglicancommunion.org/windsor2004/section_c/p1.cfm (accessed 25 May 2014).

Wirzba, Norman. *Living the Sabbath: Discovering the Rhythms of Rest and Delight.* Grand Rapids: Brazos Press, 2006.

Witt, William G. 'George Herbert's Approach to God: The Faith and Spirituality of a Country Priest.' http://willgwitt.org/george-herberts-approach-to-god/ (accessed 27 August 2012).

Woodhouse, C.M. *The New Concert of Nations.* London: Bodley Head, 1964.

World Footprint: Do We Fit on the Planet? http://www.footprintnetwork.org/en/index.php/GFN/page/world_footprint (accessed 29 May 2014).

World POPClock Projection, http://www.census.gov/population/popclockworld.html (accessed 4 November 2011).

Wray, Judith Hoch. *Rest as a Theological Metaphor in the Epistle to the Hebrews and the Gospel of Truth: Early Christian Homiletics of Rest.* Atlanta: Scholars Press, 1998.

Wright, N.T. *The Lord and His Prayer.* London: SPCK, 1996.

Wright, N.T. *Surprised by Hope.* London: SPCK, 2007.

Yoder, John Howard. *The Politics of Jesus,* 2nd ed. Grand Rapids: Eerdmans, 1994.

Zizioulas, John. 'Preserving God's Creation.' In *Christianity and Ecology,* edited by Elizabeth Breuilly and Martin Palmer, 47-63. London: Cassell, 1992.

Zizioulas, John. 'Priest of Creation'. In *Environmental Stewardship: Critical Perspectives, Past and Present.* ed. R. J. Berry, 273-290. New York: Continuum International, 2006.

INDEX

www.ingramcontent.com/pod-product-compliance
Lightning Source LLC
Chambersburg PA
CBHW060038100426
42742CB00014B/2627